D0219800

J. S. BACH'S
MUSICAL OFFERING

A page from the original edition of the *Musical Offering* (Flute part of the
Andante and the beginning of the second *Allegro* of the Sonata, No. 7)

J. S. BACH'S
MUSICAL OFFERING

History, Interpretation, and Analysis

By

HANS THEODORE DAVID

DOVER PUBLICATIONS, INC.
NEW YORK

Copyright © 1945 by G. Schirmer, Inc.
All rights reserved under Pan American and
International Copyright Conventions.

Published in Canada by General Publishing
Company, Ltd., 30 Lesmill Road, Don Mills,
Toronto, Ontario.
Published in the United Kingdom by Constable
and Company, Ltd., 10 Orange Street, London WC 2.

This Dover edition, first published in 1972, is an
unabridged and unaltered republication of the work
originally published by G. Schirmer, Inc., New York,
in 1945. The present edition is published by special
arrangement with G. Schirmer, Inc.

International Standard Book Number: 0-486-22768-5
Library of Congress Catalog Card Number: 72-165391

Manufactured in the United States of America
Dover Publications, Inc.
180 Varick Street
New York, N. Y. 10014

PREFACE

This book of commentary supplements the score and parts of the *Musical Offering* published by G. Schirmer, Inc. All together, these items make up a complete practical as well as scholarly edition of the work.

The *Musical Offering* is a most intricate and comprehensive collection of pieces. While offering rich and varied music to the listener, it contains numerous problems for the historian, the editor, the performer, and the analyzing theorist. An attempt is made here to deal with all aspects of this many-sided creation. This study was anticipated to a certain extent by the author's essay published in *The Musical Quarterly* for July 1937, which may still be found useful as a brief introduction to the work.

The author is deeply indebted to his friends, Mr. Arthur Mendel and Dr. Willis Wager, for their literary advice; and to the house of G. Schirmer—particularly its late president, Mr. Carl Engel—for the opportunity of having his research on the *Musical Offering* published in such completeness.

CONTENTS

ILLUSTRATIONS

J. S. BACH'S
MUSICAL OFFERING

I

ORIGIN

In May 1747, Johann Sebastian Bach paid a visit to Frederick the Great. It was this meeting between the *"cantor* and *director musices"* of St. Thomas' at Leipzig and the "King in Prussia" that led to the creation of the *Musical Offering.*

Bach's visit was reported in the *Spenersche Zeitung,* an early Berlin newspaper, for May 11;[1] in translation, the report runs as follows:

We hear from Potsdam that last Sunday [May 7] the famous *Capellmeister* from Leipzig, *Herr* Bach, arrived with the intention of hearing the excellent Royal music at that place. In the evening, at about the time when the regular chamber music in the Royal apartments usually begins, His Majesty was informed that *Capellmeister* Bach had arrived at Potsdam and was waiting in His Majesty's antechamber for His Majesty's most gracious permission to listen to the music. His August Self immediately gave orders that Bach be admitted, and went, at his entrance, to the so-called "forte and piano",[2] condescending also to play, in person and without any preparation, a theme to be executed by *Capellmeister* Bach in a fugue. This was done so happily by the aforementioned *Capellmeister* that not only His Majesty was pleased to show his satisfaction thereat, but also all those present were seized with astonishment. *Herr* Bach has found the subject propounded to him so exceedingly beautiful that he intends to set it down on paper in a regular fugue and have it engraved in copper. On Monday, the famous man was heard on the organ in the Church of the Holy Ghost at Potsdam and earned general acclaim from the auditors attending in great number. In the evening, His Majesty charged him again with the execution of a fugue, in six parts, which he

[1] Reprinted in C. H. Bitter, *Johann Sebastian Bach,* 2nd ed., Berlin, 1881, vol. III, pp. 216-217.
[2] This was an early designation of the modern keyboard instrument with hammer mechanism, in contrast to the harpsichord.

accomplished just as skilfully as on the previous occasion, to the pleasure of His Majesty and to the general admiration.

Bach undertook no further travelling after his trip to Potsdam and Berlin. Three years later, in 1750, he died. In an obituary written by his son Carl Philipp Emanuel and his pupil Johann Friedrich Agricola, a few lines were devoted to the *Musical Offering*. While they fail to give additional information, they confirm the story contained in the quaint report of the contemporary newspaper.[3]

A fuller and more colorful account, based on information by an eyewitness, Bach's son Wilhelm Friedemann, appeared in Johann Nikolaus Forkel's *Über J. S. Bachs Leben, Kunst und Kunstwerke*. This account is given here in an early translation:[4]

Bach's second son, Charles Philip Emanuel, entered the service of Frederick the Great in 1740. The reputation of the all-surpassing skill of John Sebastian was at this time so extended, that the King often heard it mentioned and praised. This made him curious to hear so great an artist. At first he distantly hinted to the son his wish, that his father would one day come to Potsdam. But by degrees he began to ask him directly, why his father did not come? The son could not avoid acquainting his father with these expressions of the King's; at first, however, he could not pay any attention to them, because he was generally too much overwhelmed with business. But the King's expressions being repeated in several of his son's letters, he at length, in 1747, prepared to make this journey, in company of his eldest son William Friedemann. At this time the King had every evening a private Concert, in which he himself generally performed some Concertos on the flute. One evening, just as he was getting his flute ready, and his musicians were assembled, an officer brought him the list of the strangers who had arrived. With his flute in his hand he ran over the list, but immediately turned to the assembled musicians, and said, with a kind of agitation, "Gentlemen, old Bach is come." The flute was

[3] The obituary was composed for the *Societät der musikalischen Wissenschaften*, of which Bach had been a member, and published by Christoph Lorenz Mizler, founder of that learned society, in his *Musikalische Bibliothek*, vol. IV, Leipzig, 1754, part 1, pp. 158-176; reprinted, with an introduction by B. F. Richter, in *Bach-Jahrbuch*, 1920, pp. 11-29. A translation appears in *The Bach Reader*, edited by Hans T. David and Arthur Mendel, New York, 1945.

[4] The original German version (Leipzig, 1802) has been reprinted (ed. J. M. Müller-Blattau), Augsburg, 1925. The translation was the work of "Mr. Stephenson, the Banker" and prepared for the press by Samuel Wesley (see *Letters of Samuel Wesley to Mr. Jacobs relating to the Introduction into this Country of the Works of John Sebastian Bach*, 2nd ed., 1878, p. 6). A new translation with notes and appendices by C. S. Terry was published in 1920. The old translation is reprinted in *The Bach Reader*.

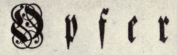

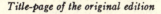

Title-page of the original edition

now laid aside; and old Bach, who had alighted at his son's lodgings, was immediately summoned to the Palace. William Friedemann, who accompanied his father, told me this story, and I must say that I still think with pleasure on the manner in which he related it. At that time it was the fashion to make rather prolix compliments. The first appearance of J. S. Bach before so great a King, who did not even give him time to change his travelling dress for a black chanter's gown, must necessarily be attended with many apologies. I will not here dwell on these apologies, but merely observe, that in William Friedemann's mouth they made a formal Dialogue between the King and the Apologist.

But what is more important than this is, that the King gave up his Concert for this evening, and invited Bach, then already called the Old Bach, to try his fortepianos, made by Silbermann, which stood in several rooms of the palace.[5] The musicians went with him from room to room, and Bach was invited everywhere to try and to play unpremeditated compositions. After he had gone on for some time, he asked the King to give him a subject for a Fugue, in order to execute it immediately without any preparation. The King admired the learned manner in which

[5] The pianofortes manufactured by Silbermann, of Freyberg, pleased the King so much, that he resolved to buy them all up. He collected fifteen. I hear that they all now stand unfit for use in various corners of the Royal Palace [Forkel's note]

Allergnädigster König,

Ew. Majestät weyhe hiermit in tiefster Unterthänigkeit ein Musicalisches Opfer, dessen edelster Theil von Deroselben hoher Hand selbst herrühret. Mit einem ehrfurchtsvollen Vergnügen erinnere ich mich annoch der ganz besondern Königlichen Gnade, da vor einiger Zeit, bey meiner Anwesenheit in Potsdam, Ew. Majestät selbst, ein Thema zu einer Fuge auf dem Clavier mir vorzuspielen geruheten, und zugleich allergnädigst auferlegten, solches alsobald in Deroselben höchsten Gegenwart auszuführen. Ew. Majestät Befehl zu gehorsamen, war meine unterthänigste Schuldigkeit. Ich bemerkte aber gar bald, daß wegen Mangels nöthiger Vorbereitung, die Ausführung nicht also gerathen wollte, als es ein so treffliches Thema erforderte. Ich faßete demnach den Entschluß, und machte mich sogleich anheischig, dieses recht Königliche Thema vollkommener auszuarbeiten, und sodann der Welt bekannt zu machen. Dieser Vorsatz ist nunmehro nach Vermögen bewerk-

Dedication of the Musical Offering, *on two pages, from the original edition*

his subject was thus executed extempore; and, probably to see how far such art could be carried, expressed a wish to hear a Fugue with six Obligato Parts. But as it is not every subject that is fit for such full harmony, Bach chose one himself, and immediately executed it to the astonishment of all present in the same magnificent and learned manner as he had done that of the King. His Majesty desired also to hear his performance on the organ. The next day therefore Bach was taken to all the organs in Potsdam, as he had before been to Silbermann's fortepianos. After his return to Leipsig, he composed the subject, which he had received from the King, in three and six parts, added several artificial passages in strict canon to it, and had it engraved, under the title of "Musicalisches Opfer" (Musical Offering), and dedicated it to the inventor.

The full title of the work is "Musical Offering to His Royal Majesty in Prussia, etc., most humbly dedicated by Johann Sebastian Bach" (see the facsimile reproduction on p. 5). After the title-page, the back of which is left blank, there appears the following formal dedication (see the facsimile reproduction above):

Most Gracious King,

In deepest humility I dedicate herewith to Your Majesty a musical offering, the noblest part of which derives from Your Majesty's own august hand. With awesome pleasure I still remember the very special

bewerkstelliget worden, und er hat keine andere als nur diese untadelhafte Absicht, den Ruhm eines Monarchen, ob gleich nur in einem kleinen Puncte, zu verherrlichen, dessen Größe und Stärke, gleich wie in allen Kriegs=und Friedens=Wissenschaften, also auch besonders in der Musik, jedermann bewundern und verehren muß.   Ich erkühne mich dieses unterthänigste Bitten hinzuzufügen: Ew. Majestät geruhen gegenwärtige wenige Arbeit mit einer gnädigen Aufnahme zu würdigen, und Deroselben allerhöchste Königliche Gnade noch fernerweit zu gönnen

Ew. Majestät

Leipzig den 7. Julii
1747.

allerunterthänigst gehorsamsten Knechte,
dem Verfasser.

Royal grace when, some time ago, during my visit in Potsdam, Your Majesty's Self deigned to play to me a theme for a fugue upon the clavier, and at the same time charged me most graciously to carry it out in Your Majesty's most august presence. To obey Your Majesty's command was my most humble duty. I noticed very soon, however, that, for lack of necessary preparation, the execution of the task did not fare as well as such an excellent theme demanded. I resolved therefore and promptly pledged myself to work out this right Royal theme more fully, and then make it known to the world. This resolve has now been carried out as well as possible, and it has none other than this irreproachable intent, to glorify, if only in a small point, the fame of a monarch whose greatness and power, as in all the sciences of war and peace, so especially in music, everyone must admire and revere. I make bold to add this most humble request: may Your Majesty deign to dignify the present modest labor with a gracious acceptance, and continue to grant Your Majesty's most august Royal grace to

Your Majesty's
most humble and obedient servant,
the author.

Leipzig, July 7,
1747

In this dedication, Bach states that he promised explicitly to work out the King's theme more thoroughly and have it published. From the various accounts we can surmise what Bach's promise meant. At Potsdam, he was asked to extemporize a fugue on King Frederick's theme and he complied. He was then asked to extemporize a six-part fugue; the implication evidently was that this fugue, too, should be based on the King's theme.[6] Bach did, indeed, improvise a six-part fugue, but on a theme of his own choice. As he evaded the actual challenge, it is altogether natural that he should at the same time have given assurance that he would later furnish the composition he had failed to extemporize. A six-part fugue on the King's theme actually forms part of the *Musical Offering*—it is likely that Bach specifically promised to write such a piece and that this was the fugue to which the *Spenersche Zeitung* alluded.

The *Musical Offering* contains a fugue in three parts as well as one in six parts. The Three-Part Fugue is not as perfect or well-balanced as might be expected of a composition by Bach written in this late period. Details indicate that it represents, exactly or approximately, Bach's original improvisation.[7] Bach thus included in the publication sent to his royal patron the nucleus from which the series of compositions based on the King's theme had sprung. In addition to the two fugues, the work contained a sonata in four movements, for flute, violin, and figured bass; and no less than ten canons.

The title page and the dedication were printed by Bernhard Christoph Breitkopf at Leipzig; for the edition of 200 copies, Bach paid, on July 10, 2 *Thaler* and 12 *Groschen*.[8] The music was engraved by Johann Georg Schübler at Zella St. Blasii near Suhl in Thuringia.[9] Schübler produced the work in four separate sections:

---

[6] The phrase in Forkel's account: *"Weil aber nicht jedes Thema zu einer solchen Vollstimmigkeit geeignet ist"* would seem superfluous if we failed to assume that Bach was expected to use the King's theme for his six-part improvisation. According to the account in the *Spenersche Zeitung*, Bach played the six-part fugue the day after his improvisation of the fugue on the King's theme, while Forkel's account gives the impression that the improvisations followed each other the same day.

[7] See the analysis of this composition in chapter VIII.

[8] Georg Kinsky, *Die Originalausgaben der Werke Johann Sebastian Bachs*, Vienna, 1937, p. 65.

[9] Schübler was also the engraver and publisher of Bach's "Schübler Chorales", originally called *Sechs Chorale von verschiedener Art auf einer Orgel mit 2 Clavieren und Pedal vorzuspielen* ("Six chorales of various kinds, to be presented on an organ with two manuals and a pedal"). This work, which consists of adaptations from cantata movements, was published between 1746 and 1750. Whether the publication of the *Chorales* by Schübler induced Bach to entrust

(1) the Three-Part Fugue and a Canon, 4 pages in oblong format, preceded by a blank page, evidently intended to receive the title (see the reproduction of the last page below, p. 11);

(2) six Canons on two single sheets, printed upright in broadside fashion (see pp. 12-13);

(3) the Sonata and one Canon, in three separate parts of 4 upright pages each, entitled, respectively, *Traversa*, *Violino*, and *Continuo* (see the frontispiece for a reproduction from this section); and

(4) the Six-Part Fugue and two Canons, 7 pages in oblong format, with separate pagination and the engraver's signature at the end (see the reproduction of the last page, p. 14).

The original edition clearly establishes the order of the three major pieces: the Three-Part Fugue at the beginning, the Sonata in the middle, and the Six-Part Fugue at the end. The position of the smaller pieces, on the other hand, seems to have been dictated largely by considerations of space.[10]

A special copy of the edition was prepared for King Frederick. The title, dedication, and at least the first two sections of the music were printed on paper of unusually large size and exceptional quality. On the blank page preceding the opening fugue, there was written an acrostic on the word RICERCAR, which began with the words *Regis Iussu* ("by command of the King")—apparently a reference to the King's request for a six-part fugue.[11] To two of the canons, complimentary inscriptions were added; thus we read at the margin of a canon which presents an original line in doubled note-values (No. 5):

> *Notulis crescentibus crescat Fortuna Regis*
> ("As the notes grow, so may the King's Fortune"),

and at the margin of the next canon, which ascends in continuous modulation (No. 6):

this engraver with the *Musical Offering*, as some writers have assumed, cannot be ascertained. Considering the fact that the *Chorales* do not display the systematic approach characteristic of all the other works brought to press by Bach, it seems at least possible that the publication of the *Chorales* was Schübler's idea rather than Bach's; perhaps it was the work on the *Musical Offering* that made Schübler wish to publish some organ music of Bach's as well, in which case the *Chorales* are not likely to have appeared before 1748. The work has been published in an excellent new edition by A. Riemenschneider.

[10] For a more detailed discussion of the original edition and the order of movements, see chapter VII, pp. 83-96.

[11] The acrostic is discussed in chapter IV, pp. 42-43.

Ascendenteque Modulatione ascendat Gloria Regis
("And as the modulation rises, so may the King's Glory").

The King's copy went to his sister, the Princess Anna Amalia, with whose library it has, at least partly, come down to us.[12] Whether Bach received any compensation for his work, we do not know.[13] He distributed the other copies of the original edition himself, as can be seen from a letter which he wrote, on October 6, 1748, to his cousin Johann Elias Bach:

I cannot oblige you with the required copy of the Prussian Fugue for the time being since the edition was exhausted just today (as I have had printed only a hundred copies, most of which were given *gratis* to good friends). But I shall have a few more printed between now and the New Year's fair; if, *Herr* Cousin, you then still desire to have a copy, you have only to give me notice by mail and to add a *Thaler*, and the request shall be complied with.[14]

The title *Preussische Fuge* ("Prussian fugue") may indicate that Bach did not intend to have the Sonata and Canons reprinted with the fugue or fugues. When he died, he owed to Schübler the sum of 2 *Thaler* and 16 *Groschen*, which may have covered reprints of the *Musical Offering*.[15] The remaining copies, or possibly the copper plates, were acquired by Breitkopf;[16] no reprint was issued prior to the 1830's.

King Frederick, it should be added, did not forget "old Bach's" visit, although his recollections may have been somewhat hazy. To

---

[12] For further details concerning the dedication copy, see chapter VII, pp. 91-92. The *Musical Offering* is generally assumed to have been produced without comprehensive plan and delivered in more or less accidental installments. This assumption, which originally was prompted by the rather irregular make-up of the first edition and, more specifically, the dedication copy, is critically examined in chapter VII, pp. 94-96.

[13] According to C. S. Terry, *Bach, A Biography*, London, 1928, p. 253, note 2, Bach's name does not figure in the exchequer's accounts; it is nevertheless possible that he received a gift or reward.

[14] The original German text is given in C. S. Terry, *Johann Sebastian Bach*, Leipzig, c. 1929, p. 310.

[15] See the *Specificatio der Verlassenschaft*, the official appraisal of Bach's estate, in P. Spitta, *J. S. Bach*, Leipzig, 1873-80 (reprinted 1916), vol. II, p. 962; English translation by Clara Bell and J. A. Fuller Maitland, London, 1884-5 (reprinted 1899), p. 356, also in *The Bach Reader*.

[16] In Johann Gottlieb Immanuel Breitkopf's *Verzeichniss musikalischer Bücher*, 2nd ed., Leipzig, 1761, p. 39, the work was offered under the heading of fugues, for 1 *Thaler* and 12 *Groschen;* probably only the oblong sections were included.

Last page of the *Ricercar a 3*, No. 1 (meas. 157-185), from the original edition; the page also contains the Canon No. 2, in abbreviated notation. Facsimile by courtesy of the Library of Congress.

11

The first of the two folio sheets with canons in abbreviated notation as they appear in the dedication copy of the original edition. The canons included are Nos. 9, 3-6, and the beginning of 12.

The second folio sheet with canons in abbreviated notation.

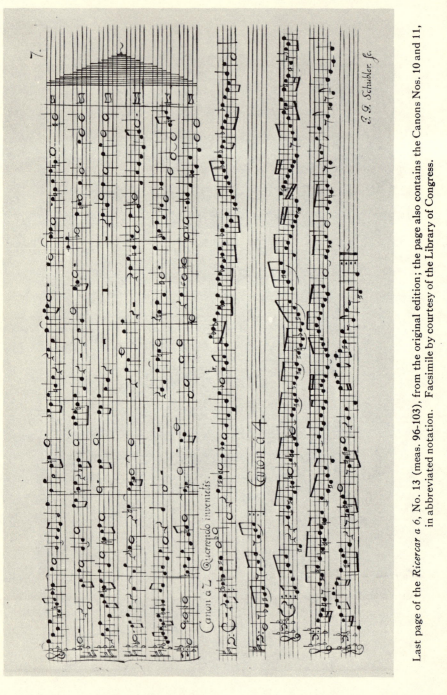

Last page of the *Ricercar a 6*, No. 13 (meas. 96-103), from the original edition; the page also contains the Canons Nos. 10 and 11, in abbreviated notation. Facsimile by courtesy of the Library of Congress.

Gottfried van Swieten, Austrian ambassador extraordinary, the King praised, in 1774, old Bach's art even beyond that of Wilhelm Friedemann, who then seemed incomparable in his "depth of harmonic knowledge and strength of performance".[17] According to van Swieten, who later induced Mozart to study Handel and Bach and to whom Forkel dedicated his Bach biography, King Frederick "sang, with strong voice, the subject of a chromatic fugue which he had given to old Bach, who immediately made it into a fugue of 4, then of 5, and finally of 8 obbligato voices"—without, it seems, mentioning the published elaboration of his theme. It does not seem likely that even a Bach, with but two hands, could have extemporized in 8 parts. And from the earlier records of the visit we may be sure that the King, who obviously looked upon Bach at the time of their meeting as a sort of magician, continued so to regard him, and embroidered in his fancy upon the events of that May evening.

[17] Quotation in A. Einstein, "Mozart's Four String Trio Preludes to Fugues of Bach", *Musical Times*, vol. 77, London, 1936, p. 209.

II

THE ROYAL THEME

BACH HIMSELF called the subject he had been given by King Frederick a· "truly Royal theme". We may assume that he was sincere in his praise, for the theme is dignified, expressive, and composed of elements which form excellent material for contrapuntal development. It appears in each of the thirteen numbers of the *Musical Offering*. The two fugues, as well as the ten canons, are based on it; the sonata uses it in full in two of its four movements while alluding to it in the others.

The theme in its original form, in C minor, makes a conspicuous entrance with three notes of an ascending triad, followed by the sixth degree and then the leading tone, reached by the downward skip of a diminished seventh. Proceeding in half-notes and cut off from the rest of the subject by a short pause, the opening motif seems to establish a 4/2 measure (a true "*alla breve*").

The second section of the theme descends chromatically from the fifth (which is expected after the sixth) to the leading-tone, thus filling in the open interval of the seventh established at the end of the first motif. The rhythm of this section seems to be somewhat arbitrary: beginning with a quarter-note up-beat, the chromatic descent proceeds in half-notes, is halted by a dotted half-note, then continues in quarters as if by diminution. The lack of coordination between melodic and rhythmic progression gives this portion an air of stiffness—the only flaw to be detected in the Royal theme.

The leading-tone reached at the end of the chromatic descent must resolve to the tonic, and does so after the introduction of passing-notes which enlarge the compass of the theme to a ninth. But the tonic, then entering on a weak beat, does not seem to form a conclusion; so the cadential formula is enlarged by a diatonic descent from the subdominant to the tonic. The last measures seem to establish a 2/2 measure, in contrast to the larger measure suggested by the opening motif.

The Royal theme appears in its original shape—as the accompanying table shows—in only three movements of the *Musical Offering:* at the beginning (No. 1) and at the end (Nos. 12 and 13). In the other movements, Bach modifies and enlivens the original subject. These alterations provide a great variety of mood and motion, establish definite relations between neighboring as well as widely separated numbers, and, in most cases, give a more convincing form to the chromatic descent within the theme.

In the Three-Part Fugue, No. 1, Bach presents the theme in the 2/2 meter suggested by its second half.

The first three Canons, Nos. 2-4, establish what might be called a first level of variation. All three vary the cadential formula, however modestly; No. 2 eliminates, in addition, one of the rhythmic changes within the chromatic descent by prolonging the up-beat. The next two canons, Nos. 5 and 6, establish a second level of variation by modifying the theme throughout. No. 5 embellishes the first, third, and fifth notes of the opening motif with passing-notes that are predominantly diatonic; No. 6, the second and fourth notes of the motif with passing-notes that are predominantly chromatic. Both canons change at least the rhythm of the chromatic descent and the cadential formula. No. 6 ends, with a modulation, on the major second above the tonic.[1]

The second movement of the Sonata, No. 7, presents the theme again essentially in its original form: thus a clear connection is established between the opening, the center, and the conclusion of the work. Here, however, the theme is offered in 2/4 meter and with halved note-values—a clear-cut diminution. The fourth movement, on the other hand, employs the most audacious variation of the theme in the entire work; couched in 6/8 meter, this variation is rendered highly vivid by passing-notes and rhythmic alteration throughout.

From the extreme of variation found in the last movement of the

---

[1] Nos. 2 and 4 are written in common time with halved note-values, but as these pieces are evidently conceived in a slower tempo than Nos. 3, 5, and 6, the difference in notation indicates a contrast of character rather than a true diminution. The distinction between common time, as indicated in Nos. 3 and 6, and cut time, as in No. 5, refers similarly to a contrast of character rather than of tempo.

The Royal Theme and its Variations

No. 1. RICERCAR A 3 *(Three-Part Fugue)*

No. 2. CANON PERPETUUS A 2 *(Canon at the Double Octave)*

No. 3. CANON A 2 VIOLINI IN UNISONO *(Canon at the Unison)*

No. 4. CANON A 2 PER MOTUM CONTRARIUM *(Canon in Contrary Motion)*

No. 5. CANON A 2 PER AUGMENTATIONEM, CONTRARIO MOTU
(Canon in Augmentation and Contrary Motion)

No. 6. CANON A 2 PER TONOS *(Modulating Canon)*

No. 7. SONATA A 3 *(Trio Sonata)*
　　Largo *(Only the opening of the theme is used in this movement.)*
　　Allegro *(First entrance a fourth lower)*

Andante *(Only allusions to the theme are given in this movement.)*
Allegro

No. 8. CANON PERPETUUS *(Mirror Canon)*

No. 9. CANON A 2 *(Crab Canon)*

No. 10. CANON A 2 *(Canon in Contrary Motion)*

No. 11. CANON A 4 *(Four-Part Canon)*

No. 12. FUGA CANONICA IN EPIDIAPENTE *(Canonic Fugue)*

No. 13. RICERCAR A 6 *(Six-Part Fugue)*

19

Sonata, a return is made to the previous levels of variation in the ensuing Canons, Nos. 8-12. In No. 8, the theme is interspersed with passing-notes as in Nos. 5 and 6; the dominant following the leading-tone which originally concluded the chromatic descent falls here on a heavy beat—a conspicuous improvement over the original version—and the end of the theme is set a fifth higher, leading to the dominant above the tonic.

No. 9 recalls the first level of variation as represented by Nos. 2-4; the theme is altered here only through syncopation of the first notes of the chromatic descent. No. 10 again introduces passing-notes within the first motif; as in No. 9, syncopation is introduced in order to improve upon the chromatic descent. Thus a transition is effected from No. 9 to No. 11, which, in turn, is quite clearly on the same level of variation as No. 8, liberally using passing-notes and extending the compass of the theme to an eleventh, exactly as in No. 8.

No. 12 uses the original form of the theme, completing the step-wise restoration which began in Nos. 8 and 9; as in the opening fugue, the theme is presented in 2/2 meter.

In the Six-Part Fugue, No. 13, Bach employs the 4/2 meter suggested by the opening of the theme. The eighth-notes in the cadential formula are omitted; the subject is thus reduced to its simplest form.

The series of variations as a whole represents gradual increase to a climax and then gradual return to the starting-point. This development is interrupted by the reappearance of the original form of the theme in the center of the work and further by a secondary increase in the degree of variation, which connects Nos. 9 to 11.[2] The choice of variations thus contributes to the coherence and unity of the work as a whole.

---

[2] Nos. 9-11 form the center of the second canon group and were meant to be separated from the surrounding Nos. 8 and 12; the interruption of the stepwise return from the highest level of variation at this point, therefore, is not accidental, but embodies a structural idea (see below, p. 37, note 4).

III

FORMS

THE COMPOSITIONS of which the *Musical Offering* is made up are based on a common theme and written in a common key, C minor.[1] In addition, they are all strictly polyphonic in texture, *i.e.* each employs a definite number of obbligato "voices" or parts. These elements give striking homogeneity to the entire work.

The *Musical Offering* contains, however, examples of three distinct forms: canon, fugue, and sonata. In the original edition only the ten Canons are so designated; the name *"ricercar"* is given to both the Three-Part and the Six-Part Fugues, and the Sonata remains without title.

CANON

A CANON is a composition in which at least two parts are identical in certain basic aspects such as melodic line and rhythmic structure. The leading part of most canons is followed by the derived part after a certain time-interval in the same direction and tempo; the following part may be kept at the same pitch as the preceding (*canon in unisono*, "canon at the unison"), or it may perform the original line at a certain interval above or below it (*e.g.*, *canon in epidiapente*, "canon at the higher fifth"). In certain canons all intervals of the original line are inverted by the following part (*canon per motum contrarium*, or *motu contrario*, "canon in contrary motion"). In others we find one part moving backward while the other moves forward (*canon cancrizans*, "crab canon"). Then

[1] No. 11 appears in the original edition as a composition in G minor; difficulties of notation seem to have prompted a transposition in this case, which evidently forms an exception in appearance rather than intention (see Appendix, pp. 176-8).

again, there are canons in which the canonic voices proceed at different speed; thus one voice may double the note-values of the original line while the other performs it as written (*canon per augmentationem,* "canon in augmentation"). All these patterns, together with a number of other, more unusual devices, are represented in the *Musical Offering,* which thus constitutes a generous demonstration of the possibilities inherent in this form.

The implication of the canon form is that all corresponding canonic parts can be reduced to, and then performed from, a single written line. When actually presented in its most concise notation, the canon is called a *canon clausus* ("close canon"). When, however, the parts are written out in full, it is called a *canon apertus* ("open canon"). In the original edition of the *Musical Offering,* all canons except one (No. 8) are given in abbreviated notation (see the facsimile reproduction of the four pages from the original edition containing canons in abbreviated notation, above, pp. 11-14).

Canons in abbreviated notation generally employ two or more clefs in order to specify the interval distance between the parts, and mark the entrance of the following parts by special signs; the specific character of the canon is also often indicated in the title. However, in reducing a canon to its most concise form, a composer might deliberately omit explaining titles and the indications of the place or pitch at which the successive voices are to enter. A canon thus presented is called a *canon enigmaticus* ("puzzle canon"). Examples are Nos. 9, 10, and 11 of the *Musical Offering;* to all three applies the inscription on the second of them: *Quaerendo invenietis* ("Seek and ye shall find").

The ten canons in the *Musical Offering* clearly fall into two contrasting sets of five. Throughout the first group of canons (Nos. 2-6), the Royal theme appears in one part, as a kind of *cantus firmus,* accompanied by two canonic parts. In the second group of canons (Nos. 8-12), the theme itself is used as canonic material and thus is presented in each number by at least two voices. This contrast in treatment is expressed in two headings found in the dedication copy of the work. The first reads:

> *Canones diversi super Thema Regium*
> ("Various Canons upon the Royal Theme"),

the other:

Thematis Regii Elaborationes Canonicae
("Canonic Elaborations of the Royal Theme").[1]

The specific contrapuntal structure of the single movements is discussed below.

No. 2. *Canon perpetuus a 2 (Canon at the Double Octave)*[2]

Like all the other Canons upon the Royal Theme, this is a three-part composition including a two-part canon. The Royal theme appears in the middle, flanked by the canonic voices. The higher canonic part sets out first, followed after a full measure by its counterpart a double octave below. Since the theme is noted in diminution, with a prevailing movement of quarters, the second canonic part enters under the fifth note of the theme.

A canon that can be repeated at will is termed *perpetuus* ("infinite"). In the *Musical Offering*, only two pieces (Nos. 2 and 8) bear the title *canon perpetuus;* actually, however, all canons in the work except three (Nos. 6, 9, and 12) return to their beginning and thus deserve to be called "continuous".

No. 3. *Canon a 2 Violini in Unisono (Canon at the Unison)*

The Royal theme is used here as a bass. The second canonic voice follows the first in identical pitch after a full measure. Since the theme is noted in its original movement predominantly of half-notes, the second canonic part enters above the third note of the theme; thus the canonic parts seem to be brought closer together than in the opening canon.

The present number represents theoretically the simplest form of a two-part canon although crossings of the canonic parts make its comprehension in performance slightly more difficult than that of the preceding number.

No. 4. *Canon a 2 per Motum contrarium* (*Canon in Contrary Motion*)

The Royal theme forms the highest part of a composition renouncing the use of the bass register. The higher canonic part is again in-

[1] In Elizabethan England, canons built around plainsong melodies were very fashionable; they bore titles such as: "Two parts in one upon *Miserere*". "Two parts in one" means that two canonic parts were presented in one line or could be so presented; the expression "upon..." has been used here for the translation of the first heading. (See also chapter VII, pp. 92-93.)

[2] The original title reads: "*Canon perpetuus super Thema Regium*"; for an explanation see chapter VII, p. 92.

troduced first, followed after half a measure by an exact inversion.
Since the theme is again noted in diminution, the second part enters,
as in the preceding canon, with the third note of the theme.

In all canons in contrary motion, there is of necessity a note common to the original line and its inversion. The common note in this
example is the third degree of the scale, that is, E♭ or E♮. Accordingly, C is answered by G, and G by C. At the beginning, Bach
avails himself of a minor licence by answering certain major intervals
with minor ones, and *vice versa*. The line G F E♭ D C is thus inverted
as C D E♭ F G. Such treatment makes it possible to preserve the
tonality of the original line in the inversion and may therefore be
called a "tonal" answer. In the further course of the canon, however,
the intervals of the leading voice are inverted exactly, forming a
"real" answer; here the line C D E♭, for instance, appears in inversion as G F E♮.[3]

No. 5. Canon a 2 per Augmentationem, contrario Motu [4]
(Canon in Augmentation and Contrary Motion)

This canon, the most intricate of the group, introduces two principles of contrapuntal complication. The second voice forms an inversion of the first, as in the preceding number, but in notes of twice
the original value. The theme appears again in the middle. The
canon proper is here, for the first time, opened by the lower voice,
followed over the second basic note of the theme by the augmented
inversion. In a canon in augmentation, the canonic parts may enter
simultaneously; here the slower-moving part enters a quarter of a
measure later than simultaneous entry of both parts would require.
The pivot of the inversion is again the third degree of the scale, and
again an initial tonal answer is later replaced by a real one.

No. 6. Canon a 2 per Tonos (Modulating Canon) [5]

This concluding number of the first canon group forms a canon in
parallel motion at the higher fifth. The theme lies on top; the lower

[3] Since the canon appears in abbreviated notation in the original edition, the
choice between real and tonal answer is left to the performer or editor. There
can be no doubt, however, that at least the opening of the following canon,
No. 5, was designed by Bach as requiring a tonal answer (see Appendix, pp.
158-9).

[4] For the inscription to this canon in the copy of the original edition sent to
King Frederick, see p. 9.

[5] Johann Christoph Oley, who was the first to work out a solution for all the

canonic part enters first, the higher after a full measure, with the third note of the theme. The composition modulates with each repetition of the basic setting a major second ("tonus") upward; six presentations of the original canon are therefore required before the tonality of the opening is reached again, while the pitch of the opening never returns. Since the following canonic part plays a fifth above the preceding one and the repetitions take place at the higher second, we find that the appearances of the canonic line throughout the composition comprise the complete cycle of fifths, expressed in minor tonalities:

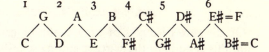

Upper canonic part: G   A   B   C♯   D♯   E♯ = F

Lower canonic part: C   D   E   F♯   G♯   A♯   B♯ = C

No. 8. Canon perpetuus (Mirror Canon)

This opening number of the second group of Canons is designated as *Canon perpetuus*, exactly as is the opening number of the first canon group. Here the Royal theme is for the first time subjected to canonic treatment. The canon proper is in two parts and contrary motion. The canonic parts have exactly the same high range and are supported by a contrapuntally free bass; the latter is figured to provide for a keyboard accompaniment.

The canonic line includes two presentations of the Royal theme, one in C minor and one in G minor; the second is a tonal inversion of the first. A short interlude separates the appearances of the theme. The second part enters two measures after the first, over the fifth basic note of the theme. The pivot of the inversion is again the third degree of the scale; the answer is real, not tonal, so that an initial E♭ appears in the inversion as E♮. Since the theme in its present variation begins on C and ends on G, the inversion opens with G and ends with C.

The second pair of entries (meas. 19 ff.) uses the third degree of G minor (B♭ and B♮) as the pivot of inversion. Here the leading voice begins on D and concludes the presentation of the theme on

canons of the *Musical Offering* (see chapter VII, pp. 96f.), called this piece *canon circularis per tonos*. The indication *per tonos* has been adapted here; the term *circularis* is somewhat misleading since it has been applied, though less appropriately, to the "infinite" canon.

For the inscription to this canon in the dedication copy of the original edition, see pp. 9-10.

G, while the answer opens with G and ends on D. This part of the canon is concluded with an isolated appearance of the opening of the theme in the bass (meas. 29), after which the first group of entries returns. Since the second pair of entries represents an inversion of the first, the canon includes the mirrored image of its own first section and is therefore properly called a mirror canon.[6]

This canon cannot be presented in abbreviated notation since the pivot of inversion changes twice in the course of the composition. The original edition, accordingly, gives it in full, in separate parts printed together with those of the Sonata, No. 7.

No. 9. Canon a 2 (Crab Canon)

Of the rare examples of crab canon or canon in retrograde motion, this is perhaps the wittiest and most easily comprehended. The original line consists of a presentation of the theme, followed by a counterpoint of the same length. Two comparatively high voices of equal range begin simultaneously, one working its way forward from the beginning, the other backward from the end. While the first part offers the theme, the second offers the reversion of the counterpoint; while the first offers the counterpoint, the second offers the reversion of the theme. Having arrived at the end, both parts turn around and play the lines they presented before, in opposite direction.[7]

In the original edition, no title helps to find the solution for this canon; the task, however, is made easier by the presence of two clefs, one at the beginning and a reversed one at the end of the one-line abbreviated notation.

No. 10. Canon a 2 (Canon in Contrary Motion)

Again the theme is offered in two-part canonic treatment without accompaniment. Like Nos. 4, 5, and 8, this is a canon in contrary motion, but here the fifth is used as a pivot—or rather, the fifth above the tonic is answered by the fourth below the tonic. The inversion is real, without any deviation. Of the two relatively low

[6] The term "mirror canon" is sometimes used to designate simply a canon in contrary motion; it seemed more economical to use the word "mirror" only in connection with such compositions as invert a whole section (like the present canon) or are themselves inverted completely (like the two pairs of "mirror fugues" in Bach's *Art of the Fugue*).

[7] The addition of a retrograde reading of the entire canon was first made by Oley. It results contrapuntally in a repetition, but seemed valuable since it gives the two players an opportunity to visualize their own lines in crab-like reversion.

voices, the higher enters first, the other following after 2 1/2 measures, under the fifth basic note of the theme. The canonic line adds a short episode between the initial presentation of the theme and the beginning of the repeat. In our realization, the entire canon is also offered in inversion with exchanged voices—the leading higher part now presents the inversion, the following lower part the original line.[8]

The title of this number in the original edition again offers no clue to the contrapuntal character of the canon, nor is the place marked where the second part is supposed to enter. The presence of two clefs, the second printed upside down, indicates at least that a canon in contrary motion was intended.[9]

No. 11. Canon a 4 (Four-Part Canon)

This canon for two high and two low parts is the only number in the *Musical Offering* containing more than two canonic voices. The parts enter at the unison and at the distance of one or two octaves below the original part.[10] The entrances are made throughout after a time-interval of 7 measures, while in all the preceding canons the entrances were kept close together. Accordingly the entire Royal theme is offered in each of the first three parts before the next part is introduced. The entire composition can be represented as a four-part setting of the theme—a setting the lines of which are continuously interchanged, as the following diagram illustrates (*Th* indicates the appearance of the Royal theme, *Cp 1* that of the first counterpoint, etc.):

	Exposition (meas. 1-28)				Center, repeated (meas. 29-56)			
First part	Th	Cp 1	Cp 2	Cp 3 ‖	Th	Cp 1	Cp 2	Cp 3 ‖
Second part		Th	Cp 1	Cp 2	Cp 3	Th	Cp 1	Cp 2 ‖
Third part			Th	Cp 1	Cp 2	Cp 3	Th	Cp 1 ‖
Fourth part				Th	Cp 1	Cp 2	Cp 3	Th ‖

Since the parts enter at varying intervals, the composition is of necessity written in four-part counterpoint at the octave.

In the original edition, two clefs are used for this number. The points of entrance for the succeeding parts are not indicated, and the

---

[8] The second version has been added, in correspondence with the second reading of the preceding canon, in order to make each player perform the inversion of his own line.

[9] The canon is inscribed "*Quaerendo invenietis*"; see above, p. 22.

[10] For a discussion of the interval distances, see Appendix, pp. 176-8.

composition is thus established as a puzzle canon, like the preceding numbers.

No. 12. Fuga canonica in Epidiapente (Canonic Fugue)

The last of the Canonic Elaborations of the Royal Theme is a canon for two high parts with accompaniment of a free bass—like the opening canon of the group, No. 8, although the present bass is not figured. The canonic parts proceed in parallel motion; the second part performs, as the title indicates, a fifth above the first. The leading part presents the Royal theme in full before the following part enters, exactly as in the preceding number; the distance between the parts is 10 measures.

The canonic line is of considerable length. The theme is presented twice, once in the tonic and once in the subdominant; both presentations are followed by extended episodes. The second canonic part quite naturally answers the entrance of the theme in the tonic by one in the dominant; and the entrance in the subdominant by one in the tonic. The two pairs of entries are separated, as in the Mirror Canon, by episodic material. Thus we seem to hear a two-part accompanied fugue while the strict canon is at no place interrupted. The second group of entries is ingeniously extended by a third entrance, in the bass; thus the two-part canon seems to broaden into a three-part fugue. The entrance of the theme in the bass reminds one of the deceptive entrance of the theme in the bass offered at a corresponding place in the Mirror Canon; the present introduction of a complete entrance of the theme in the bass appears like the final realization of a structural idea only cautiously suggested before.

RICERCAR

During the Middle Ages, the word *fuga* ("flight") was in musical terminology used to designate what we would call a canon. Later the term was applied to freer imitations or their subjects. It was not until the end of the 17th century that the word *fuga* acquired the definite meaning it had for Bach, his contemporaries, and his successors.

The fugue originated in the *ricercar* and the *canzon alla francese* or *canzon per sonar*. *Ricercar* (or *ricercare*) originally means "to search". The title *ricercar* was for a while given to free preludes in which an instrument and its tuning were tried out, but this use of the word did not persist. In general, the term *ricercar* designated those polyphonic compositions which transplanted the style of the vocal motet into instrumental music. The *canzon* on the other hand was, as its name indicated, an instrumental offspring of the French *chanson*. In accordance with their differing origins, the *ricercar* was heavier and used broader themes than the *canzon*, which was usually of a lighter and more lively character. Both *ricercar* and *canzon alla francese* were common forms of music for several concerted instruments as well as for keyboard instruments alone.

The *ricercar* was developed chiefly by Flemish masters working in Italy, like Adrian Willaert and Jacques Buus, and then by Venetians like Claudio Merulo and Andrea Gabrieli. It appeared as a standard type in the works of Gerolamo Frescobaldi. His pupil, Johann Jacob Froberger, made the form popular in Germany. Bach esteemed Frescobaldi as well as Froberger,[1] and we know that he acquired, in 1714, a copy of Frescobaldi's *Fiori musicali*, a collection first published in 1635 and including *ricercari* as well as other compositions.[2]

Frescobaldi's *ricercari* consisted of one or several sections. When there were several sections, all were based on the same theme. Compositions of this type began, and were often kept throughout, in *tempus imperfectum*, or true *alla breve*, which corresponds to our 4/2 time. The theme, which was frequently made up of a few notes only, appeared regularly at first in long notes. In those *ricercari* which included several sections, variations of the theme were introduced. Bach never used the word *ricercar* outside of the *Musical Offering*, but several of his earlier fugues are strict *ricercari*, such as the E-major Fugue in the Second Part of the *Well-Tempered Clavier* and the organ fugue in E-flat major which concluded the Third Part of the *Clavier-Übung* and has become known as the "St. Anne" Fugue; he also opened the *Art of the Fugue* with a series of four fugues in *ricercar* style.

The theme King Frederick gave to Bach for his extemporization proceeded mostly in half-notes and thus formed a fitting, though somewhat lengthy, subject for a *ricercar*. Bach worked the Six-Part Fugue out entirely in the manner of a *ricercar*. Following the tradi-

---

[1] Letter by C. P. E. Bach to Forkel, Jan. 13, 1775, reprinted in *Bach-Urkunden*, ed. by M. Schneider, *Veröffentlichungen der Neuen Bachgesellschaft, Jahrgang* 17, *Heft* 3; translated in *The Bach Reader*.

[2] P. Spitta, *J. S. Bach*, German ed., vol. I, p. 418; Engl. transl., vol. I, pp. 420-1.

tion, he even used the *alla breve* notation, and we may say that this is a *ricercar* in the strictest sense of the term—the most elaborate and profound example of its type.

Bach evidently wanted to give the same title to both fugues in the *Musical Offering*, and thus called the Three-Part Fugue also a *ricercar*. This piece is written in 2/2 time, and the title *ricercar* fits its character less well than the more general "fugue" would have. But the composition is based on the same slow-moving theme as the Six-Part Fugue, and this may be deemed sufficient to justify Bach's choice of title.

When Bach improvised his fugue upon the King's theme, those who listened had to "search" for the theme in the music they heard, and whoever was to study, to perform, or to hear the six-part fugue had a similar task before him. Thus the word *ricercar* pointed straight at the particular intention of these pieces. This evidently was the reason why Bach used the term which at that time had already become somewhat obsolete.

The *ricercar* was, to Bach's mind, a kind of fugue. The *Ricercari* in the *Musical Offering* accordingly comply with the rules Bach followed in composing his fugues. They are compositions written in a definite number of parts and based on a certain "subject" or theme from beginning to end. Each voice-part makes its first entrance with a presentation of the complete subject. The opening exposition of both *Ricercari* has, like most fugues, exactly as many entries of the subject as obbligato parts, and these entries follow each other, according to common practice, at a distance of alternating fifths and fourths, or alternately in tonic and dominant. The further development of both *Ricercari*, like that of most fugues, is determined by the contrast between entries of the complete subject (or groups of such entries) and interludes or "episodes" during which the subject is either elaborated in fragments or not referred to at all. Out of these elements, Bach creates structures of extraordinary interest. While the Three-Part *Ricercar* may serve as an example of his approach to fugue-improvisation, the Six-Part *Ricercar* stands out as one of his most elaborate and monumental fugues.[3]

---

[3] An analysis of the *Ricercari* is given in chapter VIII, pp. 104-110 and 134-152.

SONATA

THE WORD *sonata* (derived from *sonare*, "to play") at first simply indicated a piece which was played, not sung. The earliest sonatas were regularly written for an ensemble of instruments, especially of the wind group. When used more specifically, the word signified a composition which did not imitate a vocal form—in contrast, particularly, to the *canzon per sonar*.

The history of the sonata as an artistic form starts with the work of Giovanni Gabrieli, the great Venetian, who wrote sonatas in from 4 to 22 parts. During the seventeenth century, the sonata became the standard form of chamber music. Most fashionable was the *sonata a tre* ("sonata in three parts," or "trio sonata") for two high instruments and figured bass. The high parts were of equal importance and preferably played on violins; the bass, sometimes less active contrapuntally than the upper voices, was executed by a harpsichord, organ, or other harmonic instrument, often reinforced by a stringed or other bass instrument. Greatest rival of the *sonata a tre* was the sonata for a solo violin with figured bass, a form which frequently offered material for the virtuoso player rather than chamber music.

The sonata, like the violin, was developed chiefly in Italy. The later Italian composers, among whom Arcangelo Corelli excelled, distinguished between a *sonata da chiesa* ("church sonata") and a *sonata da camera* ("chamber sonata"). The church sonata regularly consisted of four movements, alternately slow and quick; the quick movements, particularly the first, were usually fugued. The chamber sonata, on the other hand, consisted of dance movements, often ushered in by a free prelude.

Bach wrote approximately 20 sonatas for an ensemble of instruments. Many of them follow the pattern of the *sonata da chiesa* although Bach liked to end with a gigue or gigue-like movement. Most of his sonatas were written for an obbligato harpsichord with violin, flute, or *viola da gamba*—combinations which were new at the time. On the other hand, there are hardly any sonatas for a single solo instrument with figured-bass accompaniment among his works, and of trio sonatas written before 1747 only two can be named: the well-known Sonata in C major for two violins and a Sonata in G minor for two flutes, both with figured bass.[1] Bach evidently was

[1] The Sonata for two flutes and figured bass was rewritten by Bach for obbligato harpsichord and *viola da gamba*. A third trio sonata, for flute, violin, and

somewhat reluctant to increase further the already vast literature of solo and trio sonatas. Why, then, should he have turned to the trio sonata when he decided to include a sonata in the *Musical Offering*?

As King Frederick played the flute, it was logical that Bach should think of this instrument in writing the *Musical Offering*. The theme on which the work was based could hardly have been used for a concerto. It would also have made a rather stiff impression in a sonata unless it was considerably changed, or accompanied by lively counterpoints. Thus it was hardly suitable for use in a sonata for flute alone with figured bass. Bach could have introduced it into a sonata for an obbligato keyboard instrument and flute, but he preferred to show it off in a *sonata a tre*. Imagining a performance at the Prussian Court, he may have wanted to include a part for Johann Gottlieb Graun, the Royal concert-master and former teacher of Wilhelm Friedemann Bach. More probably, however, he chose the *sonata a tre* because it exposed the polyphonic structure of his music more clearly than a sonata for obbligato harpsichord and flute would have done. At any rate, he worked out the sonata for the *Musical Offering* in three parts, assigning the parts to *Traversa*,[2] *Violino*, and *Continuo*;[3] and thereby he contrived the last and finest sonata he ever wrote in a medium in which he had shown little interest before.

This sonata is strictly a *sonata da chiesa*, in four movements. The opening slow movement, a *Largo* in triple time (3/4), displays an expressive interchange of rather short motifs in a manner characteristic of many first movements of sonatas by Bach. The second movement, an *Allegro* in quick duple meter (2/4), is a free double fugue; to the opening independent theme, the Royal theme is later added as a counter-subject somewhat with the character of a *cantus firmus*. The third movement, an *Andante* in common time (C), employs a continuous alternation of *forte* motifs with *piano* echoes; it is thus based on a peculiar formal pattern as many third movements of Bach's sonatas are. The last movement, an *Allegro* in compound time (6/8), is a free fugue which uses a variation of the Royal theme as

---

figured bass, in G major, has been attributed to Bach, but is in this form of doubtful authenticity; it is an arrangement of a Sonata for violin and figured bass, which might be an authentic early work of Bach's.

[2] *Traversa* or *flauto traverso* indicated the cross-flute or German flute, in contrast to the recorder which was still widely used in Bach's time.

[3] *Continuo* (originally *basso continuo*) indicated a thorough-bass; the present example is generously figured to provide for a harmonic accompaniment in accordance with the practice of the seventeenth and eighteenth centuries.

the main subject; in rhythmic texture, it is faintly reminiscent of a gigue.[4]

Though rather conservative in form, the Sonata was definitely progressive in style. The King and his musicians were much younger than Bach and cherished a style strikingly different from that of "old Bach". Some of Bach's own works had pointed out to the younger generation, especially to his sons, the way towards the future classic style, and Bach evidently attempted in this work to write as "modern" a sonata as he could without sacrificing the polyphonic strictness which was part of his artistic creed. Thus the Sonata became an act of homage to King Frederick even beyond the use of his theme and his favorite instrument.

[4] An analysis of the four movements of the Sonata is given in chapter VIII, pp. 111-134.

IV

THE WORK AS A WHOLE

STRUCTURE

Up to the middle of the eighteenth century, music publications usually included a number of separate, independent compositions. All of the works Bach himself designated for publication were such collections of pieces that could be performed singly, and the *Musical Offering* is no exception.

It was logical that composers should attempt to give a certain inner connection to the compositions that were to appear within the same book. The history of these attempts is quite interesting.[1] At first a definite scheme and order of tonalities was used to unite the separate compositions. Bach created, in addition, concrete ties between certain parts of a collection by employing similar material or corresponding principles of style and form; the result was a web of symmetrical or other relations linking all parts of a collection. When this technique of comprehensive construction had acquired sufficient strength, Bach renounced the use of tonal schemes. Four of his last works were each written in one key throughout while also based on a single theme: the *Goldberg Variations*, the *Canonic Variations on the Christmas Song "Vom Himmel hoch da komm ich her"*, the *Musical Offering*, and the *Art of the Fugue*. Each of these has a structure as strict and perfectly unified as any single movement written by Bach.

The *Musical Offering*—if arranged in the order apparently intended by Bach[2]—forms a symmetrical structure of admirable consistency.

The Three-Part Fugue, improvised at Potsdam, opens the series of movements. The Six-Part Fugue, whose presence was expected in

[1] See H. T. David, "The Structure of Musical Collections up to 1750," in *Bulletin of the American Musicological Society*, No. 3.
[2] See chapter VII, pp. 89-96.

34

the work, concludes it, so that the suspense is maintained to the end. The Sonata, most extended of the compositions contained in the work, stands in the center. The Canons upon the Royal Theme, forming a group of five smaller numbers, make their appearance between the opening Fugue and the Sonata. The Canonic Elaborations of the Royal Theme, forming another group of five smaller numbers, find their place between the Sonata and the concluding Fugue. Thus a five-part symmetry is established. The first part corresponds to the last, the second to the fourth, while the third is self-contained:

I. *Ricercar a 3*	No. 1	A⌐
II. Five canons	Nos. 2-6	B⌐
III. Sonata	No. 7	C⌐
IV. Five canons	Nos. 8-12	B⌐
V. *Ricercar a 6*	No. 13	A⌐

The relationship between the *Ricercari* is evident. The similarity of form is emphasized by the correspondence of thematic material. The *Ricercar a 6*, however, is so much richer and more carefully worked out than the *Ricercar a 3* that the six-part composition appears almost as the crowning fulfilment of promises contained in the three-part antecedent.

The Sonata is symmetrical in itself. The extended opening *Largo* is balanced by the shorter *Andante* and second *Allegro* together. The first *Allegro* thus is pushed into the very center of the structure. This free double fugue, which combines the Royal theme with a subject of its own, is built up in five sections. The first and second are roughly parallel to each other. The fourth and fifth are strict recapitulations of the first and second. The third contrasts in style and technique with all the others. In the course of the middle section, the theme peculiar to this movement makes its unique entrance in the bass, accenting the exact center of the section as well as of the movement. The symmetry of the entire work is thus mirrored in its center piece.[3]

Both canon groups are built around a center which consists of three pieces in systematic progression.

The three-piece center of the first canon group is formed by:

(1) a canon at the unison   (No. 3)
(2) a canon in contrary motion   (No. 4)
(3) a canon in contrary motion and augmentation   (No. 5)

---

[3] For further details, see the analysis of this movement, pp. 115-122.

The first of these canons represents the simplest available form of
a canon; the second contains a single element of contrapuntal complication; the third contains two such elements combined. Thus a
series results which may be said to correspond to the mathematical
series of simple number, square, and cube. Apparently it was the
wish to establish a progression as logical as this which impelled Bach
to proceed to a canon in both contrary motion and augmentation
without having first demonstrated the latter device alone.

The first piece in the first group of canons, No. 2, which precedes
the center group just described, employs the dotted rhythm of the
French overture or the *entrée*, making clear its function as an opening. The group is concluded by the Modulating Canon, No. 6, the
first of the more extended canonic forms to appear in the work; its
length and rhythmic vitality establish it as a real *finale*, a striking
counterpart to the opening *entrée*.

The three-piece center of the second canon group is formed by:

(1) a canon for two high instruments, entering simultaneously (No. 9)
(2) a - canon for two low instruments, entering at close
  time-distance   (No. 10)
(3) a canon for two high and two low instruments, entering at the distance of a full phrase   (No. 11)

Two principles of connection are employed in this group. On the
one hand, the third piece employs the same instruments as the first
and second together; thus a progression is formed which corresponds
to the simple pattern: $2+2=4$. On the other hand, the distance between the canonic voices increases from nought, through an inter-
mediary stage, that of a *stretto*, to the greatest obtainable within a
canon, that of the full length of the theme or the first complete
phrase in the opening part; thus a progress in three stages, leading
from one extreme to the opposite, is realized. In the original edition,
these three numbers are presented as puzzle canons, which emphasizes
their inner connection.

The opening and concluding pieces of this second canon group,
Nos. 8 and 12, are closely related, instead of being contrasted as
were the opening and concluding numbers of the first canon group.
No. 8 is the Mirror Canon, No. 12 the Canonic Fugue. Both are
canons for two high instruments with a thorough-bass. Both introduce two different groups of entries of the Royal theme, separated
by an episode. The parallelism of the pieces is made even more strik-

ing by the fact that the thorough-bass lines of both begin in identical manner. The thorough-bass lines of both, furthermore, refer to the theme at the end of the second group of entries. Since the two numbers are so similar, they seem to form a symmetrical frame around the center group.

Both canon groups consist of a center triad of pieces flanked by slightly more detached numbers. This correspondence of structure is strengthened by certain details. The first number in both groups is called *canon perpetuus;* the second is in both a canon at the unison; the third, a canon in contrary motion; and the last, an extended canon at the fifth. There are no other canons at the unison or the fifth in the *Musical Offering,* nor is a third number classified as infinite; and the other canons in contrary motion are clearly distinguished from those set in relation to each other, for one (No. 5) employs augmentation as well as inversion and the other (No. 8) interrupts the continuity of the canonic line by changes of the inversion-pivot. Thus the interrelations between the two canon groups are clearly set into relief.

Bach never created a finer or richer system of relations between the parts of a collection—the *Musical Offering* is one of the greatest examples of a multiple work unified by a comprehensive structure.[4]

---

[4] It will be noticed that the plan of the work as described above is partly emphasized and supplemented by thematic relations. The discussion of the Royal theme and its variations (chapter II, pp. 16-20) has shown that the theme appears in its original form at the beginning and end of the work. Thus the correspondence between the two *Ricercari* is increased. The Sonata offers the theme first in a practically unvaried diminution and then in its most extreme variation, uniting the point of departure for variation and the climax of variation in one number, although not in one movement.

The progress in variation from the opening *Ricercar* to the first canons is so slight that continuity is assured. The first three canons (Nos. 2-4) are held on the same level of variation; thus a close connection is established between the *entrée* and the structurally separated first canons of the center of the group. The last two canons of the group (Nos. 5-6) are similarly held on the same level; thus the end of the center group is tied up with the *finale* of the set. It is significant that the most conspicuous increase in variation takes place between the second and third number of the three-piece center (Nos. 4 and 5), or at the place where the coherence between pieces is most fully warranted by contrapuntal means.

The opening and concluding numbers of the second group of canons (Nos. 8 and 12), which are strikingly related in structure, use entirely unrelated forms of the theme; the variation used in the opening number refers back to the last canon of the first group, while the concluding number anticipates the thematic level of the last *Ricercar.* The three-piece center of this group (Nos. 9-11) presents by itself an increase in variation, thus achieving an even closer connection

SCOPE

WHEN BACH wrote the *Musical Offering,* six of his works seem to have already been in print. One of these was a cantata written in his youth for the inauguration of councillors of a town in Thuringia and published for their glory, not for the composer's. It was only in 1726 that he could begin to have compositions of his own choice printed. The works which he began to publish in that year amounted, together, to a survey of the contemporary forms of instrumental music.

First came a series of partitas, or suites. With the title *Clavier-Übung* ("Keyboard Practice"), Bach issued, year after year, a single partita, each with a different type of opening movement. When there were six of them, he collected them into one volume, his *Opus I.*

A Second Part of the *Clavier-Übung* followed. It included the little-known *Overture in the French Manner* and the popular *Concerto in the Italian Style.* Both represented forms which had grown up in music for orchestra, or rather for a large ensemble of instruments. The first was a reproduction of the French orchestra suite, the second of the Italian concerto for orchestra with either a single solo instrument or a *concertino* of several solo instruments. Both, however, were conceived and written for a harpsichord with two keyboards; both were, accordingly, adaptations of forms, not arrangements of particular pieces.

A Third Part of the *Clavier-Übung* presented music for organ. Here the forms of sacred keyboard music were reviewed. The work contained a *toccata* in the manner of Buxtehude and a *ricercar* in that of Frescobaldi, various types of chorale fantasies, and a series of free two-part organ pieces.

Another *Clavier-Übung*—often referred to as a Fourth Part, but not thus designated in the original edition—offered the *Goldberg Variations.* In this publication the "fantasy upon a ground" found its

---

of the three numbers than is assured by structural relations. The first piece of this center (No. 9) points forward toward the concluding number of the entire group (No. 12), the third piece of the center (No. 11) backward toward the opening number of the group (No. 8); thus the frame is connected with the center of the group although neither the opening nor the concluding number is in its thematic aspect related to the neighboring canon.

most impressive and diversified elaboration. Thus another instrumental form was represented. The work had been commissioned for a particular purpose, but while Bach fulfilled the wish of a sponsor, he seized the occasion to further a plan that had occupied him for years.

A single group of instrumental forms had not been touched upon by the four parts of the *Clavier-Übung:* those developed in chamber music, or rather music for a small ensemble of instruments. This field is represented by the *Musical Offering.* The work covers the three forms: sonata, *ricercar,* and canon. Each of these was commonly used in music for a few solo instruments. Thus the survey of instrumental music contained in the parts of the *Clavier-Übung* was supplemented and completed by the *Musical Offering.*

The sonata was the most popular form in the field of music for a few solo instruments. It originated in this field and was transplanted into that of solo keyboard music only at the end of the 17th century. Quite fittingly, a sonata occupies the center of Bach's one comprehensive work that illustrates the forms of chamber music.

The *ricercar* was used in both fields. The masters of the seventeenth century wrote *ricercari* for ensembles of instruments as well as for organ or harpsichord. *Ricercari* by Adrian Willaert, Andrea Gabrieli, and others were published in parts. Thus the term could be used for chamber music, in contrast to *fuga,* which might appear within sonatas, but was not used separately in music for several instruments.

The canon occurred in vocal as well as instrumental music, in music for ensemble as well as for a solo keyboard instrument. In the last years of his life, Bach showed a particular fondness for writing canons. Thus only one of his works published after 1735 failed to include canons. The Third Part of the *Clavier-Übung* contained a few canonically treated chorales. Another publication by Bach, the *Canonic Variations on the Christmas Song "Vom Himmel hoch da komm ich her",* for organ—issued presumably in 1747, shortly before the *Musical Offering*—demonstrated systematically the canonic treatment of the chorale fantasy; it contained, like the *Musical Offering,* pieces in which the *cantus firmus* was flanked by canonic counterpoints, as well as canonic elaborations of the *cantus firmus* itself. The *Goldberg Variations,* furthermore, included a complete series of canons at various intervals, beginning with the unison and working up stepwise to the ninth. To these canons for organ and for harpsichord, the *Musical Offering* added examples for concerted instruments. Instruments are specified in two, the *Canon a 2 Violini in unisono*, No. 3, and the Mirror Canon, No. 8, which was published in separate parts for Flute, Violin, and Continuo. The other canons, though lacking instrumental specification, were apparently also intended for an ensemble of instruments, for some of them, including the very first, are so spaced that they cannot be executed completely by a single player on the harpsichord or piano.

The canons in the *Musical Offering* cover almost the entire field of canonic art. But Bach evidently did not intend to give a complete systematic demonstration of canonic writing, for he included neither a canon in augmentation, uninverted, nor did he use intervals other than the unison, octave, double octave, and fifth in the canons in parallel motion, or pivots other than the third and the fifth scale-degrees in the canons in contrary motion. Apparently he was reluctant to repeat himself. He had expanded the series of intervals in the *Goldberg Variations;* he did not write another canon at the second, fourth, sixth, or ninth. In the *Canonic Variations on the Christmas Song "Vom Himmel hoch da komm ich her,"* he had exploited the various pivots suitable for canons in contrary motion; there we find also the uninverted canon in augmentation which is so conspicuously missing in the *Musical Offering*. In the *Musical Offering* he furnished so great a variety of patterns that a certain impression of completeness is created, but completeness in a theoretical sense was beyond the scope of the work.

INTEGRATION

THE FIRST IMPULSE for the composition of the *Musical Offering* had been given by an improvisation. When Bach worked out the series of movements, he was, it seems, inspired by a procedure which he had for decades used in improvisation. Forkel, in discussing Bach the organist, gives the following account, inserted here in the old translation: [1]

When John Seb. Bach seated himself at the organ, when there was no divine service, which he was often requested to do, by strangers, he used to choose some subject, and to execute it, in all the various forms of organ composition, so that the subject constantly remained the ground-

[1] *Life of John Sebastian Bach*, pp. 36-37.

work of his performance, even if he had played, without intermission, for two hours or more. First, he used this theme for a prelude and a fugue, with all the stops. Then he shewed his art of using the stops, for a trio, a quartet, etc., always upon the same subject. Afterwards followed Psalm tunes [*i.e.*, chorales] the melody of which was intermingled in the most diversified manner, with the original subject, in three or four parts. Finally, the conclusion was made by a fugue, with all the stops, in which either another treatment only of the first subject predominated, or one, or according to its nature, two others were mixed with it.

The description Forkel gives of Bach's non-liturgical improvisations reminds one vividly of the *Musical Offering*. Here, too, a single subject is drawn upon in a long series of independent pieces. Here, too, a fugue, although without prelude, opens the series of elaborations, and another fugue, more richly endowed, concludes it. And no less than fourteen movements of two, three, or four parts are inserted between the fugues to show off Bach's power of imagination. Thus the *Musical Offering* presents itself as a series of fantasies upon one theme corresponding to those series of improvisations which Bach was wont to offer to his admirers.

In his improvisations, Bach followed a tradition of long standing. During a visit to Hamburg in 1720, according to the obituary by C. P. E. Bach and J. F. Agricola, Bach extemporized on the chorale "*An Wasserflüssen Babylons*" for almost half an hour in various ways, "exactly as the good old organists of Hamburg used to do during the Saturday vespers."[2] Among his listeners was a pupil of a pupil of the great Jan Pieters Sweelinck, Jan Adams Reincken, then almost a hundred years old. Reincken, who was a good organist and composer himself, paid Bach this compliment: "I thought that this art was dead, but I see that it still lives in you."[3] Forkel asserts that the particular type of improvisation which he describes in the passage quoted above was the "art, which old Reincken, at Hamburg, considered as being already lost in his time, but which, as he afterwards found, not only lived in John Sebastian Bach, but had attained through him, the highest degree of perfection".[4]

If Bach indulged in elaborating a single subject in improvisations that might last twice as long as the whole *Musical Offering*, it is highly probable that he also envisioned, or at least would not have

[2] See *Bach-Jahrbuch*, 1920, p. 19.
[3] *Life of John Sebastian Bach*, p. 13.
[4] *Ibid.*, p. 37.

objected to, complete performances of the work. He had written the *Goldberg Variations* to be played singly upon occasion, but had not failed to indicate, by an *Aria da capo* at the end, that he wished complete performance as well. The *Musical Offering*, like the *Goldberg Variations*, unfolds its grandeur of conception only when the complete series of compositions is heard in succession; the work deserves to be thus presented.

Bach himself considered the *Musical Offering* as a whole. He expressed this, though somewhat cryptically, by an acrostic which, in the copy of the work sent to King Frederick, was written on the page preceding the first page of music; it was later engraved, printed on small strips of paper, and appears in all ordinary copies of the original edition on the page preceding the bulk of the canon notations, as follows: [5]

Regis Iusſu Cantio Et Reliqua Canonica Arte Reſoluta.

("At the King's Command, the Song and the Remainder Resolved with Canonic Art")

In this inscription, the word *cantio* ("melody" or "song") may have been intended to refer either to the theme given to Bach by King Frederick, or to the six-part fugue Bach had failed to extemporize. The word was occasionally used for compositions of various kinds, including *cantiones mutae* (instrumental "songs without words"). Bach probably meant to allude to the fugue rather than the theme.

Cantio et reliqua evidently cover the whole work, whether *cantio* be interpreted as hinting at the Royal theme only, or the six-part fugue. Accordingly the inscription is properly inserted before the first piece of music, as in the dedicatory copy, not before the canons, as in later copies of the first edition.

The words *canonica arte* are—perhaps intentionally—ambiguous. They could be interpreted, in a musical sense, as referring to the "art of canon writing"; or they might simply have reference to the more general meaning of the word *canon*—that is, strict rule.

Resoluta may be taken as applying to *cantio* as well as to *reliqua:*

everything is worked out as if a definite problem had been "solved"—a thought which seems to underly Bach's conception of his art.

The initial letters of the eight words of the inscription form the word RICERCAR; thus the title that had been given to the fugues is repeated here to designate the entire work.

Throughout the *Musical Offering*, the reader, performer, or listener is to search for the Royal theme in all its forms. The entire work, therefore, is a *ricercar* in the original, literal sense of the word. The *ricercar* of the seventeenth-century composers, furthermore, was often made up of several sections using the basic theme in various ways. Bach's "St. Anne" Fugue is such a *ricercar* in several sections, each of which uses a different form of the common subject. The *Musical Offering* similarly consists of various sections using the same theme in changing shapes and diversified treatment. In this respect, too, the work is appropriately called a *ricercar*.

Still, Bach's use of the word is astonishing. A *ricercar*, however many sections it included, was one composition, consisting of connected movements, while the *Musical Offering* presented itself as a series of thirteen clearly separated compositions. But to Bach, the coherence between the sections apparently seemed just as strong as their physical separation; and thus he could refer to the entire work as a *ricercar*—indicating that it lived in his mind as if it were a single composition of complete continuity, a perfectly unified whole.

V

INSTRUMENTATION

ORIGINAL INDICATIONS

ALTHOUGH THE *Musical Offering* was obviously written for instrumental performance, Bach specified in only a few of the movements the particular instruments that were to be used.

The Sonata was conceived for flute, violin, and figured bass. According to the practice of the time, an accompaniment was to be improvised from the figured bass on a harpsichord or other keyboard instrument. The bass line was preferably, though not necessarily, to be reinforced by a violoncello or a *viola da gamba*. It is even more important nowadays than in Bach's time to have a string instrument play the bass line, in addition to the keyboard instrument, because we are less accustomed to hearing polyphonic music than were Bach's contemporaries. For the accompaniment, a piano or harpsichord may be used, but it should be played throughout in such a way as not to obscure the obbligato voices.

For the Canons, performing instruments are specified in only two instances. In the Canon at the Unison, No. 3, the canonic parts are two violins; the Mirror Canon, No. 8, is written for the same combination as the Sonata. In the other canonic sections of the work, the choice of instruments was left to the performer. This was common practice up to Bach's time. On the title pages of early German publications, we read again and again *Auf allerley Instrumenten lieblich zu spielen* ("suitable for playing on all kinds of instruments"). The canons in the *Musical Offering* could similarly be played on any available instruments.

The *Ricercari* bear no explicit verbal indication of the instruments by which they might suitably be played.

The Three-Part *Ricercar* was improvised on a keyboard instrument and published in keyboard notation, on two staves. As a composition for a keyboard instrument, it forms a direct continuation of the *Clavier-Übung*. The instrument on which it was improvised was a *pianoforte* with hammer mechanism. This early *pianoforte* had a rather limited dynamic range, but, within its limits *crescendi* and *decrescendi* could be produced. The Three-Part *Ricercar* apparently takes the limited dynamic possibilities of the instrument into consideration, but it neither requires nor invites the application of a *crescendo* or *decrescendo*. Its style is essentially that of harpsichord music, based on definite contrasts of sonority or tone color rather than continuous transitions. In any case, it is better suited for a harpsichord than a modern piano. When played on the latter, its sonority should be kept rather close to a medium level.

As we have seen, the *Musical Offering* represented forms characteristic of concerted chamber music, and certain of the movements are so designed that they could not be played otherwise than by an ensemble of instruments. It would seem likely, therefore, that any other composition included in the work could also be played by an ensemble of solo instruments. This is indeed the case with the Three-Part *Ricercar*, which makes as fine a show-piece of ensemble playing as does any of the movements for which ensemble presentation is prescribed or suggested by the composer.

The Six-Part *Ricercar*, too, was written by Bach in keyboard notation. It was evidently meant to be playable on a keyboard instrument without pedals, for even in two-hand execution it does not contain intervals larger than an octave to be played with one hand. It can, accordingly, be performed by a single player on a harpsichord or piano. Its solemn character makes it even more appropriate to the organ; in playing the composition on the organ, one may give the lowest part mostly to the pedals, which makes the manual parts easier and clarifies the contrapuntal structure.

On the other hand, the Six-Part *Ricercar* was published in open score, presumably in compliance with the wishes or instructions of Bach himself. Bach may have wanted presentation of the *Ricercar a 6* in open score because the contrapuntal structure of the composition could thus be studied more easily than in keyboard notation. On the other hand, score notation simplified the task of extracting parts for performance by an ensemble of instruments, and this was possibly Bach's main purpose in having the piece printed in this form. Bach's use of score notation points back to Frescobaldi, as does his use of certain stylistic patterns and of the title *ricercar*. Some of Frescobaldi's works, including the *Fiori musicali*, of which Bach owned a copy, were printed in score. They were all intended *da sonare con ogni sorte di stromenti, da tasti ed altri* ("to be played by all manner of instruments, keyboard or otherwise"), or simply, as the *Fiori musicali* stated, "*per sonatori*", for players. They could, in other words, be played by an ensemble of instruments as well as on a single keyboard instrument. They were contrasted, on the one hand, with compositions exclusively for a keyboard instrument, which were printed in tablature, and, on the other hand, with those intended exclusively for an ensemble of instruments, which were printed in separate part-books. We may assume that the same intention was behind Bach's use of the score for the Six-Part *Ricercar:* he wanted it to be suitable for an ensemble of instruments as well as for a single keyboard instrument.

PERFORMANCE OF SINGLE MOVEMENTS

ANY OF THE THIRTEEN compositions in the *Musical Offering*, when performed singly, can be played on any instruments or combinations of instruments that have the proper range.

A single keyboard instrument suffices to play the two *Ricercari*, for which keyboard notation is provided in our edition beneath the score. Most canons are hard to play, harder to make clear, and some are even impossible, on a piano. The two-part Canon in Contrary Motion, No. 10, is comparatively easy; it makes a splendid exercise in clef-reading. The Crab Canon, No. 9, might be played on an instrument with two keyboards; one part should be played an octave lower than written, with a transposing stop ("4-foot"). The three-part canons can effectively be presented on an organ with two manuals and pedal.

There is a manuscript of the Canonic Fugue, No. 12, which, in Carl Philipp Emanuel Bach's hand, bears the words "*Fürs obligate Clavir und eine Violine*" ("for an obbligato keyboard instrument and a violin"); and another gives the same composition in a similar arrangement for flute or violin and obbligato keyboard instrument. All the three-part movements in the *Musical Offering* can be performed in similar fashion with two parts on the piano and one on any other instrument at hand (violin, flute, recorder, viola, violoncello, etc.). Such a combination corresponds to those constantly employed by Bach, as his sonatas for obbligato harpsichord with violin, with flute, with *viola da gamba* prove.

All the movements of the work can be performed by an ensemble of solo instruments. Nowadays, ensembles of string instruments are most easily available. The part books of this edition are so arranged that the four String parts together with the Flute part cover the entire work. The Flute part contains the pieces designated for flute by Bach himself—the Sonata, No. 7, and the Mirror Canon, No. 8—and, in addition, the Canonic Fugue, No. 12. If one wants to perform the Sonata with two violins—which should be done in informal presentation only—the first violin will use the Flute part, and the second violin the Violin I part. A similar shift of parts, however, is not necessary for the performance of the Mirror Canon and the Canonic Fugue with two violins, the appropriate parts for Violin I and Violin II being found in their books.

The keyboard accompaniment of the Sonata, No. 7, and the Mirror Canon, No. 8, is prescribed by Bach. In the Canonic Fugue, No. 12, it has been added by the editor; if the piece is played singly, the accompaniment may be omitted. For all these three numbers, the accompaniment will be found in the score, no separate part being provided for the keyboard player.

The following combinations are needed to perform any given section of the work, the designations of the instruments conforming with those used for the separate parts (it should be noted that the parts for Violas I and II appear together in the Viola book, and similarly the parts for Violoncello I and II in the Violoncello book):

Two instruments	Violin I and Violin II	No. 9
	Viola and Violoncello	No. 10
Three instruments	Violin I, Viola, and Violoncello	Nos. 1, 2, 5, and 6
	Violin I, Violin II, and Viola	No. 4 .
	Violin I, Violin II, and Violoncello	Nos. 3 and 12
Four instruments	Flute and Violin I (or Violins I and II), Violoncello, and Piano or Harpsichord	Nos. 7, 8, and 12
	Violin I, Violin II, Viola, and Violoncello	No. 11
Six instruments	Violin I, Violin II, Violas I and II, Violoncellos I and II	No. 13

A small string orchestra may be used to perform the *Ricercari*, Nos. 1 and 13, and the first group of Canons, Nos. 2 to 6. The second group of Canons, Nos. 8 to 12, may also be similarly performed, but such performance will prove technically and stylistically difficult. The Sonata, No. 7, should always be performed with an ensemble of solo instruments. The Six-Part *Ricercar* is magnificently suited for performance by a string orchestra or, more properly speaking, with several instruments to a part. The effect will be heightened by the discreet use of a double-bass, indications for which will be found in the Violoncello II book.

The success of a performance of the Six-Part *Ricercar* with string orchestra depends largely on the proper balance of parts. Each part should be able to stand out above the others wherever the contrapuntal structure calls for it. The six sections of the string orchestra must therefore be of equal power. It will be found useful to have more second violins than first. The total number of violins should be determined by the number of violoncellos at hand and especially by the strength of the viola sections.

A good balance may be achieved by combinations like this:

(I)	(II)	(III)
3 Violin I	5 Violin I	8 Violin I
4 Violin II	6 Violin II	10 Violin II
3 Viola I	4 Viola I	6 Viola I
3 Viola II	4-5 Viola II	7 Viola II
1-2 Violoncello I	3 Violoncello I	4 Violoncello I
1 Violoncello II	2 Violoncello II	3 Violoncello II
1 Double-Bass	1 Double-Bass	1 Double-Bass

COMPLETE PERFORMANCE

INTEGRATED PRESENTATION of the *Musical Offering* requires special consideration in the choice of instruments. First, there should, if possible, be no substitute for an instrument expressly indicated by Bach; therefore a flute is essential for correct presentation of the entire work. Second, careful balance of the voices is of the greatest importance for a complete performance; therefore the pieces with a thorough-bass should by all means be played with a violoncello in addition to the keyboard bass, even if one may leave out the violoncello in an occasional informal reading of the Sonata, No. 7, and the Mirror Canon, No. 8. Third, corresponding pieces should be performed in similar manner; therefore, the same combination of instruments should be used for the Canonic Fugue, No. 12, as for its counterpart, the Mirror Canon, No. 8: flute, violin, violoncello, and accompanying keyboard instrument, the latter, in that case, being obligatory.

FIRST SUGGESTION
Flute and Solo Strings, with Keyboard Accompaniment

If the series of movements is to appear as a whole, its instrumentation must be consistent. As the Sonata can be played only with solo instruments, the work in its entirety is best performed by an ensemble of solo instruments throughout. No doubt the easiest type of performance to organize is that with flute, two violins, two violas, two violoncellos, and harpsichord or piano. The instrumentation of the movements will then be as follows:

No. 1. Three-Part *Ricercar* — Violin I, Viola, and Violoncello
No. 2. Canon at the Double Octave — Violin I, Viola, and Violoncello
No. 3. Canon at the Unison — Violin I, Violin II, and Violoncello
No. 4. Canon in Contrary Motion — Violin I, Violin II, and Viola
No. 5. Canon in Augmentation and Contrary Motion — Violin I, Viola, and Violoncello
No. 6. Modulating Canon — Violin I, Viola, and Violoncello
No. 7. Trio Sonata — Flute, Violin I, Violoncello, and Harpsichord or Piano
No. 8. Mirror Canon — Flute, Violin I, Violoncello, and Harpsichord or Piano
No. 9. Crab Canon — Violin I and Violin II
No. 10. Canon in Contrary Motion — Viola and Violoncello
No. 11. Four-Part Canon — Violin I, Violin II, Viola, and Violoncello
No. 12. Canonic Fugue — Flute, Violin I, Violoncello, and Harpsichord or Piano
No. 13. Six-Part *Ricercar* — Violin I, Violin II, Violas I and II, Violoncellos I and II

SECOND SUGGESTION
Solo Keyboard Instrument, Flute, Solo Strings, and String Orchestra

The Three-Part *Ricercar* was originally designed for a solo keyboard instrument, and one might feel reluctant to entrust this composition tu an instrumental ensemble. If it is played on a keyboard instrument, however, a definite break will be felt between the opening *Ricercar* and the following Canons. This break can be balanced if a similar break is made between the last Canon and the concluding Six-Part *Ricercar*. The necessary second change is strikingly effected by the introduction of a string orchestra for the Six-Part *Ricercar*. In this case the homogeneity of instrumentation provided by the first suggestion is renounced in favor of a definite progression in three steps. Such performance requires, as solo instruments, flute, two violins, viola, violoncello, and harpsichord or piano, together with a string orchestra of two violin groups, two viola groups, two violoncello groups, and a double-bass *ad lib*. The instruments would be used as follows:

First level	No. 1. Three-Part *Ricercar*	Harpsichord or Piano solo
Second level	Nos. 2-6. Canons No. 7. Trio Sonata Nos. 8-12. Canons	Ensemble of solo instruments as above
Third level	No. 13. Six-Part *Ricercar*	String Orchestra

THIRD SUGGESTION

*Flute, Reed Instruments, and Solo Strings, with
Keyboard Accompaniment*

The intricate contrapuntal structure of some movements in the *Musical Offering* is difficult to grasp, especially at a single hearing. The comprehension of the work becomes considerably easier if a combination of contrasting instruments is used rather than a homogeneous string ensemble. The use of such a combination is particularly recommended for concert performance of the work or for broadcasting.

Contrasting instrumental colors are most conspicuously displayed in the instrumental portions of Bach's cantatas or in concertos like the second *Brandenburg*, which employs flute, oboe, trumpet, and violin as solo instruments. In choosing such combinations, Bach followed a Renaissance tradition which persisted longer in Germany than in other countries, as can be seen in such works as Johann Heinrich Schmelzer's sonatas for 2 trumpets, 2 violins, and 4 viols, with figured bass, and for *cornettino*, 3 trombones, violin, and 3 viols, with figured bass (published 1662); Matthias Weckmann's sonatas for *cornettino*, violin, bassoon, and trombone with *basso continuo* (written before 1674); and Johann Rosenmüller's sonata for violin and bassoon with *basso continuo* (published 1682). Organ builders and players up to Bach's time, particularly in Germany, also relied chiefly on contrasting stops or colors for rendering the polyphonic music of the period.

A combination of strings and wood-winds is sufficient to set all the sections of the *Musical Offering* into proper relief. Best results are obtained with a combination of double-reed instruments and strings. This combination produces a remarkably transparent embodiment of the contrapuntal structure and a tone color typical of Bach's own orchestration. Bach had four main reed instruments at his disposal: the oboe; the *oboe d'amore*, a minor third lower than the regular oboe; the *oboe da caccia*, a fifth lower than the regular oboe; and the bassoon. The oboe and bassoon, in somewhat improved form, are still in common use. The range of the *oboe da caccia* is accessible to the related English horn. The *oboe d'amore*, unfortunately, is only occasionally available, and hardly ever in specimens of satisfactory intonation.

The Six-Part *Ricercar* calls for a differentiation of instrumental colors more urgently than does any other number in the *Musical Offering*. The parts are best given to oboe, violin, English horn, viola, bassoon, and violoncello, in this order, descending from top to bottom of the score. Replacement of the oboe by a flute may seem feasible, but it hardly yields satisfactory results. Addition of a double-bass would upset the balance, which is logically based on the principle that each part should be entrusted to a single instrument. The combination of three reed instruments and three strings produces a sonority of particular beauty and a clarity considerably superior to that of a string ensemble without reeds.

The Canons upon the Royal Theme, Nos. 2-6, also profit greatly by performance with a mixed group of instruments. Here, the Royal theme is best enunciated by a reed instrument while the actual canon is played by strings. Accordingly the *cantus firmus* is given to the oboe in the Canon in Contrary Motion, No. 4; to the English horn in the Canon at the Double Octave, No. 2, the Canon in Augmentation and Contrary Motion, No. 5, and the Modulating Canon, No. 6; and to the bassoon in the Canon at the Unison, No. 3. An *oboe d'amore* is preferable to the English horn in the Modulating Canon, No. 6, because the end lies uncomfortably high for an English horn playing *forte*. The optional part for *oboe d'amore* is inserted in the Oboe book.

If a combination of strings and winds is employed, the entire series of movements should be played by an ensemble of solo instruments. Experience has proved that when the Three-Part *Ricercar* is played on a keyboard instrument, the gap between the sonority of the opening *Ricercar* and that of the following canons for three instruments is too great to be bridged by the audience without difficulty. Accordingly it is recommended that the Three-Part *Ricercar* be performed by oboe, English horn, and bassoon, or, if the players of the high reed instruments are less efficient, by flute, viola, and bassoon. The introduction of wind instruments in the very first number not only prepares for their appearance in the following canons, but helps to establish clearly the correspondence between the opening and the concluding *Ricercar*.[1]

The Canonic Elaborations of the Royal Theme, Nos. 8 to 12, can be performed with flute, strings, and an accompanying keyboard instrument and will be easily comprehended in such presentation. In the Sonata, No. 7, as well as in the canons for flute, violin, and thorough-bass, Nos. 8 and 12, the harpsichord will be found a more satisfactory accompanying instrument than the piano. This is particularly true of performances before the microphone.

Complete performance of the *Musical Offering* with a combination of strings and winds requires flute, oboe (preferably alternating with *oboe d'amore*), bassoon, two violins, viola, violoncello, and harpsichord or piano. Complete parts for performance with this combination are provided in the set of parts issued with this edition. The instruments are employed as follows:

No. 1. Three-Part *Ricercar*	Oboe, English Horn, and Bassoon
No. 2. Canon at the Double Octave	English Horn, Violin I, and Violoncello
No. 3. Canon at the Unison	Bassoon, Violin I, and Violin II
No. 4. Canon in Contrary Motion	Oboe, Violin II, and Viola

[1] Performance of the Three-Part *Ricercar* with a keyboard instrument is more correct historically, while artistically the performance with three instruments, which achieves greater consistency of instrumentation, deserves preference. The situation described, however, changes somewhat when a performance is transmitted through a microphone, for, in that case, the delicate sound of the harpsichord can be amplified to match that of the ensembles called upon to perform the canons following the opening *Ricercar a 3*.

No. 5. Canon in Augmentation and Contrary Motion	English Horn, Violin I, and Violoncello
No. 6. Modulating Canon	*Oboe d'Amore* or English Horn, Viola, and Violoncello
No. 7. Trio Sonata	Flute, Violin I, Violoncello, and Harpsichord or Piano
No. 8. Mirror Canon	Flute, Violin I, Violoncello, and Harpsichord or Piano
No. 9. Crab Canon	Violin I and Violin II
No. 10. Canon in Contrary Motion	Viola and Violoncello
No. 11. Four-Part Canon	Violin I, Violin II, Viola, and Violoncello
No. 12. Canonic Fugue	Flute, Violin I, Violoncello, and Harpsichord or Piano
No. 13. Six-Part *Ricercar*	Oboe, English Horn, Bassoon, Violin I, Viola, and Violoncello

VI

INTERPRETATION

GENERAL REMARKS

MARKS OF INTERPRETATION were introduced into musical notation at a comparatively late date, and their use spread rather slowly. They are rarely found in the compositions of Bach's predecessors or of most of his contemporaries. Bach occasionally furnished more detailed indications, particularly of phrasing, but even he left decisions on interpretation largely to the performer.

Why the old masters failed to indicate their wishes concerning interpretation is a matter of speculation. At that time musicians largely performed works by contemporaries—music in a style with which they were thoroughly familiar. Nevertheless, the composer who left the task of interpretation of a work almost completely to the performer could not hope for a satisfactory result unless the task of interpretation itself was comparatively simple—the lack of interpretative marks in old music, however it may be explained, suggests either that a none too elaborate interpretation was required or that the interpretation was expected to proceed along well-established lines.

During certain periods, the performer was expected to add embellishments or even to improvise a fully harmonized accompaniment from nothing but a bass with figures. Numerous textbooks explained the technique to be used in such cases. But questions like those of phrasing or the differentiation of sonorities, hardly ever touched upon in theoretical works, did not seem to offer problems requiring much consideration. This seems to indicate that, up to Bach's time, interpretation was in these latter matters meant to be rather plain and straightforward.

The detailed and often rather fancy differentiation particularly

of sonority applied to Bach's works in most modern performances is an outgrowth of romantic methods of interpretation. The deliberate or unconscious modernization of Bach's music apparently originated when, after a period of complete neglect, his compositions were revived at the beginning of the nineteenth century. It grew rather steadily for more than a century before a purist movement began to counteract it.

Most reprints of Bach's works are loaded with additions by the editor. For decades no distinction was made between the original text and the editor's share. Accordingly there are still many musicians who do not realize whether in their interpretation they follow Bach's own expressed will or an editor's whim. In the accompanying score, a clear distinction between original text and editorial additions has been made wherever feasible; the facsimiles included in this book—reproductions of pages from the chief sources of the work—will help the reader to realize how detailed a typical manuscript or edition from Bach's last period was.[1]

TEMPO

IN THE ORIGINAL EDITION of the *Musical Offering*, tempo indications are given only to the four movements of the Sonata. The choice of tempo for the other numbers is left to the performer, exactly as is the choice of instruments. However, the compass within which the tempo of any number from the *Musical Offering* can actually vary is quite limited.

Bach himself hinted at the appropriate tempo of the various movements through his time signatures. How definitely a tempo may be indicated by a time signature can be seen in the Sonata, where the use of 2/4 and 6/8 for the second and fourth movements would have sufficed to mark these movements as fast, even if Bach had not specified the tempo. All the other sections of the work are couched in duple time, in the three forms: **C** (4/4), **₵** (2/2), and **₵** (4/2). It should be noted that, in the *Musical Offering*, 2/2 meter prevails considerably over 4/4.

No matter how fast or slow the tempo chosen for the canons, they will stand out clearly as splendid examples of contrapuntal artistry.

[1] For a list of facsimiles see the table of contents, p. xi.

But only when played in certain tempi do they unfold their deeper meaning. Each movement in this work has a specific expressive character or, as Bach's contemporaries would have said, *Affect;* it is this quality which determines the tempo. The sequence of movements in complete performance limits the choice of tempi still further, for even slight deviation from what appears to be the inherent relation between the movements disrupts the continuity of the series. In addition, the tempo will be found to depend partly on the choice of instruments. The *Ricercari* require a faster tempo on the piano, and particularly on the harpsichord, than on the organ or when played by an ensemble of instruments. The Three-Part *Ricercar* may be played as fast as the passages in triplets of eighth-notes can be executed unhurriedly; in this respect the woodwinds will encounter greater difficulties than the strings. The Six-Part *Ricercar,* on the other hand, may be played rather slowly, so long as the broad contrapuntal lines are sustained properly and a continuous rhythmic flow is maintained. Here the organ has an advantage over the piano or harpsichord, and the combination of strings and woodwinds over an ensemble of solo strings, while the string orchestra may adopt an even broader tempo than the mixed group of solo instruments.

Bach himself liked fast tempi. "As a conductor," the obituary states, "he was very accurate and very sure of the tempo, which, in his choice, usually was very lively."[1] "In the execution of his own pieces," Forkel comments, "he generally took the time very brisk, but contrived, besides this briskness, to introduce so much variety in his performance that under his hand every piece was, as it were, like a discourse."[2] Such information is worth remembering. Bach's compositions should certainly not just be rushed through as if they were technical studies or show-pieces for mere velocity. But their effect is equally impaired by the heavy, dragging style of performance that is still widely applied, particularly to his choral music.

The *Musical Offering* includes quite a few numbers that should clearly be treated as fast movements—*e.g.* the Canon at the Unison, No. 3, the Crab Canon, No. 9, the Canonic Fugue, No. 12, and, of course, the Allegros of the Sonata. How fast these movements may

---

[1] *Bach-Jahrbuch,* 1920, p. 24.

[2] *Life of John Sebastian Bach,* p. 29. For exact contemporary tempo indications, see R. Kirkpatrick, "Eighteenth-Century Metronomic Indications", in *Papers Read by Members of the American Musicological Society at Washington, D. C.,* 1938, pp. 30-50; and R. E. M. Harding, *Origins of Musical Time and Expression,* London, 1938.

be played depends, obviously, on the agility of the performers. The work should throughout not only sound clear and crisp to the minutest detail, but should also be presented with a certain ease and elegance, obtainable only if extremes of speed are avoided. Particularly the Mirror Canon, No. 8, calls for a certain restraint of speed as well as sonority.

Certain movements require a slower tempo than that which would seem appropriate at their opening. Among these are the Modulating Canon, No. 6, which becomes increasingly difficult in intonation as it ascends; the last movement of the Sonata, whose gradual development into continuous sixteenth-note motion determines the limits of its speed; and the Four-Part Canon, No. 11, which offers new problems of contrapuntal interpretation with each entering part. In each of these, the tempo should be so chosen that the most intricate sections can be executed gracefully.

Lightness and naturalness of interpretation depend largely on the proper handling of the metrical structure. The difference between light and heavy beats apparently was less striking up to Bach's time than it became afterwards. In performing early music we should strive to eliminate regular accents as far as possible—heavily accented beats make many performances of Bach's compositions unbearably pedestrian.

No composition should be imagined and executed in a unit smaller than that indicated by the time signature. This rule, evident as it may seem, is often neglected even by well-known musicians. Particularly the compositions designated by the time signature ¢

should definitely be conceived and played in two beats, not in four. The first movement of the Sonata should be performed in three, not in six; the first *Allegro* in two, not in four; the *Andante* in four, not in eight. The Six-Part *Ricercar* has four half-notes to a measure; this meter is chiefly distinguished from either 2/2 or 4/4 by a considerably greater evenness of beats. If a wrong metrical unit is chosen as the basis of a movement, the impression of a faulty tempo may result; in such cases the tempo is often quite appropriate while correction of the metrical conception is actually needed.

Sometimes it may even be helpful to imagine the music as if it were written in larger metrical units. Thus the Canon at the Unison, No. 3, the *Andante* of the Sonata, and the Four-Part Canon, No. 11, will sound more convincing if they seem to progress in half-notes rather than in quarters. Similarly, the first *Allegro* of the Sonata will have greater fluency if it is felt as moving in full measures (half-notes) rather than in half-measures (quarters).

It has become customary to end compositions by Bach and his contemporaries with a considerable slowing-down. In most compositions of this period, however, a *ritardando* at the end is superfluous. If the performance presents the last cadence boldly and with authority, no change of either tempo or sonority is required. There are instances in which the last cadence is clearly set off from the main part of the movement; in this case the cadence as a whole may be taken in a broader tempo, without further *ritardando*. But if the motifs and figures of a movement run without caesura or change into the cadence, any alteration of tempo would conflict with the character of the music itself.[3] Almost all cadences in the *Musical Offering* are of this type; a single exception was indicated by Bach himself by the word *adagio* at the end of the center section in the first *Allegro* of the Sonata.

Since there are so many determining factors in the choice of tempo, the author has not hesitated to include indications of tempo and even metronome markings in his edition. While they represent an attempt at a truly objective interpretation, they have been bracketed as editor's additions.

DYNAMICS

INDICATIONS OF SONORITY in compositions of the seventeenth and early eighteenth centuries usually consisted only of occasional antitheses of *forte* and *piano*. Giovanni Gabrieli used these terms to contrast sections of differing character in his *Sonata pian e forte* for *violino* (viola), *cornetto*, and six trombones, published in 1597.

---

[3] An interesting case appears in the concluding *Ricercar a 6*. Bach specifically marked the notes of the last chord as particularly long ones, while continuous motion without a break runs right up to the final harmony. The effect will be particularly striking if the measures containing the last entry of the Royal theme are played with very strict beat or even as if they were pressing forward—so presented, the final rest will enter with overwhelming power and can actually be held much longer than it could if one tried to prepare for it by a *ritenuto*. If the composition is played with woodwinds, the players should take breath before the last note. On the other hand, the measure preceding the last entry of the Royal theme (98), with its unusual cadential formula, seems to allow, or even to require, a slight broadening. The original tempo, however, should be restored as soon as the Royal theme re-enters.

Later the indication *piano* was mostly applied to repetitions of small particles, which thus were made to sound like echoes. This mannerism became quite popular during the seventeenth century, and organists like Jan Pieters Sweelinck wrote entire fantasies for organ "in the manner of echoes", that is with continuous repetitions of phrases in softer registration. Arcangelo Corelli often concluded movements, fast or slow, with a repetition of the last phrase in *piano*. Bach still employed the echo device; a delightful example is the last movement of his *Overture in the French Manner*.

Sonorities are specified just as rarely in Bach's work as in those of his predecessors and contemporaries. No indications of sonority are given in most of his compositions for keyboard instruments. A noteworthy exception is offered in the *Concerto in the Italian Style* and the *Overture in the French Manner*, which, written for a harpsichord with two keyboards, formed the Second Part of the *Clavier-Übung;* here Bach introduces *forte* and *piano* to mark contrasts of sonorities, *i.e.* of keyboards. In his chamber music, he uses indications of sonority almost exclusively to establish echo effects. In his concertos, he marks the entrance of the solo episodes by a *piano* in the accompanying instruments. In his vocal works, he similarly adds a *piano* to the instrumental parts whenever solo voices enter and restores the *forte* when the instruments are to play alone. Even in his most elaborate choral works this practice is only occasionally extended by markings like *pianissimo, un poco piano, mezzoforte;* or a *piano* in the vocal parts.

The contrast between *forte* and *piano* apparently was modest. Gabrieli used *forte* and *piano* simultaneously in different parts. Sometimes also Bach's compositions for the harpsichord simultaneously introduce voices in *piano* and in *forte*. Similar combinations are found in the *Musical Offering*.

The 1747 edition of the *Musical Offering* includes markings of sonority in but two of the sixteen movements: the *Largo* and *Andante* of the Sonata. In the *Largo*, a single *piano* is inserted in the *Violino* part, meas. 7, to assure a smooth ending of the phrase; neither the flute nor the *Continuo* takes any notice of this reduction of the violin's tone. The *Andante* is throughout based on a contrast of *forte* and *piano*. This contrast, carried out by flute and violin, is completely disregarded in the *Continuo* part, and at least once a *piano* occurs in the flute while the violin continues *forte*. The *piano* takes up only the very end of the preceding *forte* phrases, in sequence, not in repetition. Since the *piano* ending actually rounds off the *forte* phrase, the contrast should not be exaggerated.

If, in general, Bach fails to specify sonorities, how are we to interpret his music in this respect?

The Second Part of the *Clavier-Übung* offers perfect models of the treatment of sonorities. Contrasts of style and character are heightened by contrasts of sonority, while homogeneous sections, however large, are kept on the same dynamic level. Music of the seventeenth and eighteenth centuries was, in fact, based on contrasts throughout. Most compositions of the period consist of clearly separated sections, deliberately set off against each other by differences of treatment and orchestration. Craving for contrasts created the form of the *da capo* aria, the French overture, and the concerto, with their antitheses of instrumental or *tutti* sections on the one hand and solo episodes on the other. Contrasts similarly determined the fugue in its supreme form, based on the alternation of groups of subject entries and interludes or "episodes". Instruments with two or more keyboards like the organ or the harpsichord, both unable to produce any smooth transition, were bound to use contrasting colors for various sections, while even the orchestra, the body most susceptible of a more flexible treatment, was generally used to produce simply two levels of sound, by the division into a *concertino*, a small group of solo players, and a *concerto grosso*, a full body of doubling instruments. In interpreting music of the seventeenth and early eighteenth centuries, we should, accordingly, try to establish contrasts while keeping each section on a steady level.

All forms based on contrast, rather than on continuous development in a certain direction, make extended use of recapitulation. Bach employs recapitulation more generously and more consistently than do any of his contemporaries. He uses the same material or employs similar principles in sections distinctly separated or widely distant from each other. By creating an often quite intricate system of symmetrical or asymmetrical relations which bind all parts of the form together, he achieves unity of structure. The immense variety displayed in the lay-out of Bach's compositions is one of the prime sources of their unique interest. It is therefore of the utmost importance that the structure of these compositions be strongly set into relief. Proper application of dynamic contrasts is our chief means of clarifying and emphasizing the structural ground-plan of a composition. One way of emphasizing this ground-plan is to present identical sections or elements with the same dynamics wherever they appear, while sections contrasting in style or contrapuntal elaboration are presented with differing sonorities or contrasting tone colors. Each section should be given on a steady level of sonority suited to its specific style and character.

The dynamic interpretation of such compositions of Bach's time as do not specify degrees of sonority should be determined, furthermore, by the contrapuntal texture of each individual piece. A fugue or other polyphonic composition is built on thematic and contrapuntal elements of varying importance. A main subject has greater weight and dignity than changing counterpoints or a short motif used but for a passing episode. The composition becomes comprehensible only if the contrapuntal lay-out is as clearly presented as the formal structure. This is accomplished most effectively by grading the emphasis given to the various elements employed in the course of the composition. The themes which represent the backbone of a fugue should stand out above less essential material; regularly returning counterpoints, similarly, above motifs of a more casual character; and momentary elements, while entirely perceptible, ought to remain in the background—a differentiation of sonorities which will chiefly be applied to material within sections of unchanging general sonority. It seems likely that the well-versed musician of Bach's day who performed a fugue, or other polyphonic composition, naturally emphasized the more important parts and subordinated the less important ones, without any specific indication in the parts. We could do as well today if we had not lost the intimacy with contrapuntal forms which was a characteristic of Bach's work and times.

Adequate dynamic interpretation of compositions by Bach, his predecessors, or contemporaries is a matter not of personal whim, but of serious study. The interpreter must be familiar with the basic principles employed in compositions of the period and the tools of the contemporary composer. He must, in addition, comprehend the contrapuntal development as well as the formal lay-out of the composition he intends to perform—a truth which, unfortunately, has not yet been generally recognized.[1]

---

[1] The analytical descriptions of the larger movements which are given below (in chapter VIII) have partly been inserted here in view of their possible value to the performer. They provide, in fact, an explanation of the suggestions for dynamics given in the edition.

The *Musical Offering* contains six compositions that consist entirely of repetitions of a single section: the Canons Nos. 2-5, 9, and 11. Each of these should be kept on a uniform level of sonority, chosen according to the expressive nature of the piece. Two among them, the Canon in Augmentation and Contrary Motion, No. 5, and the Four-Part Canon, No. 11, are so intricate contrapuntally that they require a definite dynamic differentiation—the parts played simultaneously must be kept on different levels of sonority if a comprehensible rendition of the music is to result. The Mirror Canon, No. 8, the Canon in Contrary Motion, and the Canonic Fugue, No. 12, contain episodes, which may and should be contrasted with the main sections. Special treatment may be accorded to the Modulating Canon, No. 6, whose ascending repetitions seem to invite a stepwise increase in sonority.[2]

The remaining movements display rich and complicated structures. In these, differentiation of sonorities is invaluable as a means of clarifying the formal and contrapuntal structure. Four of the movements are fugues, in which a distinction between thematic sections and episodes should be effected. The sections are less clearly separated and contrasted in the Three-Part *Ricercar* than in the Six-Part *Ricercar* and the fast movements of the Sonata. The first *Allegro* of the Sonata offers a most conspicuous contrast between the center section and the surrounding parts; the center section, which is light and airy in character, requires presentation predominantly in *piano*.

That Bach ever used a deliberate *crescendo* may be doubted. Forkel's comment upon his piano playing, as given in the old translation, is as follows: "When he wished to express strong emotions [*"Affecten"*], he did not do it as many do, by striking the keys with great force, but by melodical and harmonical figures, that is, by the internal resources of the art".[3] When he wanted to build up a climax in his compositions, he similarly did so through contrapuntal, artistic means. Perfect examples of such technique are found in the Six-Part *Ricercar*, in which the parts enter several times one after the other, effecting a *crescendo* even though the single parts do not increase their sonority.

---

[2] For specific problems of interpretation arising in the Canons, see the last section of this chapter (pp. 75-82).

[3] *Life of John Sebastian Bach*, p. 29.

In the *Musical Offering*, Bach may have felt more inclined towards a gradual change of sonority than in any other work. He had improvised the Three-Part Fugue on a *pianoforte*, an instrument capable of gradual changes within the rather narrow limits of its sonority. Apparently he conceived his homage to King Frederick, to a certain extent, as a progressive work, in the fashionable style of the day. Accordingly we may imagine its interpretation to have been somewhat influenced by the manner employed at the German Courts of the time. Details in the Sonata as well as the Six-Part *Ricercar* point in this direction. The performer of the *Musical Offering* may, for this reason, consider himself entitled to include, at a few suitable places, gradual changes of sonority—which he should avoid in other works by Bach.

In the present edition, suggestions for dynamic interpretation have been added in compliance with the principles outlined above. The editor has attempted—as in respect to tempo indications—to add no effects of his own invention, but to work out the dynamics in such manner that the emphasis given to any detail corresponds exactly to the importance it holds within the structure. In the version for keyboard instruments of the *Ricercari* and in the score of the other movements, the suggestions of dynamics have been given in brackets or with dotted lines.

PHRASING

THE PROBLEM OF PHRASING is perhaps more intricate than any other problem of interpretation encountered in music of Bach's time. None, however, has been more seriously neglected. Practical editions of works by Bach and his contemporaries suggest phrasing that complies neither with the practice of the composer nor with the structure of the compositions. Even so great a purist and authority on Bach as Albert Schweitzer applies phrasing which is based largely on romantic theory rather than on a minute study of Bach's holographs or reliable reprints.

Bach specified phrasing to varying degrees. His indications of phrasing consisted of slurs and *staccato* marks, the latter in the form of either strokes or dots, apparently used indiscriminately. In his compositions for keyboard instruments he rarely inserted marks of phrasing. In music for voices, too, he renounced the use of such marks almost completely, but his parts for strings and woodwinds are in most cases carefully marked.

The indication of phrasing is similarly uneven in the *Musical Offering*. The *Ricercari*, written down originally in keyboard notation, include slurs and *staccato* dots only at a few places. The Canons are slightly richer in markings. The Sonata is as completely and carefully phrased as any of Bach's compositions; it may serve as a model for additional phrasing in the other sections of the work. The Mirror Canon, No. 8, which was written out in parts and printed on the same sheets as the Sonata, offers a peculiar problem. Here, the violin part is carefully marked while the flute has only a few indications, and it is hard to decide whether the difference in treatment is accidental or intentional.[1]

To the modern performer on a string or woodwind instrument, it may seem that slurred figures are more appropriate to his instrument than a continuous *staccato* or *détaché* style. But from theoretical sources of the sixteenth and seventeenth centuries we can conclude that, in principle, each note was played with a separate stroke of the bow or was tongued separately. In Bach's time, still, slurring was mostly confined to sixteenth-notes or, particularly in fast movements, to eighth-notes.

Bach's phrasing follows closely the pattern of the music. Often his slurs connect notes in diatonic progression, while neighboring notes progressing by skips are separated. The opening theme of the first *Allegro* in the Sonata offers a very instructive example of this principle. Patterns of three slurred notes and one separate one (♫♫♪ and ♪♫♫) are common, whereas that of two and two (♫♫♪), although widely applied to Bach's works by later editors, actually belongs to the period of Haydn and Mozart.

The reed instruments should tongue separately all notes not specifically marked as slurred. The tonguing should in general be as soft as possible, except for the few places marked *staccato*. Skips may always be marked slightly more than steps while chromatic progressions should be even more carefully connected than diatonic ones. Particular smoothness is required of the reed instruments in the *Ricercari*. Where breath cannot be taken sufficiently between phrases, one may shorten suspended notes in order to take breath,

[1] See Appendix, pp. 172-3.

particularly if the suspension takes only part of a beat (𝅘𝅥𝅘𝅥𝅮𝅘𝅥𝅯𝅘𝅥𝅮𝅘𝅥𝅮𝅘𝅥𝅮).

The strings should use, as their basic stroke, a *détaché* with strict connection of the single strokes: *quasi legato.* "The bow must always be drawn strait on the strings", explains Francesco Geminiani,[2] "and never be raised from them in playing semi-quavers". The *staccato,* which is more properly described as a *martellato* executed without lifting the bow from the strings, may be used sparingly for special effects. The *spiccato* had in general better be avoided; an exception is the beginning of the canonic parts in the Modulating Canon, No. 6, where a sharp *spiccato* may serve to make the entrance of the canonic parts and of each transposed repetition stand out clearly.

There are many shades of *legato* and *staccato,* and many transitional stages between them. These are invaluable for a convincing articulation and moulding of phrases, particularly in the music of Bach's time. In a line containing steps and skips, the notes reached and left by skips may be played shorter and more sharply than those reached and left step-wise. How conspicuously the distinction can be made depends on the character of the movement. Wherever it is made, one should remember that progressions by seconds tend to the *legato* side, whether actual slurs are employed or not, and that progressions by larger intervals, on the other hand, tend to the *staccato* side. This rule will be found particularly helpful for bringing series of detached equal notes to life and having them flow naturally, a task imposed regularly on string players executing a *basso continuo.* How well a differentiation in this manner may set a bass line into relief will be seen if one imagines steps and skips treated distinctly in the opening of the first *Allegro* of the *Sonata:*

Ex. 1

Such a differentiation, however, should be made almost insensibly; any marking of the kind used in the example seems to indicate too bold a contrast and is therefore misleading.

[2] *The Art of Playing on the Violin, Opera* IX, London, 1751.

In the score and parts of this edition, slurs have been indicated wherever necessary. In the Sonata, the editor's task was confined to the elimination of errors and inconsistencies in the phrasing of the original edition.[3] In the other numbers, slurs have been added in order to assure proper phrasing. The slurs supplied by the editor appear as dotted ones in the keyboard version of the *Ricercari* and in the score of the other numbers while original slurs are invariably printed in full. An even more restricted use of slurs than that suggested in the edition may be found sufficient for players able to provide appropriate phrasing within a more continuous *détaché*, but hardly any additional slurs could be introduced without damage to the purity of style.

At a few places *staccato* marks have been added as well as slurs. The finer differentiation of strokes, however, has been, and should be, left to the performer. In the keyboard version of the *Ricercari* and in the score of the other numbers, *staccato* strokes have been used to indicate marks found in the original; dots represent additions by the editor. The score of the *Ricercari* and the parts of all numbers, on the other hand, use, following a widely accepted custom, *staccato* strokes to indicate a heavier *staccato*, and dots to indicate a lighter one.

[3] See the discussion of variant readings in the Appendix, pp. 161-171.

BOWING

THE *Musical Offering* is chamber music, written primarily for the enjoyment of the participants, not virtuoso music intended to show off the technical ability of the performers. Accordingly, a simple and straightforward manner of performance will be found most appropriate to the work—in bowing as well as in other fields of interpretation.

The violinist of Bach's time was still strongly influenced by the practice of bowing established by Jean-Baptiste Lully. The rules of bowing Lully devised have been handed down to us by one of his pupils, Georg Muffat;[1] they form an excellent basis for the violinistic interpretation of compositions of the late seventeenth and early eighteenth centuries.

[1] Preface to Muffat's *Suavioris Harmoniae Instrumentalis Hyporchematicae Florilegium Secundum*, Passau, 1698, reprinted in *Denkmäler der Tonkunst in Österreich*, year 2, pt. 2, Vienna, 1895.

Notes that opened a full measure were played with a down-bow.
Series of equal notes in even numbers were played with a continuous
alternation of down-bows and up-bows (♩ ♩ |♩ ♩ ♩ ♩ |♫♫
♫♫). Single up-beats were played with an up-bow; anticipations
of notes that would ordinarily require a down-bow, with a down-
bow (♩ |♩ ♪ ♩|♩ ♩ ♩).

Series of three notes in slow tempo were played with two down-
bows in succession, one at the end of the first group and one at the
beginning of the second (♩ ♩ ♩ |♩ ♩ ♩). In faster tempo, this
scheme could be replaced by a straight alternation (♫♫ ♫♫),
or by the use of two up-bows in succession (♫♫ ♫♫). Two
up-bows in succession were used in other cases, too, to prepare a
down-bow for the beginning of a measure or other strong beat (as
in ♩ ♫♫♫♩|).

Dotted notes followed by single shorter notes were, wherever
possible, presented with a straight alternation of down-bow and
up-bow (♩. ♪♩. ♪). If need be, however, one could use a second
up-bow for the shorter note (♩ ♫♩ ♫♩). The corresponding double down-bow (as in ♫♩♫♩) is not mentioned by Muffat
and probably was not considered good or practical. However, with
the longer modern bow, additional small notes can be played almost
as easily on a down-bow as on an up-bow, and will seem equally
well in style.

Lully's rules had been designed to unify the bowing of members
of an orchestra and to bring out the rhythms of the contemporary
dance with verve and precision. Applied rigidly, they actually set
rhythm and meter into perfect relief. When they were transplanted
into chamber music, however, they lost some of their original
rigidity. In the first half of the eighteenth century, there seems to
have developed particularly a tendency to use more liberally a
straight alternation of down-bows and up-bows without regard to
heavy beats (as in ♩ ♫♫♩). This style of playing may be applied

to Bach's works wherever the old rules would produce a stiff or crude effect.

Bowings for the violoncello corresponded to those for the violin. On the *viola da gamba* or other viols, which were played with a differently held bow, the up-bow instead of the down-bow served for the heavier beats. The modern school of cello playing and even of violin playing shows a certain inclination toward bowings corresponding to the viol technique. This might lead to a smoother style of playing, but it is apt to impair rhythmic conciseness and to weaken the metric pulse.

Special attention should be given to the bowing of adjoining musical lines or phrases. Proper bowing at such places will provide convincing punctuation as well as articulation.

In Bach's music it often happens that the last note of one phrase is also the first of the next. Even more common are cases in which a transitory note connects motifs or phrases. Wherever phrases are connected in either way, care should be taken not to let the tension of the line lapse, but rather to see that the phrases are firmly linked. The proper bowing of connected phrases is the uninterrupted alternation of down-bows and up-bows. One should try, however, to open the second phrase with a down-bow if it opens with a note which has the character of a down-beat; and with an up-bow, if the first note has the character of an up-beat (*Ricercar a 6*, top voice, meas. 41-42 and 52-53):

Ex. 2

Ex. 3

Phrases or motifs beginning with a down-beat are at least as common with Bach as those beginning with an up-beat, and one should carefully avoid the over-use of up-beats as suggested by Hugo Riemann, Albert Schweitzer, and others. Usually it is best to break lines as rarely as possible and to avoid punctuating phrases by the introduction of *sospiri* before up-beats.

There are, however, instances in Bach's music in which a new motif or line is clearly separated from the end of the previous phrase although no rest is introduced. In these cases, one should bow the new phrase as if it were preceded by a rest. According to this rule, occasionally two down-bows are required in succession: the first for the ending-note of one phrase, and the second for the opening-note of the next. In such cases it will be best to play the end of the preceding phrase as a short note and with a short stroke, lift the bow, and begin the second down-bow nearer the nut (*Ricercar a 6*, Viola I, meas. 29):

Ex. 4

This type of bowing is, of course, quite distinct from the succession of two down-bows within the same phrase which requires a smooth connection and does not allow for a lifting of the bow (as in: ♩ ♩ ♩):

A succession of two up-bows belonging to separate phrases occurs only rarely and hardly ever requires a lifting of the bow (♩ ♪♪♩ to be played as: ♩ ♪♩ ♩).

In the edition, bowing marks have been added in the parts to the *Ricercari* and the Canons, chiefly in order to facilitate reading at sight and homogeneous bowing in performance with a string orchestra. No bowing marks have been given in the Sonata, for the player who is technically and musically mature enough to handle this rather difficult composition will not need, and may even resent, practical aids of this kind. The marks follow in general the old practice, but are to be regarded as suggestions for which alternatives might be found and substituted.[2]

2 It should be noted that the dash has been used exclusively to denote the broad *détaché*, not a *tenuto* (in ♩ ♩ as well as ♩ ♩ or ♩. ♪), and the *staccato* dot to denote a short note to be played with the bow remaining on the string, not a *spiccato* (in ♪ ♩ as well as ♪ ♩ or ♩. ♩).

ORNAMENTS

THE *Musical Offering* contains a comparatively small number of ornaments; there are no indications that the performer was expected to enlarge freely upon this number.

Bach's ornamentation, like that of most of his contemporaries, was determined by French influence. Lully had set up rules stating which notes within a musical line invited ornamentation, what type of embellishment might be considered appropriate to certain notes, and how any ornament was to be executed. As in the matter of bowing, we owe our knowledge of the practice of the Lullists to Georg Muffat.[1] In French music, ornamentation continued to play a most important role, reaching a climax in the work of the *clavecinistes*, the French masters of the harpsichord.

When Bach wrote his *Clavier-Büchlein vor Wilhelm Friedemann Bach*, a note book for the instruction of his eldest son, he included, on one of the first pages, a chart of ornaments. This chart, the only by Bach we have, shows the various marks denoting specific embellishments together with their execution; it closely follows similar charts by French *clavecinistes* like Jean-Henry d'Anglebert.[2]

Bach's ornaments, as shown completely in his chart, consist of a small number of basic elements, which may be classified as follows:[3]

1. Repeating ornaments (the main note recurring after a neighboring note has been sounded):
   a. main note and higher second, major or minor (marked by ⚬⚬

   or ⚬⚬⚬), *tremblement* or *cadence*, *trillo*, *Triller*, "shake" or "trill":

---

[1] See p. 66, note 1.

[2] A facsimile reproduction is given in Ralph Kirkpatrick's excellent edition of the *Goldberg Variations* (New York, G. Schirmer, Inc., 1938), which also contains an extended discussion of ornamentation in general. Further information can be found in: J. Wolf, *Handbuch der Notationskunde* (Leipzig, 1913-19, vol. 2, pp. 279-91); E. Borrel, *L'Interprétation de la Musique Française* (Paris, 1934, pp. 52-103); A. Dolmetsch, *The Interpretation of the Music of the XVIIth and XVIIIth Centuries* (London, c. 1915, pp. 88-341); A. Beyschlag, *Die Ornamentik der Musik* (Leipzig, 1908, pp. 70-176); and E. Dannreuther, *Musical Ornamentation* (London, 1893-5, part I). The last three should be used with caution wherever they go beyond the quotation of source material.

[3] The French terms changed their exact meaning in the course of the development, sometimes from composer to composer. The old English terms are taken from Henry Purcell, Geminiani, and others.

b. main note and lower second, major or minor (marked by *pincé, Mordent*, "mordent" or "turned shake": ♪♪ or ♪♪♪)

2. Non-repeating ornaments

a. ascent or descent by a single note (mostly a second) into the main note (marked by ♩ or ♩ , respectively, or by small notes), *port de voix, appoggiatura,' Vorschlag* or *Accent*, "forefall" and "backfall": ♪ and ♪

b. ascent by two notes into the main note (marked by ⌇), *coulé, Schleifer*, "slur" or "slide": ♪♪

3. "Turns" (including the note above and the note below the main note):

a. beginning with a descent (marked by ∞ or, in connection with a shake, by ⌇⌇), *doublé*: ♪♪♪

b. beginning with an ascent (usually in connection with other elements; marked, in connection with a shake, by ⌇⌇): ♪♪♪

Any turn, in connection with a shake, was called *double cadence*.

These elements could be combined in the most varied manner. Such combinations usually centered around the trill. The latter could be executed as a "plain shake", a continuous series of beats. However, it could also be ornamented by a prefix, an added opening in the form of an appoggiatura or a turn, and by a suffix, a conclusion consisting of either a mordent or a hold. Bach explains the following versions of a shake:

		indicated:	played:
Trillo	(shake)	⌇ (or ⌇⌇)	
trillo und mordant	(shake and mordent)	⌇⌇ (or ⌇⌇)	
doppelt cadence	(turn and shake)	⌇	
idem	(the same)	⌇	
doppelt cadence und mordant	(turn, shake, and mordent)	⌇⌇ (or ⌇⌇)	

indicated: played:

idem[4]   (the same)

accent und mordant   (forefall and
                  mordent)

accent und trillo   (backfall and
                  shake)

In later life, Bach made much less use of the detailed signs introduced by the French. He took to indicating appoggiaturas by small
notes rather than by the little *accent* marks which he had used in
the 1720's. Thus, in the *Musical Offering,* all the appoggiaturas are
indicated by small notes. At several places, too, the openings of trills
are indicated by small notes and the endings of many trills are written
out in full.

The 1747 edition contains only one example of a detailed mark
in the French manner, a shake with preceding turn ( ) in the
opening of the Three-Part *Ricercar.* All the other shakes are simply
indicated by   This however was a general mark which could
indicate any form of trill, leaving the choice of the actual ornament
to the performer. Therefore a definite knowledge of compound
ornaments is necessary for a proper interpretation of the work,
although compound ornaments are not specifically required in the
work after the first presentation of the Royal theme.

Trills in general should begin with the higher note. An exception
may be made in the rare case of a trilled note reached from below.
Trills on short notes (eighth-notes in slow tempo and quarter-notes
in faster movements) are best executed as simple shakes terminated
by a hold in the manner indicated by Bach, or following a pattern
somewhat vaguely suggested by François Couperin: [5]

Longer trills may be played with a turn at the beginning (
or). The opening turn should be ascending if the main note
is preceded by a lower note, descending if it is reached from a
higher note. If the preceding note is a third higher than the main

[4] This ornament is given to a dotted quarter whereas all the others fill only
a quarter.
[5] *Pièces de Clavecin, Premier Livre,* 1713. The original reads:

note, one should put some stress on the opening note of the trill, either through a slight tenuto (♪ 𝄽) or by holding the passing note as an appoggiatura (♪ 𝄽).

Longer trills should end with a mordent (⤲ or ⤲) or with a hold. The mordent is preferable if the trill occupies one or more complete beats (as in ♩♩ ♩♩). If however the trilled note is followed by a rest, or an anticipation of the next tone, the shake should end with a hold (*cadence coupée*, to be used for ♩. 𝄾 and ♩. ♪♩). If a suffix or a continuation within the same beat is indicated in the text, the shake may simply slide into it, without a mordent or hold (as in ♩. 𝅘 or ♩. 𝅘). Trills of considerable length may start slowly and accelerate the beat toward the end.

The length of Bach's appoggiaturas is hard to determine. The musicians of the generation following him used appoggiaturas of considerably varying value. According to theorists like Bach's son, Carl Philipp Emanuel, or King Frederick's teacher, Johann Joachim Quantz, an appoggiatura before a long note would regularly take half of the latter's value if it could be evenly divided, and two thirds if it were dotted. Philipp Emanuel recommended indication of the actual value of appoggiaturas in the small notes with which they were expressed. He explained, however, that previously appoggiaturas had mostly been indicated as eighth-notes, and added that appoggiaturas had not varied so widely in value.[6] We must conclude that his theories do not cover earlier music and that the modern attempts to apply the son's rules to the interpretation of the father's music are questionable if not erroneous.

J. S. Bach apparently wrote all appoggiaturas of considerable length out in full notes. Examples are found in the *Largo* of the Sonata here (see meas. 28 and 42, in contrast to 15 and 47) and, most conspicuously, at the end of the five-part *Praeludium* which opens the Third Part of the *Clavier-Übung* (usually associated with the "St. Anne" Fugue). No indication can be found that he ever used small notes to indicate appoggiaturas longer than a quarter-note.

---

[6] *Versuch über die wahre Art das Clavier zu spielen*, Berlin, 1753-62; reprint ed. W. Niemann, Leipzig, 1906, pp. 31-32.

His conception of the *accent* probably came close to that expressed by his friend Johann Gottfried Walther, who, having mentioned that the *accents* could ascend or descend, by a half tone or by a full tone, added:[7] "Be it noted that all the kinds of *accents* mentioned above sometimes take only a little from the value of the following note, as is the case with the longer notes; but sometimes one half, as with the shorter ones." Long appoggiaturas, applied to Bach's music, tend to destroy the steady flow of the melodic lines. Bach's appoggiaturas, accordingly, should never be held longer than their actual value indicates, *i.e.*, mostly not longer than an eighth-note, and in many cases they might or should be played even shorter.

In J. S. Bach's music, small notes were used for short grace notes as well as longer appoggiaturas (Sonata, *Largo*, Flute, meas. 25):

Ex. 5

Sometimes the harmonic and contrapuntal context shows that small notes should be executed as grace notes; thus a progression of the two upper voices in unison would result if we executed the following small note as an eighth-note appoggiatura (Sonata, *Allegro*, Flute, meas. 30):

Ex. 6

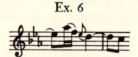

Evidently Bach meant small notes prepared in the manner of suspensions to be executed as longer appoggiaturas than unprepared ones; the latter, then, may be executed either as comparatively short appoggiaturas (sixteenth-note out of a quarter-note), or as grace notes. Care should be taken, however, that the grace note is given a certain weight and importance; the grace notes may, therefore, be slightly accented, in contrast to those in music of the immediately following period.

The execution of ornaments in modern performance should be historically correct, but also artistically convincing. Ornaments are meant to be improvised embellishments and should therefore maintain a somewhat irrational character. Most of the explanations of

[7] *Musicalisches Lexicon*, Leipzig, 1732, p. 5.

ornaments given by contemporaries are rationalizations, attempts to express rhythmically free patterns with the signs of strictly measured music; such realizations will sound pedantic or artificial unless they are presented with a certain irregularity of beat. In addition to these, there are certain realizations of ornaments which have succeeded in expressing the irrational character of an embellishment in notation. Among them are the uneven divisions of the beat as contained in Bach's trill with hold (see *Trillo*, on p. 71) or a backfall and shake suggested by d'Anglebert (*tremblement appuyé:*

♩♫♫♫♫);[8] and the realizations introducing triplets like

Bach's backfall and shake (see *accent und trillo*, p. 72) or quintuplets like Couperin's trill (*ibid.*). These patterns with their improvisatory character will always serve as satisfactory ornaments or true "graces".

In the score and parts of this edition, suggestions for the execution of all ornaments have been included. In application of the ideas outlined above, ample use has been made of irregular divisions.

CANONIC DEVICES

THE CANONS in the *Musical Offering* may be called studies in musical expression as well as in contrapuntal artistry. Their interpretation imposes a double task on the performer: to clarify their structure and to make their expression values evident. The character of each number is partly determined by its motion and melodic material, but even more so by the specific contrapuntal devices employed; accordingly, a different situation faces the performer in each canon.

No. 2. Canon perpetuus a 2 (Canon at the Double Octave)

Since the canonic lines proceed in parallel motion without any further complication, these lines should be presented in identical manner. The character of the composition as an *entrée*, which is chiefly suggested by the dotted rhythm, may be emphasized by a certain gravity; thus even the sixteenth-notes will be played with rather long strokes and full tone.

[8] *Pièces de Clavecin*, Paris, 1689, reprint ed. M. Roesgen-Champion, Paris, 1934.

No. 3. Canon a 2 Violini in Unisono (Canon at the Unison)

Here again a complete identity of style should appear in the canonic parts. Since it is usually easier to apprehend the leading part in a canon at equal pitch, it is recommended that the following part be given slightly more emphasis than the first, particularly at the opening of each phrase. The rhythmic character of this number suggests 2/2 time rather than the 4/4 (**C**) indicated in the 1747 edition. The contrast with the preceding canon will be most striking if a brisk tempo is taken.

No. 4. Canon a 2 per Motum contrarium
(Canon in Contrary Motion)

Inversion of a musical line changes its resting points into points of suspended tension and its energetic ascent into relaxed descent; thus a complete change of character is effected by inversion, although the original line seems untouched. The interpretation of a canon in contrary motion should emphasize the contrast of moods between the parts. Here, the beginning of the first part flows off smoothly while the second part enters with a certain boldness. The contrast is less outspoken later on, but should be emphasized at the beginning of each repeat. The relation between the original and the inverted voice will be easier to grasp if the following voice is, on the whole, slightly louder than the preceding one. In general, however, this canon has a very soft and delicate character. The tempo should be unhurriedly flowing. The clash between B♭ and B♮ (in meas. 3) should be brought out deliberately to make sure that the false relation is not suspected as an error of performance or editing.

No. 5. Canon a 2 per Augmentationem, contrario Motu
(Canon in Augmentation and Contrary Motion)

The change of character brought into a line by augmentation is, perhaps, even more conspicuous than that caused by inversion, for augmentation may convert a lively original into a calm and austere derivation. The contrast between original and derived lines is particularly strong in the present number, which combines augmentation with inversion.

A clear rendition of this canon is harder to achieve than that of any other canon in the *Musical Offering*, for, in addition to the contrapuntal intricacy, it introduces the Royal theme in a richly embellished variation. The faster-moving canonic line is pointed and energetic; rather conspicuous by its very nature, it may be kept on a level of sonority considerably below that required for the theme and the augmented part. The slower-moving part is majestic, with a certain aloofness; it answers, characteristically, the opening tense ascent of the original line with a smooth descent. It should be noted

that the theme moves in 2/2 (¢) time while the original canonic

line clearly expresses common time (4/4). The augmented line would be most properly written in 4/2 and should be so played. Beginning with a rest a quarter longer than a simultaneous entry of the canonic parts would yield, this line forms measures not coinciding with those of the other parts, and should be visualized and performed as if it were written thus:

Ex. 7

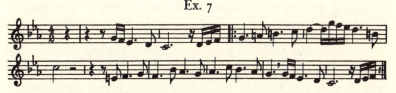

No. 6. Canon a 2 per Tonos (Modulating Canon)

This canon is again in parallel motion, which requires identical presentation of the two canonic lines. The second canonic part, harder to recognize than the first and played in a less sonorous register of the instrument, should be offered with greater energy and stronger tone than the leading part.

The canonic line, although written in 4/4 meter, has an inner rhythm which again and again creates patterns three quarters long. If the line is barred according to its inner rhythm, the following is the result:

Ex. 8

As the canonic parts play at a time-distance of four quarters and against a subject which is conceived in 4/4 meter, a continuous inter-locking of meters and accents results. Thus a contrapuntal setting of exceptional intricacy and intensity is created, most fitting for a number requiring a six-fold presentation before it can end properly. If the 3/4 patterns are deliberately brought out, the listener will be enabled to understand and enjoy the complicated metrical structure.

The six-fold ascent contained in this composition causes a gradual increase of sharpness and poignancy of tone. This effect may be heightened by the use of increasingly pointed strokes. It seems per-missible, in addition, to emphasize the implicit *crescendo* of this ex-citing composition by an increase of sonority from transposition to transposition. Whoever finds such treatment too daring may per-form the piece in a steady *mezzoforte* of all parts and sections; a competent performance might make the development toward a climax evident even without the deliberate increase of sonority.

No. 8. Canon perpetuus (Mirror Canon)

Among the canons of the *Musical Offering*, this is, perhaps, the most playful. The Royal theme, greatly altered, begins with a pattern suggesting a four-fold up-beat:

Ex. 9

In the further course, accentuation at equal distances seems to be completely avoided; accordingly the theme can equally well appear at a different place in the measure, and actually does so in the second group of entries (beginning in meas. 18).

The canonic parts, although proceeding in contrary motion, do not seem to develop contrasting character. As the inversion is exact and its pivot the third scale degree, the initial E♭ is answered by E♮; a slight emphasis on the latter is recommended in order to set the relation between the entries into clear relief. In the second group of entries, a similar correspondence exists between B♭ and B♮; again the second requires a slight accentuation.

Diatonic and chromatic phrases of two measures each alternate three times within the theme. Since the inverted canonic line enters two measures after the original one, a continuous exchange of chromatic bits is offered by the canonic parts. If this alternation is clearly brought out, the listener will have no difficulty in grasping the composition, however complicated it may look on paper.

If presented in an elegant and almost precious manner, this canon will sound delightful and form a sufficient contrast to the last movement of the Sonata, which precedes it in complete performance. The modest episode (meas. 15-18) should be well contrasted with the thematic sections. The bass part should be played lightly throughout.

No. 9. Canon a 2 (Crab Canon)

Retrograde motion is held to be the most artificial of canonic devices. This example successfully contradicts any prejudice against the artistic value of the crab canon. It can easily be understood; and when properly presented, it creates an excellent effect.

The closer the theme and its reversion are brought together in performance, the clearer becomes their relation; a lively tempo is therefore essential for the comprehension of this number. One may play it as fast as both players can execute the eighth-notes without blurring.

The theme should be introduced energetically; the cadential formula may be given in a clear *martellato*. The syncopated part of the theme will be set with strong accents against the continuous eighth-notes of the counterpoint, which, in turn, may display a certain smoothness though played *forte*. The retrograde form of the theme, which is difficult to grasp as a whole, should be brought out as intensely as possible. A minute *diminuendo* at the end, without any *ritardando*, will provide a convincing conclusion.

No. 10. Canon a 2 (Canon in Contrary Motion)

The theme, altered into a vehement chromatic ascent and a strongly syncopated descent, is full of vigor. The episodic continuation, which is softer and lighter in character, may be well contrasted with the thematic sections. As in the preceding canon in contrary motion (Mirror Canon, No. 8), no contrast in character is felt between the original line and its inversion.

In the original part, the accents resulting from the melodic and rhythmic structure of the theme coincide with those suggested by the bars. In the episodic continuation (meas. 9 ff.), on the other hand, the accents seem at first to fall on the second half of the measure and then (meas. 15-16) to form a series of shorter measures; a climactic ascent leads back into the theme:

Ex. 10

As the inverted canonic part enters at the distance of an odd number of beats, its accents fall on the second half of the measure in the theme, and on the first half in the episode. Thus the accents of the individual canonic voices conflict through most of the piece, as in the Modulating Canon, No. 6. The canonic parts should, of course, be presented in similar manner; accordingly the inverted theme will sound as if it were written thus:

Ex. 11

No. 11. Canon a 4 (Four-Part Canon)

To accomplish a clear and transparent rendition of a four-part contrapuntal composition is not an easy task for an ensemble of homogeneous instruments such as strings. In this canon, however, the counterpoints are so strikingly contrasted that all lines can actually be heard simultaneously. As suggested in the edition, the sections of the canonic line must be differentiated as to dynamics, phrasing, and expression.

In a string quartet, the carrying power of the single instruments often varies considerably. If the *forte* of the first violin cannot be matched by the viola or second violin, one may change the sonority of the entire setting from section to section. In rehearsing, one should first make the theme and the first counterpoint stand out boldly and then add as much body of tone to the other voices as can be done without covering the dominant parts. When a proper balance within each section is achieved, the canon will stand out as the most intense and impressive of the group.

No. 12. Fuga canonica in Epidiapente (Canonic Fugue)

The Canonic Fugue is, in the *Musical Offering*, the last composition that has the character of a fast movement; and it should be played in a fresh and lively manner. Conceived in a lighter vein than the preceding Four-Part Canon, it reminds one somewhat of the Mirror Canon, No. 8, which opens this group of canons; and it may be given a touch of the latter's delicacy.

This is, like the Modulating Canon, No. 6, a canon at the fifth in parallel motion; accordingly, the canonic parts should be presented in identical style. The canonic line consists, as in the Four-Part Canon, of various sections, the first voice completing the presentation of the theme before the second enters. The sections should be contrasted as distinctly as possible. As the first counterpoint to the theme (meas. 11-20 of the leading part) is later used for an episode (meas. 21-30 of the following part), outspoken contrasts of sonorities cannot be introduced. Accordingly the necessary differentiation of the sections must be accomplished through variation of the performing style. Such a differentiation has been suggested in the edition through the indications *leggero, dolce, cantabile, marcato,* and *maestoso.* They recur in the second canonic voice ten measures after their first appearance; thus a contrast of character between the canonic parts is suggested for almost any given point. *Leggero* should be taken to signify bowing with pressureless and rather short strokes, not *staccato* or *saltato.* The violoncello, in particular, should not fall into the choppy style of playing frequently applied to thorough-bass execution.

As the distance between the canonic parts is ten measures, one might expect to find a period of ten measures used as the basic unit for the entire structure. This basic meter is clearly established at the very beginning, but it is weakened as soon as the second entry of the theme is completed. The first section of the canonic line consists of the theme and a pair of transitional measures (meas. 9-10). When the transitional measures appear in the consequent (meas. 19-20), the antecedent introduces a counterpoint weighty enough to function as the opening of a metrical unit. When this counterpoint in turn is taken over by the second canonic part (meas. 27-28), little doubt remains that the beginning of the section has been shifted two measures ahead of the ten-measure norm. Thus the second group of entries begins two measures earlier than the beginning would lead one to expect (meas. 29, instead of 31). In contrast to the first half of the composition, the ten-measure distance is strictly adhered to in the second half, as if to restore the regularity impaired before. The friction created through the overlapping of large metrical units may be compared to that arising from the discrepancy between the inner rhythms of various voices, as in the Circle Canon, No. 6. It is significant that Bach gave to the concluding canon of the first canon group as well as to that of the second an added interest by dovetailing metrical units—smaller ones in the *finale* of the first group, larger ones in the corresponding number of the second. While the interpretation of rhythms which overlap bars requires special attention, the metrical shiftings on the present broader time-scale will become clear even if no particular emphasis is placed upon them; however, the player familiar with the situation may help to clarify it for the listener by paying particular attention to the *marcato* opening of the counterpoint, which actually effects the metrical shifting.

VII

SOURCES AND EDITIONS

BACH'S HOLOGRAPH

OF BACH'S MANUSCRIPT of the *Musical Offering*, only a single section has come down to us, the Six-Part *Ricercar*. The manuscript lacks an original title. It belonged to Carl Philipp Emanuel Bach, who supplied it with the title:

> *6 stimmige Fuge, von J. S. Bach u. origineller Handschrift*
> ("6-part fugue, by J. S. Bach and in his original handwriting").

Philipp Emanuel never parted with this manuscript. After his death, it was sold at auction with the rest of his library.[1] It was owned for some time by Georg Pölchau, one of the first and foremost collectors of Bach items—he also owned the copy of the first edition which is now in the Library of Congress. The manuscript finally went to the *Preussische Staatsbibliothek*, Berlin.

The *Ricercar* is written down in braces of two staves, that is, in ordinary keyboard notation. The manuscript fills four pages in a sequence often found in old letters; the order, according to customary pagination, is: 1, 4, 3, 2. The last system of page 2 (the last full page written by the composer) is continued by an additional system, containing the last measures of the composition, at the bottom of page 3 (the main part of which is taken up by the original third page). The entire manuscript is reproduced here in the original order of pages (see pp. 85-88).

The manuscript, which is, in general, of extraordinary neatness, seems to represent Bach's first draft of the composition. At two places where the notes are blurred in the manuscript, mistakes occur

---

[1] See *Verzeichniss des musikalischen Nachlasses des verstorbenen Capellmeisters Carl Philipp Emanuel Bach*, Hamburg, 1791, p. 68.

in the original edition. This leads to the conclusion that the printer either engraved from the manuscript itself or from a copy which was not corrected by Bach. Quite possibly Schübler himself copied the *Ricercar* in score before he engraved it.[2]

The holograph and the printed edition supplement each other curiously in a certain detail of phrasing. The first counterpoint to the Royal theme contains, in its first measure, a short figure which was supposed to be slurred. The holograph indicates the slurs in the first three appearances of the counterpoint (meas. 5, 9, and 13), but not in the fourth (meas. 19); the edition, on the contrary, only in the fourth. Evidently, then, the manuscript and edition were not compared when, in the latter, the slur was added to the fourth appearance of the counterpoint. The chances are that the manuscript was sent back to Bach after a copy had been made, that Bach noticed the missing slur in his manuscript and asked for the addition of that slur in the edition—without knowing that the preceding slurs had been left out in the edition.

Bach's holograph and the printed edition, furthermore, show variants at several places. A few of them are deliberate changes, evidently made in order to improve on the original version; all of these are slight and some of them have a pedantic tinge, but they actually seem to have been indicated by Bach himself. Since no corrections are visible at the places involved in the printed edition, the changes must have been communicated to the printer before he engraved the number. If Bach's holograph of the *Ricercar a 6* was returned to him after a copy had been made, but before the engraving was undertaken, Bach may have had time to ask not only for the inclusion of the slur mentioned above, but also to draw up a list of corrections to be carried out in the copy and the edition. There are no indications that Bach might have read proofs of the edition.

The readings of the holograph and the 1747 edition, strangely enough, have never been critically compared, for the previous editors of the work simply accepted the printed edition as representing Bach's own final intention as far as the score was concerned. A critical comparison shows that some of the discrepancies between

---

[2] L. Landshoff, in the *Beiheft* to his edition of the *Musical Offering*, p. 24, treats the holograph as a reduction of the score, with variants representing changes made by Bach in order to adapt the composition to the limits of the two hands. However, a closer study reveals that the variants have nothing to do with the reach of the hands; some of the variants, in addition, make it quite clear that the manuscript was the source for the edition, not an afterthought.

Bach's manuscript of the *Ricercar a 6*, No. 13, on four pages, which are reproduced here in the original order. First page, representing meas. 1-24.

Bach's manuscript of the *Ricercar a 6*, meas. 70-99.

Bach's manuscript of the *Ricercar a 6*, meas. 50-70 and 99-103.

Bach's manuscript of the *Ricercar a 6*, meas. 24-49.

manuscript and print are simply due to errors in the latter; in these cases, the version of the holograph should, of course, be restored. A more difficult situation arises when we try to evaluate the variants of those places which may have been changed in the printed edition according to Bach's own wish. Bach, not always as lucky in the improvement of his own compositions as in their creation, in certain cases improved details at the expense of other and even more important ones; in such cases a first version might prove superior to a second. Accordingly, in attempting to provide a final text of the *Ricercar a 6*, it seemed advisable to choose throughout the musically superior version, whether it was the earlier or the later. The result was mostly a return from the version of the edition to the unquestionably authentic version of the holograph.[3]

THE EDITION OF 1747

SINCE ONLY ONE SECTION of Bach's holograph has been preserved and no direct copies of any section of that manuscript are known, the edition of 1747 remains our chief source for the text of the *Musical Offering*. This original edition, too, forms our only source of information about the order of movements within the work.

Typographical aspects

The edition of 1747 consisted, as has been mentioned above (pp. 8-9), of title, dedication, and four separate sections of music. There were two sections printed on oblong sheets, and two on upright. The first oblong section contained the *Ricercar a 3*, No. 1, and the Canon No. 2; the other oblong section, the *Ricercar a 6*, and the Canons Nos. 10 and 11. Of the upright sections, one contained the *Sonata*, No. 7, and the Canon No. 8, in separate parts; the other, on only two pages, the Canons Nos. 9, 3 to 6, and 12, in this order. Why should the work have been split up in such an unusual manner?

It was fashionable at Bach's time to print music for a keyboard instrument on oblong sheets; music for an ensemble of instruments, on the other hand, was invariably printed on upright pages. Now, the *Ricercar a 3* was written in keyboard notation and the *Ricercar a 6* probably reached Schübler in the same notation even if he may have been requested to print it in score. Thus it was quite appropriate

---

[3] See Appendix, pp. 179-183.

that he would present these two compositions, as keyboard music, on oblong sheets. Bach himself may have specified such publication, for he had the dedication, which was printed at Leipzig, run off on oblong sheets. It might be recalled, too, that the First Part of the *Clavier-Übung*, containing the Partitas, had been published in oblong format, as well as the Third Part, containing music for the organ.

The Sonata, on the contrary, was presumably sent to Schübler in score, and, according to contemporary practice, he could assume that he was to print it in separate parts—if, indeed, he was not specifically asked to do so. Such parts necessarily were engraved on upright plates. The Mirror Canon, No. 8, which could not be written down in abbreviated notation (see pp. 25-26), probably appeared in Bach's manuscript, like the Sonata, in score; Schübler actually treated it as if it formed a part of the Sonata.

Most of the canons were presented in abbreviated notation and could, therefore, not very well be run in with the specified parts of the Sonata. There was, however, an indication that they were intended for an ensemble: the *a due Violini* in the title of No. 3. Thus Schübler printed them on upright sheets, separate from the Sonata.

Such considerations explain why Schübler chose three different methods of typographical presentation for the *Musical Offering*. They do not explain, however, why Schübler should have made up two sections in oblong format and paged them separately—unless the two *Ricercari* which formed the chief pieces in these sections were just as clearly separated in Bach's manuscript.

The title and dedication of the *Musical Offering* were set in type, at Leipzig. Schübler must have been informed that he was not supposed to provide an engraved title page. Accordingly he left a first page blank when he printed the *Ricercar a 3*.[1] Evidently he knew that this was to be the opening number of the work.

At the bottom of the last page of the *Ricercar a 6*, on the other hand, we find the signature *J. G. Schübler sc*[*ulpsit*]. This, then, represented the last part of Schübler's job. The two *Ricercari*, accordingly, were printed in two separate sections because they were meant to form the opening and the conclusion of the work, with the Sonata and the canon sheets to be inserted between these two layers.

---

[1] In Breitkopf's print, the *verso* of the title page was left blank and the dedication covered two pages. Accordingly it ended with a left page and could not be pasted on the page left blank by Schübler.

Schübler's treatment of the work thus was entirely logical, even if it resulted in a rather odd-looking edition.

The dedication copy

While a few copies of the oblong sections of the original edition have survived, copies of the canon sheets are extremely rare, and of the Sonata a unique copy is known to exist—in the library of the Princess Amalia.[2] This library contains a copy of all sections of the original edition, though scattered under different call-numbers.[3] That these sections originally formed parts of one copy cannot be proven although it is most likely the case. Now, parts of this copy represent, as the inscriptions quoted above (pp. 9-10) establish without doubt, the copy sent by Bach to King Frederick; these sections differ in size and quality of paper from the copies of the Sonata and the *Ricercar a 6* in the same library as well as from all other copies of the edition known. If Amalia's copy of the Sonata and the *Ricercar a 6* actually formed part of the dedication copy, how can the difference in printing stock be explained?

At first thought, one may be inclined to assume that Bach provided the paper of the copy sent to King Frederick since the same kind of paper was used for the dedication printed at Leipzig and for the *Ricercar a 3* and the canons printed at Zella St. Blasii. However, if the paper had been furnished by Bach, Breitkopf, or Schübler, there surely would have been a way of procuring at least a quantity sufficient for one complete copy of the work. Furthermore, paper of similar quality appears nowhere else in Bach's manuscripts. On the other hand, we know that Bach had promised to King Frederick the delivery of an engraved work, and we know that the King had a special interest in the manufacture of paper in his land. Thus it seems possible that the King gave paper from one of his mills to Bach during Bach's stay at Potsdam. This possibility is strengthened by the fact that paper of similar size and quality is found in contemporary manuscripts and prints produced in or near the Prussian capital.

The Princess Amalia, who played the piano, had the dedication and the *Ricercar a 3*, the only section of the work printed in keyboard notation, bound in leather. The suggestion has been made that

---

[2] This library was bequeathed to the *Joachimsthalsche Gymnasium* and then leased to the *Preussische Staatsbibliothek*.

[3] See R. Eitner, *Katalog der Musikalien-Sammlung des Joachimsthalschen Gymnasiums, Beilage* to *Monatshefte für Musikgeschichte*, Berlin, 1884, Nos. 146 and 124.

the binding, too, was provided by Bach, but this binding conforms so completely with a number of other bindings in the Princess's library that its true provenience is evident.

Indications of the primary order

The order of movements in the original edition does not correspond to the order described above (pp. 34-37). What must have been Bach's own plan of the work has been handed down by Schübler in a somewhat distorted way. The edition of 1747 affords, nevertheless, all the information necessary to reconstruct Bach's original intention.

Schübler made it clear that the first oblong section formed the first part of the work, and the second oblong section, the last (see p. 9). Where, exactly, should the Sonata and the canons fit into the scheme?

In the copy sent to King Frederick, the *verso* of the first page of canon notations bears the inscription: *Thematis Regii Elaborationes Canonicae* (see pp. 22-23). If we turn the page, we read, as title to the canon notations: *Canones diversi super Thema Regium*. There was no sense in having two similar headings for the same group of pieces, and accordingly the first was omitted in all the copies printed afterwards. But originally there must have been a meaning behind the differently worded titles. They formulate, in fact, the contrast between canons derived from the Royal theme and canons using it solely as a basis. This indicates that Bach had established two groups of canons, with separate titles. There are exactly five canons corresponding to each title. Bach, then, must have created two groups of five canons each.

In the original edition, the first Canon upon the Royal Theme follows the *Ricercar a 3,* and the first Elaboration of the Royal Theme follows the Sonata. Thus the order of the canon groups is indicated: the first was to be inserted between the Three-Part Fugue and the Sonata, the other between the Sonata and the Six-Part Fugue. The remaining four canons of the first group are found together on the first canon sheet, the appropriate title being used as heading of the page. That the first canon originally formed a part of this group is established by its title: *Canon perpetuus a 2 super Thema Regium.* Thus the first canon group is easily discernible in the original edition.

The second group, on the other hand, is scattered. The Mirror Canon (No. 8) appears where it belongs, immediately after the Sonata. The Crab Canon (No. 9) opens the series of canons on the canon sheets, contradicting the heading under which it appears. The simplicity of its title: *Canon a 2* is matched by that of the *Canon a 2* (No. 10) and the *Canon a 4* (No. 11), found on the last page of the concluding *Ricercar a 6*. That these three pieces belong together is made even more probable by the following features that they have in common: all three are puzzle canons, all three are pure canons without either a *cantus firmus* or an accompanying bass, and they are the only pieces of that description in the entire work. The consistency of their inner progression, finally, proves that they were designed to follow one another consecutively. There remains only one canon, the Canonic Fugue (No. 12), which concludes the series of canons on the canon sheets, but is distinguished from the preceding numbers by the lack of a numeral. The parallelism in form and structure of Mirror Canon and Canonic Fugue indicate that they were intended as symmetric counterparts to each other; accordingly the Canonic Fugue must have been designed to conclude the second canon group.

If there is any doubt left that the canon groups were planned as symmetrical counterparts to each other, it is dispelled by the structure of the Sonata with its unique accentuation of the center of the first *Allegro;*[4] for the ostentatious display of symmetry in this composition would seem rather arbitrary and artificial were it not supported by a surrounding symmetry of higher order.

Schübler's procedure

If the clues offered by the original edition have been correctly interpreted above, we must assume that Bach's manuscript contained two groups of canons, with distinct headings and separated by the Sonata. Why, then, was the work engraved as it appears in the edition?

When Schübler had finished engraving the *Ricercar a 3*, space for two staves of music was left. He took the first of the canons and inserted it at the bottom of the last page. At the end of the Sonata, he inserted the Mirror Canon, either because he considered the canon as a movement of the Sonata or because he could conveniently insert the parts where he did. When he had finished the *Ricercar a 6*, half a plate remained unused. This space would not have sufficed for the Canonic Fugue, presumably the last canonic composition in Bach's manuscript, but it was sufficient for the two canons which must

---

4 See above, p. 35, and, below, the analysis, pp. 115-122.

have preceded the Canonic Fugue in Bach's manuscript, the second *Canon a 2* and the *Canon a 4*.

By using up the empty spaces left on his plates, Schübler had disposed of one canon of the original first canon group and three of the second. By then, the second group had shrunk to only two pieces and, as a matter of course, the engraver decided to combine them with the rest of the first group. The canons of the first group were, it seems, numbered 1 to 5 in the manuscript. Schübler had taken out the first number. He now replaced it with the single canon of corresponding size left over from the second canon group, the Crab Canon. Thus he could pride himself on having preserved the original numbers 2 to 5 of the manuscript. He then added the long Canonic Fugue, logically enough, it seemed, at the end of the entire canonic series. Evidently Schübler tried hard to do his best, although he did not realize—as few contemporaries might have done—that here for once the order of movements in a collection of independent compositions was a matter of importance.

Erroneous conclusions

The appearance of the original edition in general and the dedication copy in particular prompted a regrettable misconception of the entire work. It was put forward by Philipp Spitta, whose *J. S. Bach*,[5] notwithstanding errors in detail, is one of the standard works of musical biography.

Spitta assumed that Bach himself had provided the fancy paper used in the first sections of the dedicatory copy and the binding of the dedication and Three-Part *Ricercar* as well. The division of the original edition into sections printed partly on oblong sheets, partly on upright ones, made him believe that Bach had devised the sections successively without a definite plan and had sent them to King Frederick piece by piece. At first, Spitta surmised, Bach sent off the parts printed on the luxurious paper mentioned above. Accordingly the title *Musical Offering* would have been intended only for the opening *Ricercar* and the canon sheets. The *Ricercar a 6*, Spitta thought, formed a second installment, and the Sonata a third. Thus the work appeared to Spitta "a motley heap of numbers thrown together, done in pieces to show a certain subject in as many elaborations as possible". And he added: "In this work, Bach renounced the introduc-

---

[5] German ed. (see above, p. 10, note 15), vol. II, pp. 671-6 and 843-5; Engl. transl., vol. III, pp. 191-7 and 292-4.

tion of any comprehensive idea which would unify the separate artistic creations."

Spitta's conclusions, however, are not correct. First, the binding, as has been stated above, was made for Princess Amalia, not for Bach. Second, the distinction between upright and oblong sections cannot possibly be due to a delay in the manufacture of the edition, and Spitta contradicts his own line of argument by assuming that oblong and upright sheets were both included in Bach's original modest *Offering*. Third, the use of paper of varying quality would be explained by a delay in manufacture only if the paper chosen for the first sections of the dedication copy had been furnished by Bach or his helpers and had unexpectedly become unavailable while Bach was still at work—a none too probable coincidence. Therefore, the assumption that the work was composed, printed, and delivered piecemeal fails to explain the appearance of the original edition. Conversely, the appearance of the original edition and dedicatory copy fails to prove that the work was altogether produced in more or less haphazard installments.

There are more forceful reasons for believing that Bach devised and dispatched the *Musical Offering* as a whole. The old accounts of his visit to Potsdam indicate that he promised specifically or implicitly to furnish a six-part fugue on the Royal theme. To have sent off the Three-Part Fugue with but a handful of canons—as Spitta says Bach did—would have been impossible under the circumstances. Bach's dedication, furthermore, stated, with evident satisfaction, that Bach considered his original intention "fulfilled as well as possible". Bach could not have used such words had not at least the Six-Part Fugue been included in his *Offering*.

The Sonata, furthermore, preceded the *Ricercar a 6* in Bach's manuscript, as can be deduced from the fact that Schübler put his signature at the end of the *Ricercar a 6*, and nowhere else. We must conclude that Bach did not fail to include the Sonata as well as the Six-Part Fugue when he had the *Musical Offering* sent to His Majesty in Prussia. A consideration of etiquette, finally, confirms this conclusion. The *Musical Offering* was sent by a "most obediant servant" to a Royal patron, and a delivery in pieces "without further formality", as Spitta suggests, would certainly have been considered indecorous by Bach as well as by the monarch whom he addressed.

Spitta's line of argument, unfortunately, has been accepted without scrutiny by most writers on Bach. Albert Schweitzer,[6] for instance, followed closely Spitta's report, and even Georg Kinsky, who wrote a special study on the first editions of Bach's works,[7] took no exception to Spitta's reasoning.

The *Musical Offering* has accordingly been treated as a minor work of Bach's. Spitta himself called it "a half abstract accomplishment, the appraisal of which is dominated by technical considerations". And Schweitzer refers even to the *Ricercar a 6* as "a product of Bach's last creative period, in which the contrapuntal technique, though not actually an aim in itself, nevertheless plays the leading part, the invention taking a subordinate place". The work has, at best, been considered as "a study for something greater", a kind of "entrance hall" through which Bach entered into the temple of the *Art of the Fugue*. Such characterization overlooks not only the inherent unity of the work, but also the basic difference in aim between the comprehensive representation of chamber music in the *Musical Offering* and the systematic demonstration of fugue writing in the *Art of the Fugue*.

[6] *J. S. Bach*, English translation by Ernest Newman, 2 vols., Leipzig, 1911, vol. I, pp. 417-22.

[7] *Die Originalausgaben der Werke Johann Sebastian Bachs*, Vienna, 1937, pp. 62-66.

CANON SOLUTIONS

THE ORIGINAL EDITION of the *Musical Offering* presented nine of the ten canons as *canones clausi*, or in abbreviated notation. Their solution has been attempted by various musicians.

Johann Christoph Oley, a great admirer of Bach, solved all the canons as early as 1763. Said to "owe his strength and ability almost completely to his own industry", he was, according to Ernst Ludwig Gerber, the son of a pupil of Bach's, "an able man on the piano and on the organ, in fugues as well as fantasies."[1] Oley served as organist at Bernburg and later at Aschersleben, both in Thuringia. The work he did on the *Musical Offering* gives great credit to his musicianship. Oley was, for instance, the first to write out the Modulating Canon, No. 6, with all transpositions. It was, furthermore, Oley's idea to supplement the Crab Canon, No. 9, with its own reversion. The Four-Part Canon, No. 11, which was written down

[1] *Historisch-Biographisches Lexicon der Tonkünstler*, Leipzig, 1790-2, vol. II, column 43.

by Bach in two clefs without further explanation, was interpreted by Oley as a composition for three high instruments and a single bass.

Johann Friedrich Agricola, a pupil of Bach's, composer to the Prussian Court, and later director of the Royal chapel, worked out the solution of the Canon at the Double Octave, No. 2, and two different solutions to one of the puzzle canons, the *Canon a 2*, in Contrary Motion, No. 10.

Johann Philipp Kirnberger, another pupil of Bach's, followed with the first publication of canon solutions to the *Musical Offering*. As teacher of composition and master of the chapel of Princess Amalia, he had easy access to the dedication copy. In his *Die Kunst des reinen Satzes*,[2] he included solutions of the Canon at the Double Octave, No. 2; the Canon in Contrary Motion, No. 4; the Modulating Canon, No. 6; and the Crab Canon, No. 9. Kirnberger knew and used Agricola's manuscript.

Undoubtedly the most generous reference to the canons to appear in print in the course of the eighteenth century was offered by Augustus Frederic Christopher Kollmann, the German-born "Organist of His Majesty's German Chapel at St. James's" in London. In his *Essay on Practical Musical Composition*, which was published in 1799, Kollmann included the abbreviated notation of the nine canons that had been so presented in the original edition. He also commented on the solution of all of them and added in score the first measures of the solution of the Canon in Contrary Motion, No. 4, the Canon in Augmentation and Contrary Motion, No. 5, the Crab Canon, No. 9, and the Four-Part Canon, No. 11, interpreting the last as a canon for two low voices followed by two high ones. None of the authors to be mentioned below, however, seems to have been aware of Kollmann's publication.

The *Allgemeine Musikalische Zeitung* of Leipzig twice offered discussions of canons from the *Musical Offering*. The first, opened by Johann Gottfried Fischer of Freiberg in Saxony and continued by an unknown "*Kontrapunktist*", dealt with the puzzle canon No. 10.[3] The second, prompted by the publication of the first reprint of the work in 1832, was included in a detailed review of this edition by Joseph Klauss, then a well-known organist and theorist, who discussed the solution of all the canons.[4]

[2] Two vols., Berlin and Königsberg, 1774-9.
[3] Vol. 8, 1805-6, columns 269-72, 288, and 496, footnote.
[4] Vol. 34, 1832, columns 3-9.

When the *Musical Offering* appeared in the edition of Bach's complete works issued by the *Bach-Gesellschaft*,[5] solutions of all the canons were included. Alfred Dörffel, the editor, used Agricola's manuscript and the printed sources mentioned above. As Oley's manuscripts were not known to him, he supplied his own solutions of the Canon at the Unison, No. 3, the Canon in Augmentation and Contrary Motion, No. 5, and the Four-Part Canon, No. 11; in the last, he used two high voices of equal pitch and two low voices of equal pitch, in alternation. His solutions were correct with the exception of the Canon in Augmentation and Contrary Motion, No. 5. This canon was so devised by Bach that the Royal theme was accompanied by the original canonic line in full length and by the first half of its augmentation. Dörffel undertook to use the full length of the augmented line, as an accompaniment to two complete appearances of the theme and the original line. The second half of the resulting combination was studded with impossible progressions; Dörffel eliminated some of them by rather questionable emendation, but even so, failed to reach an acceptable result.

Dörffel's solution of the Canon in Augmentation and Contrary Motion was justly criticized by Friedrich Smend in a short article published in the *Zeitschrift für Musikwissenschaft*.[6] Smend indicated the correct solution. He suggested, however, that the piece be supplemented by an inversion in double counterpoint—a treatment which contradicts Bach's own repeat marks and which would spoil the homogeneity of the entire canon series.

An edition of eight canons for String Quartet, edited by Gustav Lenzewski, Sr.,[7] was based on Dörffel's solutions. Following a suggestion made by the latter in the preface to his edition, Lenzewski wrote out the Four-Part Canon, No. 11, in three octaves, instead of the two indicated in the original edition; the parts enter here in the order: high, middle, high, low. Lenzewski also edited the Canonic Fugue, No. 12, for Flute or Violin and Piano.

An interesting arrangement of the canons from the *Musical Offering* for Piano was given by Ferruccio Busoni;[8] here the Four-Part Canon, No. 11, is offered with a convincing new order of entries: high, middle, low, high.

---

[5] Vol. 31, pt. 2, Leipzig, 1885.   [6] Vol. 11, Leipzig, 1928-9, pp. 252-5.
[7] In the series *Musikschätze der Vergangenheit.*
[8] *Kanonische Variationen und kanonische Fuge über das Thema König Friedrich des Grossen,* in vol. VII of Busoni's *Bearbeitungen und Übertragungen* of works by Bach.

Ludwig Landshoff, in his edition of the *Musical Offering*,[9] first published those of Oley's solutions which differed from solutions suggested otherwise. Thus Landshoff became the first to print the entirely correct solution of the Canon in Augmentation and Contrary Motion, No. 5, and to include the second section of the Crab Canon, No. 9. In the Four-Part Canon, No. 11, Landshoff used Oley's distribution of voices.

The question of how to end the canons formed a stumbling-block to the few editors who made editions of these pieces for practical use and were thus forced to deal with this problem. The Royal theme, quite clearly, should in no case be cut short by the ending of a canon, and no extension of the original structure could possibly be allowed. Even Landshoff, whose edition is otherwise very creditable in matters of scholarship, fails to observe these elementary principles.

The five canons of the first group end naturally and necessarily on the last note of the Royal theme, which is also the first note of the repetition of the theme; the last of these canons, the Modulating Canon, No. 6, comes to a halt when the end of the Royal theme reaches the original tonic for the first time, that is, after the sixth presentation. The canonic counterpoints should stop together with the theme, with as little change from the original line as feasible.

Two numbers of the second canon group, the Crab Canon, No. 9, and the Canonic Fugue, No. 12, are complete in themselves. In the Mirror Canon, No. 8, the end can only be given after a recapitulation of the first group of entries; the final cadence coincides with the end of the theme in the second canonic part. The Canon in Contrary Motion, No. 10, should end at the first suitable place after the completion of the theme in the second voice; in the first version, the end may be given either on the tonic or on the dominant. The Four-Part Canon, No. 11, will logically be concluded when all voices have played the theme the same number of times; one may, however, add one more appearance of the theme in order to end with a typical bass cadence in the lowest part.

[9] C. F. Peters, Leipzig, 1937.

THOROUGH-BASS REALIZATIONS

THE *Musical Offering* included three compositions for two high instruments and a thorough-bass: the Sonata, No. 7, the Mirror

Canon, No. 8, and the Canonic Fugue, No. 12. In the original edition, the bass of the first two was figured.

An old realization of both the Sonata and the Mirror Canon has been preserved. Evidently it was a student's work, looked through by a teacher who indicated mistakes with short comments. They usually refer to wrong or incomplete rendering of the original figures or to five-note chords.

The realization of the Sonata, but not of the Mirror Canon, was copied by a certain Röllig. He attributed it to Kirnberger, and it was accordingly published in Friedrich Hermann's edition of Bach's Trio Sonatas, as well as in the edition of the *Bach-Gesellschaft*, as a work of Kirnberger. It seems, however, that Kirnberger was neither the author of this realization nor even the teacher who corrected it.

Kirnberger himself published a realization of the third movement of the Sonata as a final example in his *Grundsätze des Generalbasses*.[1] This proves his interest in this particular problem, but no connection can be found between his solution and that of the anonymous student.

The old realization has been severely critized by Robert Franz, Max Seiffert, and Ludwig Landshoff, and each of these men has written his own realization for the Sonata. It must be conceded that the old realization is by no means a masterpiece. Nevertheless, it remains one of the rare eighteenth-century examples of a thorough-bass realization for a complete composition, and, as such, it deserves to be known. If the accompaniment is played as delicately and unassumingly as any such accompaniment ought to be, it certainly fills its place quite properly.

The present edition includes Kirnberger's realization of the *Andante* from the Sonata. For the other movements of the Sonata and for the Mirror Canon, the realization by the unknown student has been used. The text has been taken from the original manuscript, not from Röllig's copy, which served as manuscript to both Hermann's and Dörffel's editions. The five-note chords of the original have not been eliminated, notwithstanding the objections of the one who corrected it. Nor did it seem advisable to change the original where it is incorrect in minor details such as the omission of a seventh in a

---

[1] Berlin, 1781. I should like to acknowledge that my attention was first called to this source by Mr. Ralph Kirkpatrick. The realization, without the violin and flute parts, has been republished by F. T. Arnold, in his monumental *The Art of Accompaniment from a Thorough-Bass*, London, 1931, pp. 790-2.

dominant chord. A few changes nevertheless proved necessary.[2] Both Kirnberger's authentic contribution and the realization of the Mirror Canon are now made generally available for the first time.

The parallelism between the Mirror Canon, No. 8, and the Canonic Fugue, No. 12, called for identical instrumentation of both pieces. The bass part of the Canonic Fugue has therefore been treated as an unfigured bass. The part of the accompanying keyboard instrument has been supplied by the editor.

[2] See the Appendix, *passim*.

REPRINTS

THE FIRST REPRINT to follow the edition of 1747 was published by Breitkopf & Härtel in Leipzig in 1832. The edition was prefaced and revised by a member of the *Gewandhaus* orchestra, Christian Gottlieb Müller.[1] It offered the Sonata and the Mirror Canon, No. 8, in score, but did not complement the original edition in any other way.

The publishing house of C. F. Peters followed in 1866 with an edition of the work by Friedrich August Roitzsch, meritorious co-editor of the first comprehensive series of editions of Bach's instrumental works. To the material included in Müller's edition, Roitzsch added the Six-Part *Ricercar* in an arrangement for organ and a score of the Canonic Fugue, No. 12. For more than seventy years, this edition remained the only separate publication of the work on the market.

The *Bach-Gesellschaft* edition[2] included a reprint of Bach's manuscript of the Six-Part *Ricercar* in keyboard notation, with indications of the variants; solutions of the canons; and the realization of the figured bass of the Sonata then believed to be Kirnberger's. The original edition of the Sonata and the Mirror Canon were not available to the editor. Instead, a copy was used which had been compared with the original edition by Ferdinand Böhme. The edition of the *Bach-Gesellschaft* is widely considered as the last word in correctness. But the technique of scholarly editing had scarcely been inaugurated when the first volume of that edition appeared, and its texts became entirely reliable only after years of experimenting and experience. The various editors of the series were, in addition, not

[1] See *Allgemeine Musikalische Zeitung*, vol. 34, Leipzig, 1832, columns 108-9.
[2] See above, p. 98, note 5.

equally accurate, and the especially difficult questions of phrasing
were often solved according to the editor's fancy rather than according to the letter of Bach's text. The editing of the Sonata was
among the worst in the volumes of the *Bach-Gesellschaft*.[3]

In 1937, C. F. Peters replaced Roitzsch's edition with one prepared
by Ludwig Landshoff. This edition offers a reprint of the original
edition, with the addition of the Six-Part *Ricercar* according to Bach's
manuscript. A *Beilage* includes canon solutions and the Six-Part
Fugue in an adaptation for instruments. A *Beiheft* discusses sources
and questions of performance. The text of the edition is carefully
prepared, and the *Beiheft* is a valuable source of critical information.
The order, unfortunately, is based on Spitta's description of the
original edition, and the interpretation, particularly of tempi and
phrasing, is questionable. Landshoff also provided a practical version
of the Sonata in his edition of Bach's Trio Sonatas.

The edition of which the present volume of commentary forms a
part is the first practical as well as scholarly one of the entire work.
It differs from the preceding editions chiefly in its order of movements: it presents the *Musical Offering* for the first time in the form
in which Bach apparently created the work, and thus restores the
monumental unity of a composition whose scope and importance
have never before been fully grasped and acknowledged.

---

[3] Sections of the *Musical Offering* were published in several practical editions,
which were based on those mentioned above without making any scholarly contribution to our knowledge of the work. In the 1830's, the two *Ricercari* were
included in C. F. Peters' edition of the *Art of the Fugue*, which formed part of
the *Edition nouvelle* of Bach's *Oeuvres complettes* for the "pianoforte". The
Six-Part *Ricercar* has also been adapted for various orchestral combinations by
Georg Lenzewski, Edwin Fischer, Anton von Webern, Eliot B. Wheaton, and
Howard Ferguson.

The Sonata appeared in collections of Bach's Trio Sonatas edited by Friedrich
Hermann and Henri Rabaud, and in separate editions by Robert Franz and Max
Seiffert. It was arranged for Violin, Violoncello, and Piano by Alfredo Casella.

After the first performance of my adaptation of the *Musical Offering* in 1928,
arrangements of the entire work were presented by Hermann Diener (see H. J.
Moser and H. Diener, *Bach's Musikalisches Opfer*, in *Jahrbuch der staatlichen
Akademie für Kirchen- und Schulmusik*, vol. 2, Berlin, 1928-9), Robert Vuataz
(version published by *Ars Viva*), and Johann Nepomuk David. All of these
took over principles of the order or instrumentation—or both—from my adaptation.

VIII

ANALYSES

OF THE SIXTEEN MOVEMENTS within the *Musical Offering*, ten, the canonic ones, are rather short and follow comparatively simple structural patterns. The interest they offer is contrapuntal rather than formal, although a few among them—particularly the Modulating Canon, No. 6, the Mirror Canon, No. 8, and the Canonic Fugue, No. 12—introduce formal elements beyond the straightforward repetition of a basic setting characteristic of the first four canons.[1]

The six larger movements within the work, on the other hand, are most intricate structural creations, undoubtedly as worthy of a detailed analytical study as any of Bach's compositions written in his last period and worked out for publication. In each of these movements, unity of form is accomplished by different means, and thus the work as a whole offers an amazing variety of structural patterns. Inner relations between the movements make a study of them particularly interesting.

The general procedure in the ensuing analyses has been to take up the features of the music in the order in which they present themselves to the listener, and to furnish him with detailed explanation of the formal significance of these features. Obviously, a reading of the following pages without constant reference to the music would defeat the purpose for which they were written.

These analyses start from the axiom that the basis of Bach's form is the mutual balancing of passages that offer the same or similar material. Such reappearances determine the pattern of the musical structure, and an appreciation of the way in which they occur is fundamental to a comprehension of the music itself.

The exact references to measures, given in parentheses, utilize certain signs to indicate the degree of similarity of passages. The equal-

[1] See chapters III, pp. 24-28, and VI, pp. 77-79 and 81-82.

sign (=) is used for identical passages; the parallel-sign (‖) for passages employing the same material with slight variation, *e.g.* transposition or inversion in double counterpoint. Where the relation between two passages is freer, verbal indications such as "corresponding to" or "*cf.*" are used.

For practical purposes, measure numbers are given for the first and last full measure of any section or other part of form, although the actual lines often begin after a first beat and usually extend into a following measure. In the score, measure-numbers appear at all points where new structural elements begin.

In the following analyses and the Appendix, a typographical distinction has been made between note names indicating the degree of the scale without regard to pitch, which are printed in roman capitals (C D E); and note names including the indication of pitch as well, which are printed in italics. The octaves are indicated as follows, ascending from the contra-octave:

(1) '*C* to '*B*; (2) *C* to *B*; (3) *c* to *b*; (4) *c'* (middle C) to *b'*; (5) *c''* to *b''*; and (6) *c'''* to *b'''*. Accordingly *C* indicates the lowest note of the great octave, while C refers to that note in the abstract.

RICERCAR A 3 (THREE-PART FUGUE)

THE THREE-PART *Ricercar* is a strict fugue with the Royal theme as sole subject. Elaboration of all particles of the subject and recapitulation of all elements introduced in the opening sections determine the style and form of the composition. Of its four sections, the second is partly recapitulated by the third, and the first in certain respects by the last. A striking departure from this general scheme takes place in the course of the third section.

The Royal theme is made up of three melodic elements, which are developed separately in the course of the composition:

(1) the opening motif (hereafter called "a"):

Ex. 1

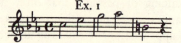

(2) the chromatic descent, first in half-notes ("b"):

Ex. 2

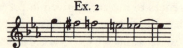

and then in quarter-notes ("β"):

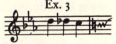

Ex. 3

(3) the cadential formula ("c"):

Ex. 4

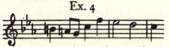

The entries of the subject throughout the composition are restricted to tonic, dominant, and subdominant.

The first section (meas. 1-37) introduces, in accordance with the convention established by the classics of fugue writing, the three obbligato voices, each with an entry of the theme, on tonic, dominant, and again tonic. The parts enter in descending order, the second using a varied tonal-answer form of the theme (see meas. 10-11). The first counterpoint to the theme begins with a conspicuous *staccato* motif (meas. 10-11, hereafter called "d"):

Ex. 5

and then introduces patterns of running eighth-notes, starting a motion which dominates the further course of the composition. The ensuing transitional measures are based upon a transformation of the *staccato* motif (meas. 18-19):

Ex. 6

and eighth-note patterns, modulating from the dominant back to the tonic (meas. 18-22). The counterpoint itself returns almost completely to accompany the third entry of the subject.

The first episode (meas. 31-37) utilizes the chromatic descent in quarter-notes (β). In passing modulations, it leads to a weak half-close.

The second section (meas. 38-86) includes, like the first, altogether three entries of the subject. In this section, however, the entries occur in ascending order, in modulating sequence (dominant, tonic, subdominant), and at greater distance from each other; in addition, a new pair of counterpoints is introduced with each entry.

The section opens in a quite original manner with an elaboration of the head of the Royal theme, giving for a moment the impression of an evasive entrance (meas. 38). A variation of the first three notes of the subject, or rather of the answer, is offered by the bass in a descending sequence:

Ex. 7

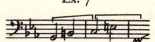

This is accompanied by a motif in eighth-note triplets, treated in imitation in the upper voices, and modulates by descending fifths as far as E-flat minor (meas. 38-41). The bass then takes up a variation of the first five notes of the subject, that is, of the complete first motif (a):

Ex. 8

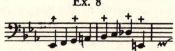

This, elaborated in an ascending sequence, brings about a modulation to the minor dominant (meas. 42-45).

The bass follows up the preliminary development of the subject-opening with an entry of the full subject itself, the first of the section (meas. 46 ff.). This is extended by a few transitional measures too inconspicuous to be felt as an independent episode (meas. 54-58).

The second entry of the subject (meas. 59 ff.) ends with a deceptive cadence (F minor V $\frac{6}{5}$, instead of C minor I, meas. 67).

Here, again, come a few transitional measures rather than a full episode (meas. 67-71), which feature an inversion of the chromatic descent (b), in the bass (meas. 69-71).

The third entry of the subject (meas. 72 ff.) ends with another deceptive cadence (G minor V 9, instead of F minor I, meas. 80). Presently the last two measures of the subject (c) are repeated a tone higher, the diatonic descent in half-notes being changed into a chromatic descent in quarter-notes:

Ex. 9

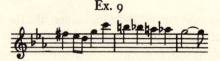

Thus the last of the three thematic elements, the only one not previously elaborated separately, is called into service. The concluding measures of the section (meas. 82-86) recapitulate the preceding group of transitional measures in another key and with the upper voices exchanged (meas. 82-86 ‖ 67-71).

The third section (meas. 87-140) starts with a strict recapitulation of the first part of the second section. The elaboration of the head of the subject in the bass, with the accompanying triplets, reappears in full, though transposed and with an exchange of the upper voices (meas. 87-94 ‖ 38-45). It is again followed by an entrance of the subject in the bass, now in the tonic, accompanied by the same counterpoints as during the corresponding first entry of the second section (meas. 95-102 ‖ 46-53). Thus the section is clearly established as a recapitulation—or, in terms of Bach's technique of formal construction, as the beginning of the second half of the whole.

The theme ends with the evasive progression heard in the previous entry and is again extended by a sequential variation of its last two measures (meas. 103-104, bass, corresponding to meas. 80-81, treble). Now, however, Bach goes further. The chromatic descent in quarter-notes introduced into what originally had been the cadential formula of the subject (c), is reminiscent of the one in the middle of the subject (β), but, on account of its pitch, represents even more clearly a diminution of the descent in half notes from the middle part of the theme (b; the descent in meas. 74 and 80 beginning on C; in meas. 97 and 103, as in the theme itself, on G). Bach proceeds to work the motif out in what may be called a short *fantasia*—this was the term he originally used for his three-part *Inventions*—inserted in the actual fugue (meas. 105-128).

At first, the chromatic motif is presented in a sort of secondary exposition: a three-fold imitation at the octave (meas. 105-108). Then, a modulating episode is introduced in which the motif from the first counterpoint (d, see meas. 18 ff.) appears in the bass (meas. 109-114). Next, the beginning of the subject itself (a) is offered in diminution ("α") by the bass, in a descending sequence, accompanied by imitations of the chromatic motif in a further diminution, in eighth-notes (meas. 115-117). Continuing to lead the way, the bass takes up the chromatic descent in quarters (β), working it out in an ascending sequence, accompanied by imitations of the same motif ascending and descending in eighth-notes (meas. 118-121).

Finally, the chromatic motif enters again, in imitation at the octave (meas. 122 f. and 125 f.); thus, a second group of entries within the *fantasia* is formed (meas. 122-128). In two out of its four appearances, the motif assumes the form of a diminution of the greater part of the theme (b combined with c), as if to bring the number of entries in this section, including the complete entry, up to three, as in the first and second sections of the composition. The chromatic descent in eighth-notes, which would appear in an unvaried diminution of the theme, is now eliminated, but appears in the accompanying voices. A few isolated eighth-note triplets set the end of the *fantasia* off against the continuation of the fugue proper (meas. 127-128).

The order of modulation in the *fantasia* section is rather complicated. The exposition establishes G minor (partly expressed as the dominant of C minor). A descent in seconds follows: G minor, F minor, E-flat major, after which a barely touched C minor leads to A-flat major. The development of the theme-opening in the bass, though digressing widely, leads only from A-flat major to its dominant. The elaboration of the chromatic descent in the bass effects a gradual ascent in seconds, balancing the previous descent and leading back to the tonic: A-flat major, B-flat major, C minor, each being preceded by its dominant. The end turns to the subdominant.

The entire *fantasia* differs considerably from the main part of the fugue. Greater use of quarters and eighths results in the impression of 4/4 motion rather than of the 2/2 maintained throughout the rest of the fugue. Generous application of diminution and double diminution gives to this *fantasia* the character of exceptional intensity and agitation; and there is, in addition, such an abundance of chromatic lines and such wide range of modulation in this part that it forms easily the most expressive and exciting piece within the composition.

The fugue now resumes its original character, and continues the interrupted recapitulation with a transposed presentation of the first episode, with exchanged upper voices (meas. 129-134 ‖ 31-36). The present episode receives an extension during which various other elements of recapitulation are introduced, particularly reminiscences of the *fantasia*. Thus we hear, in the bass, another variation of the diminished opening of the theme (α, meas. 135, 137, and 139; *cf.* the bass of meas. 115 ff.) and, in the middle voice, a single appearance of the chromatic descent in eighth-notes (diminution of β, meas. 137; *cf.* the upper voices of meas. 115 ff.). The episode modulates from the subdominant back to the tonic, which prevails for the rest of the fugue.

The last section (meas. 141-185), like the first and second sections, introduces three complete entries of the subject. They appear in exactly the same order and pitch as in the first section (compare meas. 141 ff. with 1 ff.; 153 ff. with 10 ff.; 169 ff. with 23 ff.), and this constitutes a strong element of recapitulation. The second entry is in the tonal-answer form, like the second entry of the first section. The entries are separated, however, like those of the second section. All three employ the same pair of counterpoints, using the accompaniment first heard with the second entry of the second section (see meas. 59-66). Thus certain connections between the second and fourth sections supplement the stronger relations between the second and third sections on the one hand, and between the first and fourth on the other. It should be noted, however, that the third pair of counterpoints does not reappear.

The first interlude, introduced with an evasive cadence reminiscent of that bridging over the end of the second entry of the second section (F minor $V \, {}^4_2$ instead of C minor I; compare meas. 149 with 67), corresponds in weight and character to the groups of transitory measures within the second section (compare meas. 149-152 with 67 ff. and 82 ff.).

A true episode is inserted between the second and third entries of the subject (meas. 161-168). It is based on an elaboration of the motif from the first counterpoint (d), presented here in free imitation. Bach thus seems to provide a recapitulation of the first counterpoint, although he neither re-introduces the entire counterpoint nor uses it as a counterpoint to the subject again—a quite unusual procedure.

The last entrance of the theme is followed by a few transitional measures supported by a diatonic descent of the bass from the tonic to the dominant (meas. 177-179). The upper voices again recall the interludes of the second section (compare particularly the emphatic use of the seventh in the treble, meas. 57-58 and 178-179, hinted at also in meas. 136-138). A strict recapitulation of the opening of the *fantasia* completes the composition (meas. 180-184 || 105-108).

Within the *Ricercar a 3*, the most interesting and original part, musically, is the *fantasia*. Structurally, however, it constitutes the weak point of the composition; for it differs so strongly in treatment and character from the surrounding sections that it becomes an isolated portion within the whole. Such isolated sections of contrasting material and treatment are felt as legitimate if they appear at the very center of a structure, surrounded by symmetrically related parts. Here, however, the portion that should represent the center of the structure is introduced after the opening of the recapitulation—that is, clearly within the second half of the form. Yet it is so extended that the beginning of the recapitulation, which should mark the beginning of the second half of the piece, is thrown back into the first half. Thus a serious lack of balance results—a shortcoming rarely occurring in Bach's work. It leads to the conclusion that the composition actually represents, as has been surmised, an improvisation, not a fully worked-out and finished composition. The conclusion is strengthened by two other unusual features of the composition. The one is the astonishing length of passages during which the bass alone carries and elaborates thematic material. The other inconsistency is the treatment of the counterpoints introduced in the second section; for out of three pairs, two are recapitulated, while the third simply disappears after a unique, but entirely unaccented appearance.

If the Three-Part *Ricercar* actually represents the fugue improvised by Bach at Potsdam, that fugue, it is true, observed all the rules of fugue writing, and it deserves credit as a rich and varied piece. Its balance, however, is not beyond criticism. We may conclude that Bach was serious and not merely bent on flattery when he said, in his dedication of the *Musical Offering* that "for lack of necessary preparation, the execution of the task did not fare as well as such an excellent theme demanded".[1]

---

[1] Philipp Spitta (*J. S. Bach*, German ed., vol. II, pp. 672-3) was the first to suggest that Bach, while writing down the Three-Part *Ricercar* "referred to the fugue improvised by him at Potsdam (for it had pleased the King very much) and retained more of his momentary ideas in the piece than he might have considered permissible under other circumstances." Bach presumably went even further than Spitta thought, for if the composer published the fugue in a form which could not possibly have satisfied him, he could hardly have had another reason for doing so than the desire to represent as closely as possible the original improvised fugue. There can be little doubt that Bach was capable of reproducing the original fugue in all essential points afterwards, and particularly so since the fugue was based on a comparatively simple plan.

Spitta's discussion of the fugue, nevertheless, calls for criticism. While trying

SONATA (TRIO SONATA)

THE CENTER PIECE of the *Musical Offering* is a *Sonata a 3*, for Flute, Violin, and *Basso continuo;* it is written in four movements, alternately slow and fast, and represents rather strictly the *sonata da chiesa*.[1]

LARGO

THE OPENING MOVEMENT of the Sonata may be called a free fantasy on certain principal motifs, inspired largely by the opening of the Royal theme. Thematic development of a rather loose and almost casual character builds up a structure of unusual metrical interest.

The movement comprises three periods of sixteen measures each. The first is repeated. The second is felt as a somewhat contrasting middle section. The third carries elements of recapitulation. The second and third are repeated together.

Reference to the Royal theme is restricted to its opening motif, and appears exclusively in the Continuo part.

A variation of the first motif from the Royal theme is offered in the first four measures of the bass:

Ex. 10

The first two measures of this bass, altered to an answer form and followed by a sequential repetition, support the opening of the second section (meas. 17-20):

Ex. 11

The other two measures of the bass quoted above, unaltered, but

---

to prove the improvisatory character of the fugue, he points out several features as being somewhat strange. He particularly objects to the "almost unorganic" character of the episodes meas. 38-45 and 108-115. However, as has been pointed out in the foregoing analysis, these sections are thematically justified. The shortcomings of Bach in the present fugue are obvious, but they are much subtler than those suspected by Spitta.

[1] See chapter III, pp. 31-33.

again followed by a sequential repetition, support the opening of
the third section (meas. 33-36):

Ex. 12

In addition to these partial recapitulations of the opening bass,
Bach introduces a complete second presentation of the variation of
the opening motif of the Royal theme, in answer form, at the beginning of the second phrase of the second period, that is at the beginning of the second half of the entire movement (meas. 25-28):

Ex. 13

The most conspicuous element in the opening motif of the Royal
theme is the skip of a diminished seventh. This skip seems to represent the melodic nucleus of the whole fantasy; for again and again
we hear, in the top voices even more strikingly than in the bass,
skips of a diminished or a minor seventh, and of other diminished
intervals.

The first section introduces, while the variation of the opening
motif from the Royal theme is first presented by the bass, a first
principal motif in the upper voices (meas. 1-4):

Ex. 14

This motif, in various forms, is used for imitations throughout
the movement. The rhythm of the first measure is, in addition, recalled by all cadences within the movement (meas. 5, 15, 27-28,
41-42, and 47); appearing in 20 out of 48 measures, it constitutes the
dominating rhythmic pattern of the fantasy.

In its first appearance, the motif opens with an ascending sixth,
followed by a descending diminished fourth. It is imitated at the
fourth above, after two measures, accompanied now by a counterpoint in sixteenth-notes (see the preceding example). A third
entrance, in the bass, containing an ascending octave and a descending diminished fifth, is incomplete. Forming a half-close, it throws

the metrical accent from the fifth measure to the sixth, causing the first half-phrase to be felt as a five-measure pattern. The dominant is held as an intermittent pedal-point for three measures (meas. 6-8). It supports a threefold appearance of the second principal motif—a sixteenth-note figure, derived from the counterpoint to the second appearance of the first motif (Violin, meas. 6; cf. Violin, meas. 3) and accompanied, in turn, by a tiny ornamental figure which returns occasionally in the course of the movement (meas. 6; see also meas. 7, 21, 22, 43, and 44):

Ex. 15

The complete phrase consists of eight measures, composed of a five-measure group and a three-measure group.

The second phrase, to the contrary, consists of two regular four-measure groups (meas. 9-12 and 13-16). The first group, beginning with an evasion of the expected tonic, modulates to the subdominant of the relative major (A-flat major); the second then offers a full-sized cadence in the key of the relative major (E-flat major). The first group uses at first the varied first motif, accompanied by the second, then the second alone, both in imitation. The elaboration of the first motif now employs only the first measure, with an ascending minor seventh and a descending third, imitated at a distance of a single measure; such liberty of treatment prevails throughout the movement and accounts for the impression of fanciful licence it conveys. In the second group of measures, a third principal motif is introduced, a play on large skips, imitated in contrary motion (Flute, meas. 13, and Violin, meas. 14):

Ex. 16

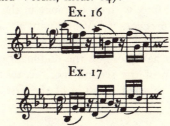

answered by:

Ex. 17

The second section uses inversions of the first motif. This section has, otherwise, a structure similar to that of the first. Two phrases of eight measures each (meas. 17-24 and 25-32) enter with imitations of the first motif. The first phrase, again, displays imitation at the distance of two measures, with the opening interval of a sixth; the second phrase, at the distance of a single measure, the opening interval now being an octave. As in the first section, the first phrase seems to be composed of groups of five and three measures (meas. 17-21 and 22-24), the second phrase of two regular four-measure groups (meas. 25-28 and 29-32).

In both phrases, only the first measure of the first motif is elaborated upon. In the first phrase, the opening of the first motif is followed by variations of the second and the third motifs in succession; thus a three-measure melodic line of great expressive intensity is built up, which is imitated canonically at the second above, after two measures (Flute, meas. 17-19, Violin, meas. 19-21). After striking modulations, this group of measures ends on the tonic. It is followed by a transition to a half-close on the dominant of the dominant (meas. 24), from which the parts move into the corresponding tonic (G minor I, meas. 25).

In the second phrase, the first measure of the first motif is followed by a reminiscence of its first counterpoint, in inversion (Violin, meas. 26, derived from meas. 3); the imitation, at the fifth below, again makes the impression of canonic treatment. The first half-phrase ends with a clear cadence in the minor dominant (meas. 28-29). The second half-phrase, based on the third motif, carries out modulation through the tonic to the subdominant.

The third section opens in a manner clearly recalling the first. The first motif returns in its original direction and shape, accompanied by its original counterpoint (meas. 33-36). The entrances are identical in pitch with those of the first phrase, but introduced in reverse order: the Flute, with an entrance in the subdominant (centering around f''), precedes the Violin with an entrance in the tonic (centering around c''). This opening four-measure group of the section ends with a half-close on the dominant of the tonic.

Then, a variation of the second motif is taken up, extended by a new variation of the first measure of the first (Flute, meas. 37f.):

Ex. 18

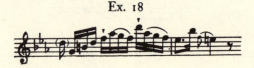

This figure is imitated three times, descending through the cycle of fifths. Thus another modulation to the relative major is effected, but the new tonality is at once abandoned in favor of a strong cadence in the tonic, rhythmically reminiscent of the cadence in the second phrase of the second period (meas. 41-42; cf. meas. 27-28). The cadence provides a clear-cut point of division after six measures of uninterrupted flow (meas. 37-42). It is bridged over, however, by a deceptive bass (going to A♭ instead of the c expected at the beginning of meas. 43) and a suspension (indicated by the figure 7 in the Continuo). Two measures based on the second motif (meas. 43-44) lead into a recapitulation of the last half-phrase from the first period (meas. 45-48 ‖ 13-16). No break is felt between the transitional measures and the recapitulation with which the movement concludes; thus the entire section seems to be composed of 4, 6, and 6 measures, in contrast to the two preceding sections, which were built up in periods of 8 measures. The opening and conclusion of the third section are definitely established as recapitulatory; thus the entire section is felt as a sphere of recapitulation, although exactly half of it is devoted to the introduction of new material or, rather, to different treatment of material introduced before.

The elements of recapitulation within the last section make the structure of the whole, to a certain degree, symmetrical. The metrical irregularity of the last section, on the other hand, establishes the form as asymmetrical. Since the last section deviates from a norm established by the opening two sections, the form seems to dissolve toward the end, thus pointing forward, as befits a movement opening a larger composition. On the whole, the movement displays a wonderful combination of liberty and regularity: possessing the character of a free fantasy, it is at the same time a masterpiece of formal structure. Thus it is particularly suited to form—as it does within the Sonata—the prelude to a fugue. Its relation to the following *Allegro* is emphasized by a thematic tie, for the last of its main motifs is taken up in the course of the *Allegro* in widely used patterns (see pp. 117 ff.).

ALLEGRO

THE SECOND MOVEMENT of the Sonata stands in the exact center of the entire *Musical Offering*.[1] The placing and function of the move-

[1] *Cf.* chapter IV, pp. 35ff.

ment within the whole are clearly expressed in its form, which is more rigidly symmetrical than that of any other part of the work. Contrapuntally, the movement may be classified as a somewhat free fugue with two subjects; structurally, as a strict *da capo* form.

The two subjects employed in the movement are treated quite distinctively. The movement opens with the subject that does not appear in any other part of the work. This subject establishes the brisk two-beat character of the meter and introduces the sixteenth-note motion which pervades the movement. The subject has three basic elements: a conspicuous opening, a middle section formed by a descending series of suspensions expressed within a single melodic line (sequence of 6—7—6—7—6 progressions in meas. 5-7), and an ending which forms an inversion of the beginning, embellished with trills (compare meas. 9 with meas. 1). These elements are employed throughout the movement in imitations and sequences, as material for episodes as well as counterpoints. The opening subject thus determines the character of the entire movement. The Royal theme, on the other hand, enters late, as a counter-subject to the first subject. It appears in diminution, but otherwise unchanged.[2] As it fails to appear without the first subject, and is not developed in any way, it keeps completely aloof from the commotion characteristic of the movement and, therefore, gives the impression of being a kind of *cantus firmus*, even if it does not proceed in slow motion. When the subjects are combined, the first subject of the movement enters a measure before the Royal theme, while they end simultaneously (Violin and Flute, at the beginning of the recapitulation, meas. 160-169, the appearance of the first subject in the Violin being identical with the beginning, meas. 1-10; the transitional figure at the end of the subject in the Violin has been included in the following illustration because it is developed in the course of the movement):

Ex. 19

2 See chapter II, pp. 17ff.

The subjects can be exchanged in double counterpoint at the octave. In the course of the movement, they are presented exclusively in tonic and dominant.

The first section (meas. 1-45) consists, as is usually the case in fugues, of exposition and first episode. Only the principal subject of the movement is introduced. It appears first in the Violin (meas. 1-10), and then in the Flute, a fifth higher and in a tonal-answer form which changes the interval of the up-beat from a fourth to a fifth (meas. 11-20). A third entrance, in the tonic, is expected in the bass. The opening of the subject is, in fact, offered by the bass, but the continuation is replaced by a sequential elaboration of the first measure of the subject, accompanied by counterpoints derived from its center and the transitional figure at its end (meas. 21-28; Flute, meas. 21, cf. meas. 5, or the fifth measure of the example given above; meas. 22, cf. meas. 10, or the last measure quoted above). Transitional measures, employing the same material as the preceding counterpoints, lead to a half-close (meas. 29-33; Continuo, meas. 29-31, cf. Violin, meas. 10; top voices, meas. 32, cf. meas. 5 ff.).

The episode, clearly set off from the exposition by the half-close, opens in the manner of an independent interlude and possesses a more playful character. New melodic patterns appear, recalling the third principal motif of the *Largo*, though in different phrasing (Flute and Violin, meas. 34, see exx. 16-17):

Ex. 20

At first the Flute leads (meas. 34-37), then the Violin, in a combination of the new pattern with the transitional one attached to the subject (meas. 38 ff.):

Ex. 21

After this, the top voices are interlocked in sequentially descending suspensions (meas. 41 ff.). A full cadence in the dominant key concludes the section with great definiteness (meas. 44-45).

The second section employs almost throughout the same material as the first, adding, however, the Royal theme as an important new element. The section is ushered in by an entry of the two subjects in the dominant; while the first subject is presented by the Violin, the Royal theme appears in the bass, with a slightly altered ending (meas. 46-55). Transitional measures follow, based in the upper voices on imitations of the figure from the middle section of the first subject (meas. 56-60). Then the evasive entrance of the first subject in the bass is taken up with its original counterpoints, though transposed and with exchanged upper voices (meas. 61-66 ‖ 21-28). Next, the two subjects are combined for the second time, now in the tonic: while the Flute takes over the first subject, the Royal theme reappears in the bass (meas. 67-76). Finally the interlude returns, without alteration except exchange of the upper voices and transposition; the concluding cadence now occurs in the tonic key. Quite clearly, then, the second section contains the same formal elements as the first: a subject entry in the tonic, a subject entry in the dominant, an evasive elaboration of the first subject in the bass, a small group of transitional measures (though composed of different material), and an episode. The order of these particles, however, is so changed that the dominant entry now precedes the tonic entry and that the continuous series of subject entries is split into two units, separated by transitional measures and the evasive entry, while the clear separation previously existing between subject entries and episode is not recalled. The second section thus is established as a sphere of continuation, in contrast to the opening exposition. Aside from that, the sections display a complete analogy, most conspicuously through the return of the evasive elaboration of the subject opening and of the entire episode. Similar relations between first sections are sometimes found in *da capo* arias of the period.

The third section (meas. 89-159) begins in the key of the relative major—in striking contrast to the minor key in which the preceding section ended. At first the new section plays with the relation between opening and ending of the first subject. Violin and Flute enter canonically in contrary motion with a line headed by the opening of the subject; as the Violin plays without ornaments while the Flute adds trills, the motif in the Violin appears as the opening of the subject, its inversion in the Flute as the concluding motif of the subject. The graceful and sprightly imitation brings about, almost casually, a modulation a second upward, to the subdominant key (meas. 89-96). The middle part of the subject is taken up in undulating parallel lines by the higher instruments, modulating another second upward, to the dominant key (meas. 97-100 and, sequentially, 101-103); then the bass takes over the motif, adopting motion in sixteenth-notes for the first time, though only for a few measures (104-106). Next, the Flute, accompanied by a series of trilled notes in the Violin, elaborates patterns from the episodes which, in turn, recall a motif from the *Largo* (meas. 107 ff.; see the preceding examples):

Ex. 22

Finally a second group of imitations in contrary motion is presented, corresponding to the first measures of the section. Now, however, the imitations open with the ending of the subject with its characteristic trills, instead of the un-ornamented beginning of the subject. In addition, this group of entries is shorter and more condensed than was the first group to which it corresponds (meas. 113-116, *cf.* 89-96; containing 4 entries of the motif in 4 measures instead of 8). The motif taken from the subject is now followed by a version of the pattern from the episode which makes its derivation from the *Largo* motif thoroughly evident (Violin, meas. 113-114):

Ex. 23

The imitations effect a modulation back to the tonic.

As soon as the tonic is reached, the first subject makes its first and only entrance in the bass, fulfilling an expectation that had been kept alive through two full sections and a considerable portion of the third. The entry is made all the more conspicuous by the fact that for the first time the bass has a whole row of measures in continuous sixteenth-note motion. The Royal theme appears in the Violin, taking for the first time to one of the upper voices (meas. 117-125). The end of the entries is bridged over in a most striking manner, for the subject in the bass leaves out the ending motif, closing a measure earlier than the Royal theme. While the bass alters the course of the first subject, the motif from the *Largo* is quoted just once with its own inversion in the Flute (meas. 124):

Ex. 24

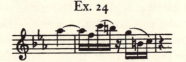

After the isolated appearance of the two subjects, the section resumes its former, more delicate character, and passes in review the elements introduced prior to the presentation of the subjects. Canonic imitation in contrary motion returns. As it begins with the descending motif evaded in the bass entry of the subject, it points back to the imitation in contrary motion immediately preceding the entry of the subjects (meas. 126 ff., recalling 113 ff.). It is, however, more extended and thus carries a weight balancing the beginning of the section (meas. 126-133; cf. 89-96). There is a further extension, consisting of canonic imitation in parallel motion of the descending motif with a new derivation from the *Largo* motif (meas. 132-135). The sequential imitations again bring about a modulation, this time to F minor; from here, transitional measures lead to B-flat minor, using the *Largo* motif in a free imitation in contrary motion (136-137). Then a considerable stretch of the first part of the section is recapitulated. The elaboration of the figure from the middle portion of the first subject returns in full, first with slight alterations of the undulating figures in the high instruments, and then in the bass (meas. 138-147 ‖ 97-106); as before, this passage accomplishes a modulation up a major second, and thus it leads back to the tonic. Next, the reminiscence of the episodes with the accompanying trills returns, with an exchange of the upper voices (meas. 148-151 ‖ 107-110), followed again by transitional measures based on the same material, though recalling the original *Largo* motif more clearly than before (meas. 152-154; cf. 111-112). For the last time, the ending of the first subject appears in imitation in parallel motion as in the extension of the preceding canonic imitation (meas. 155 ff., recalling 134 ff.), but balancing rather the short imitation which preceded the entry of the subjects (meas. 155-159; cf. meas. 113-116). To the motif derived from the subject the *Largo* motif is coupled as before, but the shape and phrasing of the motif are now more strongly reminiscent of its origin than in any previous appearance. The imitation takes place over an intermittent pedal-point on the subdominant, preparing a half-close which is emphasized by a momentary change of tempo (*Adagio*, meas. 158-159).

The entire section is symmetrical in itself, flanking the isolated appearance of the two subjects by free passages of corresponding size (first: 28 measures; second: 34 measures). At beginning and end of each of these passages, imitations of the opening and ending of the first subject are introduced, longer ones at the beginning of each, shorter ones at the end, the central portions of the two being almost identical. Thus the section displays a strictly symmetrical three-part form, with a comparatively short center-piece (9 measures) and no incisions between the parts; and the whole section accordingly forms an ideal center-piece for a symmetrical structure. It contains, however, an element of progressive development, which eliminates the danger of its making a pedantic or artificial impression. This development is based on the motif from the preceding episodes, which is derived ultimately from a motif in the preceding movement. Introduced at first as a seemingly insignificant pattern, it is more and more clearly set into relief in the course of this section; and thus a vague reminiscence is by degrees turned into a conscious reference— a striking and rather unusual feature.

The fourth section (meas. 160-206) recapitulates the first. When, after the half-close, the original tempo is resumed, the Violin offers the first subject again. It is now coupled with the only entry of the Royal theme in the Flute (meas. 160-169). Then a pair of transitional measures modulate to the dominant (meas. 170-171). After these, the second entry of the first subject returns, in the Flute, as before, but without the tonal-answer mutation (meas. 172-181). The introduction of the transitional measures and the change in the opening of the entry help to establish this group of entries, like those of the second section, as a group of middle entries, in contrast to the exposition, which they actually recapitulate. The entry of the first subject in the Flute is accompanied by the same counterpoints as in the first section, not by the Royal theme. From here on, the first section returns without further change; in the 1747 edition, the recapitulation is, in fact, not written out, but simply indicated by the inscription *da capo al Segno*.

The fifth section (meas. 207-249) is identical with the second. The movement ends with the same cadence in the tonic that preceded the beginning of the center section.

The movement as a whole has a *da capo* form of three elements: opening, center, and recapitulation. However, strong cadences are so distributed that the movement falls into five distinct sections. The first and second sections correspond in material and size (45 and 43 measures). The fourth section is almost identical with the first, the fifth completely identical with the second. The first and fourth end with a cadence in the dominant key, the second and fifth with one in the tonic key; all four use the same cadential pattern. The third section, freely symmetrical in itself, begins in the relative major and ends with a half-close on the dominant of the principal key. The third section is longer than any other single section (70 measures against 45), and approximately the same amount smaller than the sum either of the sections preceding it or of those following it (70 measures against 90). Thus it fits the three-part *da capo* form as well as the more conspicuous division of the movement into five sections.

The distribution of the subjects throughout the extended structure enhances its balance. The principal subject of the movement appears nine times: once in both Flute and Violin in each section except the third, and once in the bass, in the exact center of the form. The Royal theme appears six times: twice in the bass, in the second and last sections; once in the Violin, in the exact center of the form; and once in the Flute, at the beginning of the recapitulation. Thus a truly magnificent balance is achieved. Bach rarely created a form of equally strict symmetry. He must have laid out the movement deliberately in such manner that it would form a perfect center-piece for the greater whole of which it was to be a part.[3]

---

[3] Spitta suggests that the counterpoint accompanying the entry of the Royal theme in the bass and that of the first subject in one of the upper voices is reminiscent of a motif from the Three-Part *Ricercar* (Flute, meas. 48-49; *cf. Ricercar a 3*, meas. 42, top voice):

Ex. 25

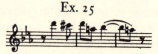

The relation, which is not in any way emphasized, is probably accidental rather than intentional.

It should be noted, however, that the *Allegro* has another, more definite, and more important relation to the *Ricercar a 3*. Both movements contain a contrasting section in which thematic elements are elaborated, opening and ending with clear-cut imitative treatment of these elements. In the *Ricercar a 3*, the contrasting section appears off center and thus impairs the balance of the form; in the *Allegro*, it constitutes the center-piece of a form balanced through complete symmetry. Thus the *Allegro* offers a solution to the problem felt in the improvised fugue, and it is possible that Bach deliberately devised this move-

ANDANTE

IN COMPOSING the slow third movement of a sonata in four movements, Bach often applied a specific stylistic device. Both the Sonata in A major for obbligato harpsichord and violin and the Trio Sonata in C major offer a canon of the upper voices at this place. The Sonata in E major for harpsichord and violin employs a *basso ostinato*. The F-minor Sonata from the same set introduces two-part writing for the violin, accompanied by broken chords in the harpsichord. And the C-minor Sonata from that set makes use of the "echo" manner popular in the seventeenth and eighteenth centuries.[1]

This *Andante*, too, is based on an echo contrast of particles in *forte* and others in *piano*. Here, however, the complete phrases are mostly *forte*, while only a figure of three sixteenth-notes is given *piano*. The *forte* phrase, which opens and dominates the movement, ends with an appoggiatura pattern, a "sigh". In using this pattern, Bach yielded, perhaps deliberately, to a mannerism which was just then in fashion. It is this sigh which returns *piano*, repeated in identical rhythm and melodic pattern, but different pitch. The *forte* phrase is almost a measure long, but incomplete without the tiny echo, which continues and completes the melodic line, and thus has an importance rarely given to echoes in music of the period (Flute and Violin, meas. 1):[2]

Ex. 26

ment in order to present the formal idea introduced unsatisfactorily in the *Ricercar a 3* in an entirely flawless representation. However, the form of the *Allegro* may have been determined entirely by its central position in the ground-plan of the *Musical Offering*.

[1] *Cf.* chapter VI, pp. 58-59.

[2] This movement offers a striking example of metrical units reaching to the beginning of the measure in which the following unit begins. The principal motif begins with the second eighth of a measure and ends with the first eighth of the following measure, and this pattern is maintained practically throughout the movement. Accordingly it might seem more correct to indicate the first appearances of the motif as extending from measure 1 to 3, and the following ones from measure 3 to 5, etc. Such indication, however, would suggest that the structural elements are each three measures long, whereas they actually fill only two. Accordingly the measure numbers are given, for this movement as well as for the others, as indicating the first and last full (or nearly full) measures rather

As the principal motif is presented by the higher voices in parallel motion, the movement is more homophonic than the other movements of the Sonata. Its rhythmic character is determined by a gentle flow. It is written in E-flat major, the relative major of the basic tonality of the Sonata. From the beginning, which inclines toward the subdominant, tonalities shift almost constantly as if to create deliberately a fanciful indefiniteness of harmony. The form of the movement is built up in comparatively small, asymmetrically related segments.

The Royal theme does not appear in the movement, but its influence is felt in certain melodic features. While in the *Largo*, it was exclusively the opening motif of the Royal theme that stimulated Bach's imagination, the *Andante* draws chiefly on the chromatic descent. However, the only direct allusion to the Royal theme occurring in the movement refers, again, to the opening motif.

The principal motif of the movement appears in the upper voices, as quoted above, and is repeated instantly with exchanged voices. one a fifth higher and one a fourth lower. While Flute and Violin are outlining an initial cadence-formula in the tonic key (I—dominant seventh of IV—IV—V—I), an intermittent pedal-point is offered by the bass, which keeps aloof from the dynamic contrast as well as the harmonic progression offered by the upper voices (meas. 1-2). Then the bass assumes the lead, offering twice, in continuous *forte*, a variation of the principal motif in sequence, modulating through F minor to B-flat minor; the upper voices accompany with holds and sighs, also throughout in *forte* (meas. 3-4). In this opening group of entries a regular metrical pattern, based on a unit of two measures, is established—so firmly, in fact, that one expects the two-measure norm to be maintained in the further course of the movement.

Instead of proceeding to the tonic of B-flat minor, the bass turns to its sixth degree, and then sinks chromatically. The upper voices continue and intensify the imitative play of *forte* and *piano* particles, introducing a characteristic new element (see the 32nd-note run, meas. 6). The opening ascent from the principal motif is avoided; thus these measures are felt as an episodic continuation of the initial group of entries. After the bass has descended chromatically through

---

than the measures in which the lines begin and end; the reader may assume that practically any formal particle appearing in this movement ends at the beginning of the measure (or half-measure) following the one quoted above as the last of that particle.

two measures (5 and 6), a full cadence in B-flat major, the dominant, is added. The cadence, which clearly marks the end of an important section, takes up half a measure (first half of meas. 7); thus the second structural element of the movement comprises two measures and a half, in clear contrast to the two-measure norm which seemed so firmly established at the beginning of the movement.

A second elaboration of the principal motif follows, such as often opens the second section of a movement. The upper voices again present the motif twice in parallel motion; the second time they begin a third higher.[3] The opening of the motif is freely imitated by the bass, which abandons the pedal-point pattern accompanying the first appearances of the motif in the upper voices. Modulation through F minor to C minor takes place, and a cadence in the latter tonality—the basic tonality of the entire work—provides the second strong point of division in the movement; thus this passage is isolated from both the preceding and following parts of the form. Again in disregard of the metrical norm, it comprises three measures and a half (meas. 7, second half, and 8-10).

A reminiscence of the Royal theme now appears, as a contrasting new motif; accompanied by the sigh pattern, it is immediately answered by its own inversion (Violin, then Flute, meas. 11):

Ex. 27

This imitation is followed by a single entry of the principal motif, introduced as a continuation to the new motif and accompanied by the pedal-point bass which was missing in the preceding set of regular entries. Thus a strange combination of episodic and thematic elements within the same form segment is achieved. The two-measure formation, which modulates from C minor to F minor, is then repeated a fifth lower with exchanged upper voices, leading from F minor to B-flat minor; thus the entire passage accomplishes a descent from the tonic C to the tonic B flat. Metrically, the norm of two measures established in the first measures of the movement is

---

[3] The completely diatonic pattern of the Flute, meas. 7-8, is taken up by the Violin, meas. 8-9, whereas Violin, meas. 7-8, and Flute, meas. 8-9, both contain a skip; thus the impression of an imitation prevails over that of a sequence.

again strictly adhered to in this passage—for the second time within the movement, though with material of contrasting character.

The next segment has the concluding qualities of a codetta. It descends sequentially and is so filled with alterations that it seems to be thoroughly chromatic although, in fact, it contains no continuous chromatic line. For two measures it seems to move within the tonal circle of B-flat minor, but in the third it modulates to A-flat major, in continuation of the diatonic descent from C to B flat effected in the preceding section. Thus we have proceeded from the related minor to the subdominant of the basic tonality. Contradicting once more the metrical norm of the movement, it is composed of three measures (15-17).

Up to this point, then, five structural elements have been introduced: (1) an exposition of entries of the principal motif, (2) a continuation with episodic material, (3) a second group of entries of the principal motif, in different treatment, (4) a somewhat contrasting passage with a motif from the Royal theme, and (5) a codetta of new episodic material. The first and third of these are related. Strong cadences mark the end of the second, third, and fifth, while the first seems to slide into the second, and the fourth into the fifth.

The rest of the form is given over to recapitulation. First, the opening four measures return in full, establishing once more the metrical norm of two measures, in double presentation. The restatement begins in the subdominant and is therefore not felt as a final recapitulation of the material; in the second half the upper voices are exchanged (meas. 18-21 || 1-4). Next comes the passage with the chromatically falling bass, transposed and with upper voices exchanged. It is extended by a measure and a half; filling four measures, it now complies with the metrical norm. The extension leads back to the tonic key, ending with an unemphatic half-close (meas. 22-25 || 5-7). Third, the codetta appears again, transposed and with exchanged upper voices. Only the first two measures return, so that this passage, too, falls metrically into line; harmonically it simply leads from the dominant back to the tonic (meas. 26-27 || 15-17). Fourth, a final recapitulation of the opening is presented, with exchanged upper voices, but in the tonic key. It balances the third structural element of the first part of the form, in that it brings the number of appearances of the main motif in two-part presentation within the recapitulation up to four, the number they had reached before the C-minor incision (meas. 28-29 cf. 7-10). Altogether, the recapitulation comprises 12 full measures, built up in a clear series of two-measure links—returning to the metrical norm established but then abandoned in the course of the earlier parts of the form.

A strangely complicated and yet perfectly lucid structure results. Of the five formal elements introduced in what might be called the arsis of the movement, three—the first, second, and last—are clearly recapitulated during the thesis of the formal development. To these is then added a second recapitulation of the first element. Accordingly the thesis of the form contains, as did the arsis, exactly two groups of entries of the principal motif. The only element, then, that has no counterpart in the recapitulation is the contrasting fourth one. Such isolated contrasting parts of form are usually given as center pieces within a movement. Here, however, the contrasting structural element is followed by the codetta which, in turn, reappears in the recapitulation. The structure may therefore be described as one in which the second part represents a selective and reshuffled recapitulation of the elements of the first. The result is a perfectly balanced form which, nevertheless, contains a contrasting section off center and continues to introduce new material beyond the middle of the form.[4]

This unique construction is made even more interesting and convincing through its treatment of metrical patterns. Of the five particles introduced before the opening of the recapitulation, only two show metrical regularity: the very first, and the contrasting section, which is not to be recapitulated. All parts of the recapitulation, on the other hand, agree with the metrical norm established at the opening of the movement. Two of the irregular patterns contained in the arsis of the form are afterwards adjusted and the third balanced by a metrically regular counterpart; thus a predominantly irregular exposition is recalled in a thoroughly regular recapitulation.[5]

[4] The *Ricercar a 3* suffered from the introduction of an insufficiently balanced contrasting section. In the *Allegro* of the Sonata, Bach created a thoroughly symmetrical form, which introduced a contrasting section as a center-piece, clearly without endangering the balance of the whole. The movement thus offered a solution to the problem arising in the *Ricercar a 3*, simply through complete symmetry. The *Andante* displays both asymmetry and balance, thus solving a problem much more puzzling than that of the *Allegro*. It may be doubted, however, whether the relation between this movement and the improvised fugue was intentional.

[5] This is by no means the only composition by Bach in which a metrical norm is first established, then contradicted, and finally restored; a simpler application of the same principle is found, within the *Musical Offering*, in the Canonic Fugue, No. 12 (see chapter VI, pp. 81-82).

ALLEGRO

THE LAST MOVEMENT of the Sonata, like the second, is entitled *Allegro*. The common title indicates that the two movements display certain similarities, but they are nevertheless strikingly contrasted. Both use the sixteenth-note as the smallest unit of continuous motion, but the first is conceived in 2/4 meter, the second in 6/8. Both are fugues employing the Royal theme as a subject, but the first introduces the Royal theme in its original shape and couples it throughout with another subject, while the second uses the Royal theme in an extreme variation and as its sole subject. In addition, the movements are contrasted as follows:

(1) The first fugue contains licences such as the evasion of the bass entry of the first subject during the exposition and the twofold appearance of the Royal theme in the bass prior to its entry in another voice; the second fugue shows considerably greater regularity.

(2) The first fugue restricts the entries of the subjects to tonic and dominant; the second fugue offers its one subject in a rather wide range of tonalities.

(3) The first fugue, much more extended than the second, builds up a structure of the greatest symmetry through generous recapitulations; the second fugue creates unity of form, on a much smaller scale, through an intricate system of asymmetrical relations.

The Royal theme in its present variation ends with an inversion of its beginning, as did the first subject of the earlier *Allegro* (Flute, meas. 1-9):

Ex. 28

The theme appears altogether eight times: three times within the first third of the form, three times within the second, and twice within the last. The third and sixth entries—that is, the last entries within the first and second thirds of the form—are given to the bass, the other appearances of the subject being evenly divided between the upper voices. Four of the entries are offered in the tonic; two in the first third of the movement, and two in the last; the other four entries represent four additional tonalities.

The first three entries, in tonic, dominant, and tonic, form a regular exposition; no melodic distinction is made between subject and answer. The first entrance of the middle group is given in the relative major key, E flat. From here on, the entrances follow each other in a continuous series of ascending fifths until the tonic is reached again: E-flat major, B-flat major, F minor, C minor. The tonic at the end of this tonal ascent is strengthened by the introduction of two entries of identical pitch.

The order of modulation as expressed by the entries of the subject is strongly emphasized by cadences. The first break is made by a complete ending in E-flat major, concluding the first third of the movement (38 measures out of 113). The next break is made by a cadence in B-flat major at about the middle of the fugue (meas. 60-61). Another point of division of similar force is created by a cadence in F minor at the end of the second third (meas. 76-77). Finally the pattern of the E-flat major cadence returns as the concluding cadence in the tonic key. Thus the cadences, too, represent an ascent in fifths from the relative major to the tonic. The cadence in E-flat major precedes the subject entry in the same key, while the cadences in B-flat major and F minor coincide with the ending of the subject entries in these tonalities. The modulation from B-flat major, the dominant of the relative major, to F minor, the subdominant, marks the transition from the dominant side to the subdominant side, a transition frequently marking the beginning of the second half in compositions by Bach. This general scheme, which by itself assures a definite unity of structure, is worked out with a wealth of varied and ingenious details.[1]

The first section (meas. 1-38) introduces the subject in the three voices, according to regular fugal practice, and adds an episode. The first entry of the subject, in the Flute (meas. 1-8), is supported from the beginning by the Continuo, which moves, like the subject, in quarter-notes and eighth-notes. The Continuo actually opens the

---

[1] Various sections within the present movement are so dovetailed that it has seemed necessary to deviate here from the principle of figuring any measure as belonging to only one section. The same holds true of certain places in the following analysis of the Six-Part *Ricercar*.

movement, with a broken triad in eighth-notes, a pattern which returns several times at conspicuous points within the movement ("a" in the following example); the bass then alludes to the opening of the subject ("b") and continues with a diatonic descent which is an inversion of the opening of the subject and an anticipation of its conclusion ("c"; the following quotation gives Continuo, meas. 1-6):

Ex. 29

The second entry of the subject, in the Violin (meas. 9-16), is accompanied by a brilliant first counterpoint including a descending scale-run in sixteenth-notes, covering a ninth; and a bass line which, again, imitates the beginning of the subject (b, in meas. 10) and then ascends, through a series of trilled notes. The end of the entry is emphasized by a short cadence in G minor, marking approximately the middle of the first section (meas. 16-17).

Transitional measures, so neatly imitative that they seem to replace an episode, employ the broken-triad motif in the bass (a, in meas. 17, 19, and 21) and introduce new material in the upper voices. The lines of Flute and Violin are interchanged in double counterpoint after two measures (cf. meas. 17-18 and 19-20). There is a digression from G minor through F minor to E-flat major, but then the tonic returns, indicating that the modulation was only intended to break the tonal monotony of the regular exposition.

The expected third entry of the subject, in the bass (meas. 23-30), is accompanied by a new version of the first counterpoint in the Violin and an entirely new counterpoint in the Flute; the first is characterized by increased sixteenth-note motion, while the latter takes over the initial allusion to the subject opening (b, Flute, meas. 23-24).

The following episode begins modestly, as if it were to represent only another group of transitional measures. A new motif, reminiscent of the subject-opening, is introduced by the Violin (meas. 31):

Ex. 30

This motif is worked out in imitation at the third above, after one measure; it is coupled with a counter-motif in double counterpoint.

The ascending imitation brings about a modulation to the dominant of E-flat major (meas. 31-33). Then the bass takes the lead with an ascending sequence of descending scale-runs in sixteenth-notes, accompanied in the upper voices by free imitations of the end of the motif quoted above (meas. 34-36). The conclusion is made by the cadence in E-flat major, which interrupts the 6/8 flow of the movement with a clear 3/4 pattern (meas. 37).

The second section (meas. 38-61) opens with an elaboration of the subject-ending. The motif appears here in two forms, which, again, are interchanged by the upper voices in double counterpoint (meas. 38-44). These imitations support a series of modulations, which separate the E-flat cadence from the impending E-flat entry of the subject. The entry, in the Violin, is accompanied by the counterpoints heard with the second entry of the subject in the exposition—an entry also played by the Violin and the first one in the entire movement to be accompanied by two clear-cut counterpoints (meas. 44-52 ‖ 9-17). Transitional measures with a sequence of the subject-ending in the Violin (meas. 52-53, reminiscent of 8-9) prepare the entry in B-flat major, in the Flute (meas. 53-61). This entry employs the same counterpoints as the preceding entry, with a slight change of the bass at the end to set the cadence in B-flat major into sharper relief (meas. 59-61, another allusion to the subject-opening, now forming an inverted anticipation of the subject-ending and immediately preceding the skips of the final cadence).

The third section (meas. 61-77) opens with surprising vivacity. The Violin recalls once more the initial broken-triad figure; then the upper voices offer scale-runs and broken chords in sixteenth-note motion, while the bass accompanies in eighth-note broken chords. Some sixteenth-note motion appeared in the first two sections, but, except for the scale-runs in the bass before the end of the first section, only sporadically; thus the motion seems to be increased suddenly at this point. The upper voices imitate each other, again in double counterpoint. The bass at first supports them lightly, then alludes to the opening of the subject (meas. 65-68). The allusion is taken up by the Violin (meas. 69), and then the F-minor entry of the subject is presented by the bass. It is accompanied by the same counterpoints as the last entry of the exposition—which was also an entry in the bass and the second presentation of the subject with two clear-cut counterpoints (meas. 69-77 ‖ 23-31).

The last section (meas. 77-113) recapitulates at first the opening of the third, in transposition and with exchanged upper voices (meas. 77-81 ‖ 61-65). The episode, however, is now extended. In the earlier episode, motion in sixteenth-notes was predominant, but not entirely continuous; now an uninterrupted flow of sixteenth-notes is presented, first by the Violin (meas. 82-85), then by the Flute (meas. 85-88), and then by the two instruments alternately (meas. 88-89). At the beginning of the extension, the key of the movement is momentarily recalled (meas. 82-83), but left again. While the Flute plays its arabesques, the tonic is brought back to mind through a pedal-point in the Violin (meas. 85-88). Once more the bass alludes to the subject-opening, in the tonic (meas. 88-89), and now, finally, the subject itself returns in the tonic key, offered by the Flute (meas. 89-96). The subject is accompanied by new counterpoints. The bass, rather insignificantly, supports the upper voices in eighth-note motion, as it supported the opening entry. The Violin, on the other hand, maintains the continuous motion in sixteenth-notes, reached immediately before in the episode, and thus this entry becomes clearly the climax of the movement.

Before the subject ends, the bass takes over the sixteenth-note patterns (meas. 95), and in the same measure the Violin cuts in with another entry of the subject in the tonic, at the same pitch as the Flute. Thus the two entries are firmly interlocked to form a final block.[2] The entry in the Violin is accompanied by the same counterpoints as the preceding entry in the Flute, a quite unusual detail, which further tightens the connection between the two entries (Flute, meas. 97-100 = Violin, meas. 91-94; Continuo, meas. 97-101 = 91-95).

The end of the entry in the Violin is bridged over by a modulating evasion (G minor II 7 as suspension before an inversion of the diminished-seventh chord, instead of C minor I). Thus a coda is introduced which recalls elements from the first section with increasing definiteness. First, the Violin offers a derivation from the last counterpoint while the Flute adds a new eighth-note figure; after

---

[2] Technically the overlapping of the two entries may be called a stretto, but the second entry comes so late that the impression is one of structural overlapping rather than contrapuntal intensification.

two measures, the two instruments are interchanged—recalling the structural principle of the transitional measures, though without an actual thematic allusion (meas. 103-106, *cf.* 17 ff.). The bass reaches the tonic at the beginning of the second, unaccented measure within the metrical unit (meas. 104), but in the next measure the evasion is repeated, and at the beginning of the next particle (meas. 107), another evasion is introduced (C minor VI instead of I). At this point, the one-measure imitation at the higher third is taken over from the first episode; now the motif used reappears as well as the principle of treatment (meas. 107-108, recalling 31-33, without the counter-motif and in but twofold imitation). Then, finally, a true recapitulation is offered: the end of the first episode returns, with its scale-runs in the bass and its imitations in the upper voices (meas. 109-113 || 34-38). The passage is slightly altered, but concluded with the same 3/4 pattern in the final cadence. This, then, is not only the strictest piece of recapitulation offered, but also the recapitulation of the last conspicuous element from the first section which remained to be restated.

The treatment of counterpoints in this fugue is strikingly exceptional. The first entry of the subject is supported by a bass-line too casual to be recognized as a true counterpoint, and accordingly not recurring. The pair of counterpoints to the second entry returns twice, with the two entries of the middle group entrusted to the upper voices. The pair of counterpoints to the third entry returns once, with the concluding entry of the middle group. Thus the counterpoints of the exposition are all used again within the second third of the movement. The last two entries, on the other hand, employ identical counterpoints and are thus interrelated. Now, the introduction of new counterpoints toward the end of a movement is apt to disturb the unity of form. Bach eliminates this danger by establishing the last counterpoints as the conclusion of a rhythmic development. He begins the movement in eighth-note motion; then adds sixteenth-notes sparingly; builds up an episode with sixteenth-note motion predominating; enlarges the recapitulation of this episode with an extension in continuous sixteenth-note motion; and finally uses this extreme of motion for the counterpoints to the last entries of the subject—the counterpoints entering after the recapitulation of the counterpoints previously introduced. Thus the movement acquires unity although the last pair of counterpoints lacks recapitulation, and accomplishes, at the same time, a development to a climax.[3]

[3] In the *Ricercar a 3*, the last of three pairs of counterpoints was not taken up again. No particular reason could be seen for such discriminating treatment, and accordingly it was felt as a shortcoming in the structure. The concluding *Allegro* of the Sonata offers a convincing solution to the problem left open in the improvised fugue. Possibly Bach was prompted to create the present form by the inconsistency he had failed to eliminate or justify in the *Ricercar a 3*.

RICERCAR A 6 (SIX-PART FUGUE)

THE SIX-PART *Ricercar*, magnificent finale of the *Musical Offering*, is a strict fugue with the Royal theme as the sole subject—like the Three-Part *Ricercar* with which the work opens. As in the Three-Part *Ricercar*, the Royal theme is used in duple time and quiet motion, without embellishing or intensifying variation. As in the Three-Part *Ricercar*, certain particles of the theme are worked out separately. As in the Three-Part *Ricercar*, the sections are carefully interrelated. The structure of the *Ricercar a 6*, however, is considerably more involved and, at the same time, more minutely balanced than that of the three-part model.

While at Potsdam, Bach improvised a fugue on the Royal theme, and this fugue apparently was the Three-Part *Ricercar*.[1] Bach declined to improvise a six-part fugue on the same subject although he seems to have been specifically asked to do so. With the Six-Part *Ricercar*, he met the challenge. Evidently he intended to make this fugue a masterpiece in every respect; and it is, in fact, one of his greatest works. Its contrapuntal intensity, its beauty of sound, its depth of expression stand out even among the representative creations of Bach's last period, and its structure is a perfect example of monumental conception and impeccable delivery.

The Royal theme is used almost exactly in its original shape; however, the isolated pair of eighth-notes in the concluding passage is eliminated:

Ex. 31

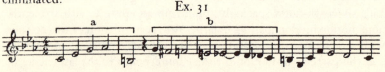

Of the three melodic elements contained in the theme, only the first

[1] See chapter I, pp. 5-8, and above, p. 110, with note.

(a) and second (b) are elaborated upon in this fugue. Of the first, furthermore, only the opening triad is employed. The second, the chromatic descent, is used in two forms, neither of which refers to the diminution included in the theme itself. Thus the thematic material is reduced here to a minimum of essential forms, in contrast to the Three-Part *Ricercar*, where all elements of the theme are subject to contrapuntal elaboration.

Twelve entrances of the theme are offered in the course of the composition. Six entries make up the exposition (meas. 1-28), and an equal number are distributed through the rest of the movement. The subject appears six times in its original subject form, the third note of which is a fifth above the opening note; and six times in a tonal-answer form, which replaces the fifth by a fourth. Subject and answer alternate throughout the fugue, although in the exposition, the subject leads off, while in the rest of the movement it follows the answer.

Each of the six parts presents the subject twice: once in the exposition and once later on. In the exposition, the parts are introduced in such order that (if we designate the highest part as i, the next highest as ii, etc.) odd and even numbers alternate, the scheme of entrances in the exposition being: iii, ii, v, iv, i, vi. Later the entrances are given first to the three "odd" parts and then to the three "even" parts; thus the order of parts in the seventh to twelfth entries is: v, iii, i; iv, ii, vi. Among this second half-dozen entries only two are brought together so closely that they seem to form a group. These two entries are the third and fourth within the half-dozen (i and iv) —the last of the three odd-part entries and the first of the three even-part entries. Thus the gap between the group of odd entries and the group of even entries is bridged over.[2]

As the later entries of the subject are more distant from each other than those of the exposition, 7 out of the 12 entries occur in the first half of the movement (meas. 1-51). Throughout this first half, the subject appears exclusively in tonic and dominant. The seventh entry

[2] In the instrumentation for reeds and strings suggested for representative performance of the *Musical Offering* (see chapter V, pp. 50-52), the odd numbers are represented by reed instruments, the even numbers by string instruments. Accordingly the entries in the exposition display alternation of tone colors while afterwards the three instruments of the reed family precede with their entries the three entries of the subject in the strings, the last entry in a reed instrument being succeeded within the same group of entries by the first of the concluding presentation of the subject by strings. Thus it becomes evident that the differentiation in the treatment of the odd and even parts is by no means of merely academic interest.

(meas. 48-51) thus is brought into close connection with the six entries of the exposition. But this entry is separated from the preceding ones by long stretches of episodic character; it is, moreover, set off against the entries of the exposition by the fact that it offers an answer form following another answer form—interrupting, for the first and only time, the continuous alternation between subject and answer otherwise strictly adhered to.[3]

The seventh entry of the subject, on G, is followed by an entry on F (meas. 58-61) and this, in turn, by one on E♭ (meas. 66-69); thus the three first middle entries are brought together as elements of a continuous diatonic descent. The answer-shape of the last of these entries, however, is so clearly established that the tonality is felt predominantly as A-flat major. This entry is followed by one in B-flat minor (meas. 73-76), and this by another answer in C minor (meas. 86-89); thus a diatonic ascent is carried out which unites the third to fifth entries exactly as the diatonic descent had united the first to third of this second group of six. It should be noted that the third entry forms the last link of the descent as well as the first of the ascent, and that the descent is carried by the scale degrees while the ascent is expressed by tonalities.[4]

[3] We expect continuous alternation or variety in the presentation of the subject in the course of a fugue. Accordingly the subject cannot appear twice in succession at the same pitch or in the same voice without indicating a break. Sometimes Bach uses such repetition to emphasize that we have passed from one section of form to another; Tovey, in his *Companion to Bach's "The Art of Fugue"*, London, 1931, p. 14, comments upon an "extreme case" of such "deliberate contempt for a rule about which some eighteenth-century theorists were very strict." Here, the implication is quite clearly that we have passed from the first half of entries to the second. In all such cases, Bach does not simply disregard the sensible old rule in order to gain greater freedom of action—he uses the momentary suspension of the rule as a means of formal construction.

[4] In the exposition, the answer opens in all three appearances without a leading-tone, using B♭ instead of the B♮ which is characteristic of the ascending C-minor scale; since the answer appears in all instances without a preparatory modulation to G minor and twice even above the tonic C, it appears as a modal variation rather than a dominant form. The seventh entry likewise introduces B♭ before a modulation to G minor has been carried out. The entry on E♭, on the other hand, and the last entry on G contain the leading-tone in the first measure and emphasize this by accompanying the opening note with a major third and minor seventh; both entries are thus formed to represent an unmistakable dominant. All the answer entries quite naturally turn toward the dominant, but only the sixth, seventh, and eleventh entries, all on G, end with a full close in G minor, while the second and fourth evade the concluding tonic G-minor chord. The ninth entry, on E♭, ends, as it began, with a dominant chord (E♭ harmonized as A-flat major V$\frac{6}{5}$.) and thus maintains its dominant character to the end, which helps to set the diatonically ascending order into relief.

It might be mentioned that a diatonic descent from G to E♭, followed by a

After the tonic has been recalled by the opening of the C-minor answer—which then turns to the dominant, so strongly expressed within the first half of the movement—a single additional entry is introduced, the concluding appearance of the subject in the tonic (meas. 99-103). This, the twelfth appearance of the theme, takes place in the lowest part, like the sixth, which concluded the exposition. The eleventh as well as twelfth entries recall pitches used during the exposition and thus carry an additional element of recapitulation.

The first section (meas. 1-39) is opened, as usual, by the exposition, which fills almost a third of the entire form (meas. 1-28), and is rounded out by the first episode, which is correspondingly of unusual length (meas. 29-39).

The subject moves predominantly in half-notes (first entry, iii, meas. 1-4). It contains quarter notes, but, in contrast to all previous appearances of the Royal theme, not a single eighth-note. A subject in slow motion, it will be recalled, was characteristic of the *ricercar* of the sixteenth and seventeenth centuries.[5]

The second entry of the subject (ii, meas. 5-8) is accompanied by an independent counterpoint, which, together with the theme, establishes continuous motion in quarters. The counterpoint starts with a conspicuous series of skips, evidently of *staccato* character (iii, meas. 5-6; cf. *Ricercar a 3*, motif d):

Ex. 32

---

diatonic ascent from Eb to G appears in the *Ricercar a 3*, preceding the second group of entries (meas. 38-46). Both descent and ascent were expressed by the principal notes of the bass, partly supported by modulation. The transition from the descent to the ascent was not accented by changes in general treatment and, for this reason, not thoroughly convincing. In the *Ricercar a 6*, the points connected by the two branches of diatonic progression are widely separated and the descent, as indicated above, is expressed by other means than the ascent; in addition to this, the ascent does not use the same degrees of the scale as the descent (G F Eb—Ab Bb C). These elements suffice to make the present inversion of the basic line entirely convincing. The treatment in both cases is somewhat unusual, and there is, at least, a possibility that the somewhat awkward use of a diatonic descent turning into a diatonic ascent in the *Ricercar a 3* gave Bach the idea of applying the same principle to the *Ricercar a 6*, on an enlarged scale and in an improved form.

[5] See chapter III, pp. 28f.

After this opening, the counterpoint introduces eighth-notes at two places (meas. 6 and 7). The eighth-notes do not form a continuous or predominant motion (as in the *Ricercar a 3*), but appear for a long time mostly in pairs. The cadence at the end of the entry is evaded in a progression typical of the somewhat archaic harmony employed in this *ricercar* (G minor I—II—V—IV).

The first counterpoint returns with the next two entries of the subject (ii, meas. 9-12, against the theme in v; v, meas. 13-16, against the theme in iv). The other voices begin to introduce pairs of eighth-notes with increasing frequency, establishing a kind of intermittent pulse; this pulse is at first of a predominantly dactylic character (♩ ♫♩), but then relies more and more on anapaestic patterns (♫♩).[6]

At the end of the fourth entry, the first clear-cut cadence seems to develop, but the tonic is evaded (G minor VI instead of I, meas. 17). A pair of transitional measures intervene (meas. 17-18). Opened by a short imitation (iii and ii in meas. 17) and supported by a resolutely ascending bass (v, meas. 17-18), they accomplish the required return from the dominant to the tonic in sustained lines, enlivened by the dactylic pulse and ending, as they began, with a deceptive cadence (C minor VI instead of I, meas. 19).

The next entry (i, meas. 19-22) is accompanied by mere remnants of the first counterpoint (see meas. iv, meas. 19-20), while the dactylic pulse becomes more and more conspicuous. Again the concluding cadence is evaded (F minor V 2 instead of C minor I; *cf. Ricercar a 3*, meas. 67). A second pair of transitional measures is introduced (meas. 23-24). Opening with another short imitation, in anapaestic rhythm (ii and i in meas. 23), and supported by a slowly descending bass (v), these measures build up tension for the last appearance of the theme within the exposition (notice the flourish of i in meas. 24).

The subject (vi, meas. 25-28) is now accompanied by sustained upper voices locked together in suspensions (i and ii in meas. 25-27)

[6] Mr. Arthur Mendel has raised the question whether the stress on the dactyls might have anything to do with the omission of the eighth-notes in the subject. I doubt whether we shall ever know enough about the inner workings of Bach's mind to answer such a nice point, but the question itself may invite fruitful speculation.

and an almost continuous imitative play of the dactylic pulse. The original first counterpoint has completely disappeared; it does not return with any further entry of the subject. The end of the theme supports a secondary cadence in G minor (meas. 28-29; V is represented by a second inversion: $\frac{4}{3}$). The six parts introduced during the exposition continue without considerable rests to the end of the section.

The first episode, beginning quietly with no motion faster than that in quarter-notes, is built over a dominating chromatic line, a free inversion of the second particle from the Royal theme. The parts separate into two groups, a lower and a higher choir. The top part of the lower choir (iv) leads, accompanied in parallels by diatonically ascending basses; the progression is that of a series of triads and first inversions in alternation (in thorough-bass figuring: 5 6 5 6). The voices of the higher choir descend diatonically in imitation of a new motif (i in meas. 29; iii and ii in 30; i again in 31):

Ex. 33

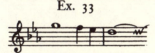

While the new motif is taken up by the leading voice (iv, meas. 31-32) and the chromatic ascent emerges for a moment in the higher choir (ii, meas. 32), the anapaestic version of the rhythmic-pulse figure (♪♪ ♩) enters in the top voices, bringing the motion back to the level reached at the end of the exposition (see i and ii in meas. 31; i, then iii in 32; cf. meas. 23). During a bridged-over cadence in C minor, the figure passes through the leading voice (iv, meas. 33) and then attaches itself to the first bass (v, meas. 33-35).

The key of C minor having returned, a second ascent of the lower choir begins, led again by the chromatic top voice and accompanied by the upper choir in contrary motion. Again the voices of the lower choir move in parallels, though each now has a different rhythmic pattern, and again the diatonic descending motif pervades in slow imitation the voices of the upper choir (ii, then i in meas. 34; ii again in 35; i and iii in 36). As in the first phrase of the episode, the motif is then taken up by the lower choir (iv in meas. 36; vi in 37), while the anapaestic pulse once more animates parts of the upper choir (meas. 36 ff.). The relative major is reached, and a broad cadence in

E-flat major ends the section; this, the first complete and fully em
phasized cadence within the movement, marks the close of approximately the second fifth of the whole (meas. 39).

The second section (meas. 39-52) opens with elaborations of material derived from the Royal theme (meas. 39-44 and 45-47); these
are followed by the first middle entry of the subject itself (meas.
48-52).

The parts reenter successively, mostly at the distance of an octave
or fifth, in what may be called a secondary exposition—a thematic
elaboration clearly set off against the preceding episode as well as
the following entry of the full theme.[7] The subject of this elaboration is a chromatic motif, related to the middle part of the subject,
accompanied and in general followed by a counterpoint motif (iv
and ii, meas. 39-40):

Ex. 34

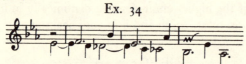

After the two-part opening, the voices enter successively until the
full body of six parts has been brought into action again. Once more
an initial motion of quarter-notes is accelerated through gradual introduction of the rhythmic-pulse figure. Modulation to the dominant
of E flat takes place. The new tonality, B-flat major, is emphasized
by a passing cadence, apparently of minor importance, marking the
end of the elaboration of the chromatic motif (meas. 44-45).

As soon as the tonic of B-flat major is reached, the opening broken

[7] Bach, in many fugues, does not content himself with introducing simply
entries or groups of entries on the one hand, and episodes on the other, but adds
a third type of contrapuntal treatment which is as distinct from the one as from
the other. It seems advisable to distinguish in such cases between "episodes",
which are always of a transitional nature and employ sequences to a considerable extent, and "thematic elaborations", which are more self-contained and may
be built up as groups of entries of secondary material. The present example is
a model of such treatment: the contrast between the sequential episode, which
ended with the E-flat major cadence, and the introduction of the chromatic
motif in voice after voice, exactly in the manner of a fugue-opening, is just as
evident as the contrast between the elaboration of the motif and a true entry
of the subject. It would be impossible to call the elaboration of the chromatic
motif an episode, and it would be just as impossible to consider the episode as
comprising the entire section from measure 29 to 44 or 47. The contrast between
the episode and the thematic elaboration becomes even more striking if we consider that both are based on the same material—the chromatic descent from the
Royal theme.

triad of the Royal theme enters, accompanied from the beginning by
a new counterpoint motif (vi, in our example transposed an octave
upwards, and i in meas. 45):

Ex. 35

Three times these motifs appear in imitation at the higher fifth
(vi with i, and v with iv in meas. 45; ii with iii in 46). The entries of
the broken triad are felt as deceptive entries of the subject itself.
They carry a modulation toward C minor, in harmonization of modal
character. An additional entry of the triad in the bass (vi, again with
i, in meas. 47) prepares the actual return of the Royal theme.

This entry of the answer (v, meas. 48-51) proceeds over a bass
which, at first, descends diatonically in slow motion to a pedal point
and then imitates the chromatic descent from the subject. The higher
voices are dominated by the dactylic pulse. The end of the entry is
accompanied by an incisive cadence in G minor, the dominant, marking the end of the first half of the form with a characteristic bit of
imitation (ii and iii in meas. 51):

Ex. 36

The third section (meas. 52-62) begins with a secondary exposition, similar to that introduced at the beginning of the second section
—an element of recapitulation which indicates that the second half
of the movement has been reached (compare meas. 52-57 and 39-44).
Again the parts enter successively in imitation, and again a main motif
is derived from the chromatic descent of the Royal theme. The
chromatic motif, however, appears now in a new rhythmic shape. It
is, in addition, coupled with an equally important diatonically ascending countermotif, and this countermotif precedes in most parts
the entrance of the chromatic motif itself (i and iv, meas. 52-53):

Ex. 37

The entries follow each other mostly at the higher fourth or lower fifth, modulating sooner and more definitely than those of the preceding secondary exposition. Thus, the parallelism between the sections is noticeably reduced by variation. The second elaboration of the chromatic motif presents, at the same time, an increase in intensity over the first, for it works out, from the beginning, three motifs instead of two. The third motif introduces series of four eighth-notes, establishing a new level of rhythmic motion (ii in meas. 52-53, simultaneously with the parts quoted above):

Ex. 38

In six entrances of the main motifs, against five in the previous section, modulation to the subdominant is effected; such a swerve from the dominant side to the subdominant side often takes place in movements by Bach at the beginning of the second half.[8]

The F-minor entry of the subject, which constitutes the second formal element of the section, is accompanied largely by counterpoints derived from the third motif of the preceding secondary exposition (compare i in meas. 53 with i in meas. 58 and 59, vi in 59 and 61, and ii in 60). Thus the dactylic pulse previously set against the theme gives way to an almost continuous flow of eighth-notes, carried by various parts in alternation and marking a new phase in the rhythmic development of the movement. The end of the entry is marked by a condensed cadence in F minor, concluding the third fifth of the form (meas. 61-62; subdominant and dominant are each given the length of a quarter-note).

The incision caused by the cadence is ingeniously bridged over. Repeating the notes reached with the tonic chord, the higher voices attach the opening triad from the Royal theme in inversion (i) and in diminished inversion (ii, imitated by iii, meas. 62-63). Forming a descending sequence, they seem to flow off easily, dissipating the energy carried over through the cadence. The continuous motion now reaches a new level in the lower voices. Runs of eight eighth-notes in succession are exchanged between the two basses, forming practically a single, entirely continuous line; while the second bass descends, moving throughout in diatonic steps, the first breaks a diatonic ascent with a single skip (v and vi, meas. 62-63):

[8] An example is found in the last *Allegro* of the Sonata; see p. 129.

Ex. 39

The figure introduced by the first bass ascends into higher parts (iv, then ii in meas. 64; iii, then v and ii in 65). The undiminished inversion of the subject opening disappears; the diminution, no longer appearing in imitation, lingers for a short while in the second bass (vi, meas. 64-65) and then is also eliminated. The thematic importance of all parts is thus reduced to a minimum. Ample rests are introduced, and a new character seems to assert itself. The garlands of eighth-notes form what appears to be a background for a more significant thematic development rather than an important detail in itself. The few measures following the F-minor cadence thus offer a transition that is, in fact, a great *diminuendo*, realized entirely through contrapuntal means.[9]

The last third of the form (meas. 66-103) begins with a recapitulation of exceptional structure. While three parts drop out (iii in meas. 66 with an allusion to the ascending head of the theme in diminution), the subject enters again (i, meas. 66-69). It is accompanied by only two voices (ii and vi). They introduce completely new counterpoints, forming continuous runs of eighth-notes with little rhythmic or thematic relief; thus a climax of motion is reached. The subject, moving calmly in strong contrast to the lively counterpoints, gives the impression of a new beginning. It seems to open a second exposition; thus it recalls the opening of the movement itself and, for that very reason, is felt as the beginning of the recapitulation.

The recapitulating function of the second exposition is emphasized by various details. The entry of the Royal theme ends with an evasive cadence similar to that opening the second group of transi-

[9] In the *Ricercar a 3*, Bach made use of the chromatic descent in both original direction and inversion, while he did not introduce the head of the theme in inversion. The *Ricercar a 6*, accordingly, is thematically richer and, since it introduces both elements in both forms, more consistent, even if the inversion of the theme-opening appears only in this one rather unimportant passage.

The *Ricercar a 3* introduced both the theme-opening and the chromatic descent in diminution, the latter in quarters as well as eighth-notes. The *Ricercar a 6*, on the other hand, uses the theme-opening, descending and ascending, in diminution, while it avoids the metric ambiguity resulting in the *Ricercar a 3* from the use of the chromatic motif not only in half-notes and quarters, but also in a diminution of both.

tional measures in the exposition proper (meas. 70, last note of the theme harmonized as the root of a dominant seventh chord, as in meas. 23). Here, too, transitional measures follow; they recall the diminution of the theme opening (i, meas. 70-71, first ascending, like iii in 66; and then inverted, like ii and iii in 62-63), while the bass continues in uninterrupted eighth-note motion.

At the end of the transitional measures, a fourth part enters (v, meas. 72) with a deceptive entry of the theme-opening, reminiscent of the deceptive entry preceding the seventh appearance of the theme (*cf.* vi, meas. 47). The real entry is provided by a fifth part (iv, meas. 73-76). The entry is given at the fourth below the preceding one—an interval typical of fugue expositions, although the relation between the entries is here weakened by the fact that the order of subject and answer is reversed. The counterpoints abound in reminiscences of material previously exploited. The first measure is accompanied by a chromatic descent containing quarter-notes, recalling the chromatic motif elaborated in the first secondary exposition (ii, meas. 73; *cf.* meas. 39 ff.). The chromatic descent in the theme is coupled, in the bass, with the diatonic counterpoint motif with which it was worked out in the second secondary exposition (vi, meas. 74; *cf.* meas. 53 ff.). Then the chromatic descent is imitated in the bass as in the seventh entry (vi, meas. 75, recalling 50; compare also v, 75, with iii, 10 and 25). The counterpoints also keep up, to a certain extent, the eighth-note motion characteristic of the immediately preceding passages (*e.g.*, i, meas. 73; *cf.* vi, 66). The eighth-note patterns, however, alternate again between the parts. Thus they make a first step toward dissolution of the continuous motion reached at the beginning of the section, and, at the same time, recall the counterpoints to the F-minor entry of the theme and the transition following this entry rather than the later A-flat major entry or the transitional measures between that entry and the present one (see v, meas. 73, which refers back to v, meas. 62, 63, and 65).

The end of the entry in B-flat minor is bridged over by an evasive cadence similar to that employed at the end of the preceding entry. Again a pair of transitional measures are attached, balancing rather clearly the second group of such measures introduced in the exposition (meas. 77-78; see meas. 23-24). A bass line, which first ascends chromatically and then descends diatonically, supports a play of eighth-note patterns derived again from the transition after the F-minor cadence (compare meas. 77-78, upper voices, with meas. 62-65). Characteristically, a return to F minor takes place, and that tonality is firmly established by the first cadence introduced since the conclusion of the previous cadence in the same tonality. The cadence itself is of secondary strength, an indication that it does not mark the conclusion of a section; it strongly recalls the secondary G-minor cadence concluding the exposition (iv and vi, meas. 28 and 78, second half, are identical).

The similarly shaped cadences are followed by similar structural parts: here as well as after the original exposition, a six-part episode ensues—the second and last true episode introduced in the course of the entire movement (meas. 79-82, corresponding to meas. 29-39). Nowhere is the recapitulatory character of a part more strongly emphasized. Again the voices proceed in contrary motion, separating into a higher and a lower choir. Again the lower choir is led by a chromatic ascent, while the higher choir is dominated by the diatonic descending motif known from the first episode. The rhythmic shape of the passage is at first somewhat different from the corresponding earlier one, for the alternating motion of eighth-notes still persists, introducing an element of imitation into the lower choir (iv and v, meas. 79-80). Soon, however, the continuous motion is abandoned and the anapaestic pulse returns, while once more the diatonic motif descends into the bass (meas. 81-82; cf. 36-37). Another broad cadence unfolds, in A-flat major. It is the second cadence in a major key within the movement, concluding the recapitulation of the first episode at the end of four-fifths of the entire composition, just as the first cadence in a major key had concluded the first episode itself at the end of the second fifth (meas. 82-83, corresponding to meas. 38-39). The recapitulation, however, is much more concise than the original episode (4 measures as against 11).

The last fifth of the form (meas. 83-103) elaborates, at first, the broken triad of the theme, recapitulating in a free manner the elaboration introduced within the second section (meas. 83-85, corresponding to 45-47). The triad is again imitated as the fifth. Only two appearances of the motif are given at the beginning; and the conspicuous appearance at the end, which has already returned (see meas. 72), is eliminated. The recapitulation, therefore, seems less weighty than the original elaboration, although both are of the same length.

The main motif is accompanied by two voices offering a counterpoint motif in parallels (ii and iii, meas. 83):

Ex. 40

Thus an increase in contrapuntal intensity over the corresponding passage is afforded. The new counterpoint motif is related to the one with which the triad was previously associated (ii and iii, meas. 83; see i, meas. 45; also ii, 19 and 58, and v, 59). The counterpoint motif contains the dactylic pulse rhythm, but its more restrained motion soon gives way to renewed eighth-note runs.

The section continues with the last tonal-answer entry of the subject (ii, meas. 86-89). The counterpoints form, for the last time, alternating series of eighth-notes, recalling those employed in the preceding entry in B-flat minor and, even more clearly, the earlier entry in F minor. The first two measures are accompanied by a bass which descends, in chiefly diatonic waves, the distance of a tenth (vi, meas. 86-87); and the chromatic descent is ornamented by a garland winding its way through four voices, covering more than two octaves (i, iii, iv, and v, meas. 87-88). The end of the entry is emphasized by a condensed cadence in G minor, which strongly recalls the first cadence in F minor (meas. 89-90, cf. 61-62)—this second G-minor cadence corresponds to the first F-minor cadence exactly as the second F-minor cadence corresponded to the first G-minor cadence.

A most ingenious further piece of recapitulation now unfolds. Slow motion returns and is not interrupted by any considerable groups of eighth notes. For the third time, the chromatic motif is worked out in imitation (meas. 90 ff., see meas. 39 ff. and 52 ff.). It returns in the shape it was given in its second elaboration, at the beginning of the third section, and is accompanied by the diatonic counterpoint associated with it in that section; thus the second and third elaborations are more closely related to each other than to the first. The present elaboration begins in four-part writing; thus it tops the second elaboration as the second topped the first. The chromatic motif appears seven times, against six times in the second elaboration and five in the first; in this respect, too, the last elaboration forms the climax of a graded development. The first elaboration covered five measures, the second six, the third nine; thus the decrease in weight found in the episodes is balanced by an increase in the contrapuntal elaborations of the chromatic motif and its counterpoints.

Of the four parts with which the elaboration opens, one, an inner voice, is insignificant. The top voice, however, introduces a new counterpoint of primary importance, a variation of the *staccato* opening of the first counterpoint (ii, meas. 90, see the quotation from iii, meas. 5, ex. 32):

Ex. 41

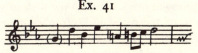

The counterpoint was gradually dissolved in the course of the exposition; it was, in a way, replaced by the dactylic pulsation which it had itself introduced. Now the beginning of the counterpoint returns, in a form containing the dactylic rhythm as well. Thus a recapitulation of conspicuous material from the exposition is effected without literal quotation—a striking structural detail.[10]

The imitations of the three principal motifs within this final elaboration are irregular, but of great contrapuntal intensity:

(1) The chromatic motif appears five times in imitation at the fourth above (or fifth below), after a full measure (iii, meas. 90; followed by ii, v, iv, and vi). A fifth voice enters with the third appearance of the motif. The fourth entry is accompanied by a flourish in the top voice, indicating a slight incision, evidently in anticipation of an important new development. The next entry, in the bass, introduces the sixth voice again; the imitative treatment of the motif now gives way to a three-fold repetition in the same voice in diatonically ascending sequence (vi, meas. 94-96).

(2) The diatonic counterpoint to the chromatic motif appears

---

[10] In the *Ricercar a 3*, Bach introduced the opening motif of his first counterpoint as material for an episode in the last quarter of the form and thus achieved an impression of recapitulation without actually offering more than a reminiscence (*cf.* meas. 10 and 161 ff.; see also above, p. 109). In the improvised fugue, however, Bach abandoned the counterpoint motif before he reached the subject again, and therefore the return of the counterpoint motif seems almost accidental. In the *Ricercar a 6* Bach deliberately employs the same device—once having taken up the counterpoint motif again, he retains it (as will be seen) up to the very end of the composition, reuniting the counterpoint motif with the subject and thus turning a casual invention into an artistic device.

only twice, just often enough to establish a clear relation between its elaborations (meas. 90 ff. and 52 ff.); the first time it enters simultaneously with the chromatic motif, the second time at a distance, thus emphasizing the looseness of connection.

(3) The motif derived from the first counterpoint, on the other hand, pervades the entire elaboration, entering at least once in each measure, at irregular intervals. It accompanies the last appearance of the chromatic motif in parallels (i and iii, meas. 96) and dominates alone the ensuing two measures, which embody a rather unusual plagal cadence (see vi in meas. 97, with parallels in v and then iii; followed by an entry of the motif in i, after less than a measure, with parallels in ii and iii, meas. 98).

The last entry of the subject (vi, meas. 99-103) is accompanied in all parts and almost exclusively by figures derived from the opening of the first counterpoint. Under a slowly falling top voice the motif is tossed from one part to another in continuous imitation which makes use of inversion as well as variation. Thus the remnants of the first counterpoint are reunited with the subject itself with which it had originally appeared. The counterpoint in its entirety never returns, but the contrapuntal treatment accorded here to its opening motif far outshines the importance the counterpoint possessed when it first appeared. The final cadence recapitulates the short imitation which emphasized the cadence at the end of the first half (iv and v, meas. 102-103; see ii and iii, meas. 51-52, ex. 36):

Ex. 42

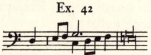

The cadences concluding the halves of the composition are thus conspicuously related to each other.[11]

The counterpoints to the last entry move predominantly in quarter-notes, with hardly a reminiscence of the dactylic pulse. Thus a last phase of rhythmic development is presented. In the course of the composition, initial motion in half-notes and quarter-notes was

[11] Immediately before the final cadence (in meas. 101), there are heard the notes B♭, A, C, B♮, which, in German nomenclature, spell out the name BACH. They are distributed between two voices (ii and i), but displayed conspicuously enough to make it at least possible that Bach deliberately included them at the end of the work as a kind of signature. Cf. Hans T. David, "Themes from Words and Names", in A Birthday Offering to Carl Engel, New York, 1943.

gradually accelerated by the introduction of the dactylic pulsation and then of alternating eighth-note runs. A climax was reached at the beginning of the recapitulation with its continuous eighth-note motion in the counterpoints. Then a contrary development set in. The alternating eighth-note runs returned, remaining dominant through the next-to-last entry of the subject. This was followed, in the final elaboration of the chromatic motif, by the return of the dactylic pulse as the limit of motion; and finally, in the concluding entry of the subject, by the return of the original motion of half-notes and quarter-notes. However, the importance assumed by the motif from the first counterpoint modifies the rhythmic character of the last measures; for the motif, with its immanent *staccato* character gives increased emphasis to the quarter-notes and thus replaces the loss in motion by an increase in weight.

The *Ricercar a 6* as a whole is one of the best balanced and most exactly proportioned compositions ever conceived. The first half of the form is composed of an exposition containing two groups of transitional measures, and an additional entry; an episode in compact six-part writing; an imitative elaboration of the middle section of the theme, and a similar elaboration of the opening of the theme. The second half is similarly composed of an exposition including two groups of transitory measures, and additional entries; a recapitulation of the episode in compact six-part writing; an imitative elaboration of the middle section of the theme, and an imitative elaboration of the opening of the theme. Thus a perfect equilibrium of contrapuntal material is achieved. The first half contains a greater length of entries and of episode; the second offsets the loss by introduction of an additional elaboration of the middle section of the theme, which simultaneously recapitulates the first counterpoint introduced in the first half. This additional elaboration is closely related to the one previously offered within the second half, more so than to the first of its type; accordingly, the recapitulation is felt to be carried by the last third of the movement rather than by the entire second half.

The intricate and yet easily apprehended system of relations between the parts of the form is sharply set into relief by the shape and tonal order of incisions. After the opening in C minor, the first fully developed cadence is given in E-flat major, when two fifths of the entire composition have been heard. The next cadence, in G minor, concludes the first half. F minor is established at the end of the third fifth, A-flat major at the end of the fourth, and C minor, of course, at the conclusion of the whole movement. After the opening in C minor, the cadences form an ascent through the tonic triad in the first half (C—E♭—G), balanced by an ascent through the subdominant triad in the second (F—A♭—C). The cadence at the conclusion of the composition takes up the cadential pattern introduced at the end of the first half, and the cadence at the end of the fourth fifth the pattern applied to the end of the second. Only three other incisive cadences are distributed throughout the form. A secondary cadence in G minor closes the exposition; a secondary cadence in F minor, of similar shape, the group of entries forming the first part of the recapitulation; and a last cadence in G minor, recalling the F-minor cadence at the end of the third fifth, splits the last fifth, setting off the next-to-last entry of the theme from the final elaboration of the chromatic motif and the return of the first counterpoint. Thus the cadences are arranged in symmetrical pairs, each forming the counterpart to one in a distant section, exactly as the sections themselves form symmetric counterparts to each other.[12]

The sequence of tonalities employed for the entries of the Royal theme (see above, pp. 135-137) does not coincide with the order of modulation represented by the cadences. The entries of the first half do not go beyond the tonic-dominant relation, and the entries in A-flat major and B-flat minor pass without cadences, surrounded on both sides by cadences in the same tonality, F minor. Thus two tonal plans, each of which supports the coherence and unity of the form, are interlocked—another unusual element in the structure of the *Ricercar a 6.*

Various important details in the *Ricercar a 6* recall the *Ricercar a 3,* aside from the fact that they use the same subject and motifs derived from it. In both compositions, the first episode is based on a leading chromatic line, a rhythmically free derivation of the chromatic descent in the theme (the fine descends in the *Ricercar a 3* and

---

[12] The proportions mentioned above are of almost mathematical exactness. Every single one is based upon a norm of not less than 99 and not more than 104 measures, while the actual composition has 103 or, if we count the last chord as held through two measures, as Bach has notated it, 104. We may be sure that Bach, in composing the *Ricercar a 6,* did not stop to count measures, but was led by his instinctive perception of musical weights and balances. All the more remarkable is the fact that the variations between the proportions are not greater.

ascends in the *Ricercar a 6*). In both, the second section is ushered in by an elaboration of elements from the theme; in both, that elaboration draws on the theme-opening (as sole motif in the *Ricercar a 3*; after an elaboration of the chromatic motif in the *Ricercar a 6*). In both, secondary expositions are introduced, formed by imitations of the chromatic descent in the theme (without rests in the *Ricercar a 3*, entering the parts successively in the *Ricercar a 6*). And in both, the first counterpoint is recapitulated by an elaboration of its first motif (in a late episode in the *Ricercar a 3*, in the last episode and with the last entry of the subject in the *Ricercar a 6*).

The formal treatment of the secondary expositions, however, shows a significant contrast between the two compositions. In the *Ricercar a 3*, which opens the second section with a homophonic elaboration confined to the bass, the secondary exposition, apparently an afterthought, opens the *fantasia* section, a contrasting center-piece which, appearing off center, destroys the symmetry and balance of the form. In the *Ricercar a 6*, secondary expositions are distributed through the entire form, the first appearing at the beginning of the second section; thus the introduction of a contrasting middle section is avoided, and the secondary expositions are comprised in the system of symmetrical relations. At the beginning of the second section of the *Ricercar a 6*, Bach combines two ideas introduced in the *Ricercar a 3* at widely distant points: that of opening a section with an elaboration of motifs derived from the theme, and that of using imitation at perfect intervals for elaboration of these motifs. The new treatment makes the elaboration of the thematic motifs, particularly of the theme-opening which might be used for pseudo-entries, more conspicuous and ensures to the *Ricercar a 6* the equilibrium which is impaired in the *Ricercar a 3* by the belated introduction of the *fantasia* section.

Bach himself apparently intended the *Ricercar a 6* to form clearly a counterpart to the *Ricercar a 3*, and the parallelism between the two compositions is so strong that they serve most convincingly as outermost bulwarks of the strictest symmetrical structure ever offered in music. But Bach sought, at the same time, to give the six-part composition the perfection he had failed to achieve within the three-part model. The *Ricercar a 3* is an impressive composition, astonishingly rich and consistent for an improvisation, and in parts unquestionably a work of genius; but the *Ricercar a 6* surpasses it to the full extent that we might expect a deliberately worked-out creation of the greatest master of fugue to surpass a mere study by him in fugue extemporization.[13]

[13] The *Ricercar a 6* solves the problem of balance raised by the *Ricercar a 3* through elimination of the center piece which endangered the equilibrium in the three-part composition. A contrasting piece of thematic elaboration, corresponding in principle to the *fantasia* section of the *Ricercar a 3*, appears in the first *Allegro* of the Sonata, forming the exact center of the form and thus beyond reproach (see the analysis, pp. 118ff. and pp. 121-2, with note 3). A passage of contrasting development is also introduced in the *Andante* of the Sonata; here, Bach manages to introduce that isolated piece off center without impairing the balance of the form (see pp. 123ff. and p. 127, with note 4). The *Ricercar a 3* suffered, in addition, from a certain inconsistency in the treatment of the recapitulation of counterpoints; a deliberate and perfectly satisfying differentiation of the counterpoints as to recapitulation is contained in the second *Allegro* of the Sonata (see pp. 129ff. and pp. 133-4, with note 3). Thus the larger movements in the *Musical Offering* are all, in certain respects, tied up with Bach's original improvisation.

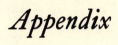

Appendix

Textual Criticism

No. 1. RICERCAR A 3 (THREE-PART FUGUE)

THE TERM *Ricercar* is discussed in chapter III, pp. 28-30.

The title of the *Ricercar a 3* as well as of the *Ricercar a 6* has variously been given as *Ricercare* and *Ricercata*. Both forms are historically possible, but neither represents the spelling of the original edition or, in fact, Bach's own spelling, as is shown by his acrostic on the word which ends with an *R* (see chapter IV, p. 42).

The original edition offers the *Ricercar a 3* in keyboard notation. The last page of the composition, as it appears in that edition, is reproduced above on p. 14. The score in the present edition—*i.e.*, the version for an ensemble of instruments—has been added by the editor (see the discussion in chapter V, pp. 44f., 49f., and 52, with footnote).

The readings differ mostly in accidentals. In looking through the pages reproduced here from Bach's manuscript and the 1747 edition, one should remember that up to Bach's time an accidental applied only to a single note or to the immediate repetition of that note. Accordingly an original:

is to be read as Bb Bb A, while: is to be read as Bb A Bb. In his later years, Bach usually, though not always, cancelled accidentals in the manner which later became customary.

A few accidentals originally missing in the plates of the 1747 edition were inserted by hand in the dedication copy and afterwards added on the plates. The ♮ before *e'* in meas. 45, middle voice, appears in only a few copies of the original edition, added by hand. The ♭♭ before *b'* in meas. 132, treble, is missing in the original edition.

The treble in meas. 80 includes an augmented second according to the original edition whereas the corresponding bass in meas. 103 eliminates the augmented interval. The readings of the original edition have been preserved in our edition, the first because the use of an E♭ instead of the expected E♮ helps to avoid a false relation, the second because it forms a perfect sequence. The editor wonders, however, whether the ♮ before *B* in meas. 103 was not due to an accident, for at first the ♮ before *A* was missing on the plate. Perhaps the engraver had originally placed the ♮ before *B* instead of *A*; in this case, an augmented second may have been Bach's own version at this place, too.

The rhythm of meas. 154, treble, has been reproduced wrongly in all previous editions. Bach apparently wrote:

This was erroneously engraved as: ♩♩♩♩. ♬♬♪　　The engraver noticed his mistake and "corrected" it to read: ♩♩♩♩. ♬♬♪

This, however, still failed to fill the measure. All later editions changed the rhythm to: ♩♩♩♪ ♬♬♪ , but if this rhythm had actually appeared in Bach's manuscript the version of the original edition could not possibly be accounted for.

The last note of the bass in meas. 166 possibly represents an error in the 1747 edition, for *g* would seem more consistent and natural than the *d* found here.

Ornaments are found in the original edition only at two places: meas. 8, treble, has a *double cadence* (⌣); meas. 102, bass, two ✶

The *double cadence* in meas. 8 is best played with a *mordent* at the end (⌣ instead of ⌣); both versions have been written out at the bottom of the page—in accordance with Bach's table of ornaments in the *Clavier-büchlein vor Wilhelm Friedemann Bach* (see chapter IV, pp. 70f.). A similar ornament should be played wherever such treatment is possible. Accordingly, ornaments have been added, in brackets, to meas. 17, 30, and 176, while at all other corresponding places the execution of the ornament seems too difficult to have been intended by Bach.

The first ✶ in meas. 102, apparently was added by mistake, particularly since it creates an ugly false relation. The second could not possibly be executed with a mordent, because such an ending would bring either E♭ and C♯ or C♮ and C♯ too close to each other. Accordingly the first ✶ has been eliminated in our edition, and for the second a *double cadence* without mordent has been indicated.

Whether the scattered ornaments were authentically Bach's or merely additions by the engraver cannot be ascertained. They are, in any case, not essential in performance with several instruments and have therefore not been included in the open score or the parts.

The phrasing found in the original has been minutely reproduced in the keyboard version. In the open score, ordinary slurs have been inserted for the use of stringed as well as wind instruments. Brackets (⌐¬) indicate additional slurrings for the wind instruments.

Octave-transpositions are necessary at several places of the score because the range of the instruments at our disposal is insufficient for playing the parts as Bach wrote them down. None of the transpositions can be said to impair the contrapuntal quality of the section in which they occur, while at several places definite improvements over the keyboard version result from the separation of parts originally played with one hand.

A single passage requires adaptation for performance with stringed instruments. The ending originally included twice a $B\natural$ in the middle part (meas. 180 and 182). Accordingly the Viola has been transposed into the higher octave, meas. 179-183. A return to the original position in meas. 182 would have destroyed the intensity of the ascent, while by remaining in the upper octave the Viola would top the Violin, with an anticipation of the latter's c''. Accordingly, the Violin has also been transposed, meas. 181-184.

In addition to this necessary change, one might consider transposition of the Violoncello in meas. 154-159. This transposition would not only eliminate the extraordinarily high pitch of the bass, but would restore the distance of parts to that of meas. 60 ff.

Performance with wind instruments requires a few more changes. Upward transposition of the English Horn has been suggested for meas. 37-41. This results in a distance of voices corresponding exactly to that found in meas. 87-90. Downward transposition of the same instrument has been suggested for meas. 47-53; here the result is the elimination of an unusually large distance between the bass and the upper voices, and of the strange skip of an eleventh in meas. 53. The end of the composition will be played as with strings; the English Horn, however, must start the upward transposition of the original line in meas. 177, a change which eliminates the gap between the treble and the lower voices found in the original. The transposition of meas. 154-159, indicated as optional in the Violoncello, has been made obligatory in the Bassoon part on account of the somewhat precarious original range.

CANONES DIVERSI SUPER THEMA REGIUM (VARIOUS CANONS UPON THE ROYAL THEME)

THE TITLES of the canon group as well as of the single pieces are discussed in chapter III, pp. 21-28.

The original edition presents all canons of this group in abbreviated notation. The original notation of No. 2 is found on p. 11, that of Nos. 3 to 6, on p. 12. The order is discussed in chapter VII, pp. 92-94.

The interpretation of these canons is discussed in chapter VI, pp. 75-78. The solution of the canons has been indicated by Bach himself; for sources of written-out solutions, see chapter VII, pp. 96-99.

No. 2. Canon perpetuus a 2 (Canon at the Double Octave)

The original title added *super Thema Regium* (see chapter VII, p. 92). The indication *Th* for *Thema* appears in the original edition of all canons of this group except the present one, where it has been added by the editor.

Meas. 5 of the theme is reproduced exactly as it appears in the original edition: ♩ ♩ ♪. ♪♪♪ ♩ .The editors of other editions have interpreted this, following certain eighteenth-century writers, as: ♩ ♩♪♪♪♪ ♩

Bach, however, used the latter manner of notation in the Canon in Augmentation and Contrary Motion, No. 5; it is therefore likely that he meant here to indicate triplets of 32nds rather than straight 32nds.

No. 3. Canon a 2 Violini in Unisono (Canon at the Unison)

The sixth measure of the canonic line is inaccurately phrased in the original edition; the context establishes the correct phrasing.

No. 4. Canon a 2 per Motum contrarium (Canon in Contrary Motion)

In this as well as in the following number the question arises whether an exact or a tonal answer was intended by Bach (see chapter III, p. 24).

Here the first three measures are preferable with E♭ in the second part, *i.e.*, with a tonal solution. In the first half of meas. 4, E♮ deserves preference because it avoids the melodic progression of an augmented fifth in the second part and, at the same time, a disagreeable false relation to the other canonic part. In the second half of the measure, E♭ is preferable because it avoids a false relation to the theme as well as to the other canonic part. We must conclude that Bach intended the beginning to be executed as a tonal inversion, and the last measure as an exact one.

In meas. 3, a clash between B♮ and B♭ occurs. In the dedicatory copy, the *b♮* of the original has been corrected to *b♭* by an unknown eighteenth-century hand. This correction, which is not found in other copies of the original edition and therefore seems not to have been inserted by the engraver, has been accepted by various editors. The original voice-leading, however, is so far superior to the "corrected" one that the authenticity of the former can hardly be doubted. Composers up to Bach's time were much less afraid of false relations and clashes than were the theorists of the late eighteenth and nineteenth centuries.

No. 5. Canon a 2 per Augmentationem, contrario Motu
(Canon in Augmentation and Contrary Motion)

The complimentary inscriptions added to this and the following canon in the dedication copy are translated in chapter I, pp. 9-10.

The original canonic line begins on the fourth sixteenth. The augmented line is accordingly expected to begin on the fourth eighth; instead, it starts—as the entrance mark in the abbreviated notation makes clear—a quarter later. Thus all the notes appearing on the first and third beats of the original line are given on the second beat in the derived line, a metrical shift of great expressional importance (see pp. 76-77).

The beginning of the derived part is established as a tonal answer even more clearly than in the preceding number, for the third in meas. 1, played within a descending scale and simultaneously with an E♭ in the theme, could not possibly be meant as E♮. In meas. 3, E♭ is still preferable, and in meas. 4 it is understood. In meas. 6, however, E♮ is preferable melodically, harmonically, and in consideration of the E♮ in the other canonic part. Thus the same transition from tonal to exact inversion is outlined in the two neighboring canons in contrary motion.

In meas. 6 of the Royal theme, the rhythm appearing in the dedication copy: ♩. ♪ ♩. ♪ ♩. ♪ ♩. ♪ was later corrected on the plate of the original edition to the superior version: ♩ ♩ ♩. ♪ ♩. ♪ ♩. ♪ , which has been used.

The Royal theme is richly ornamented in this number. All ornaments are indicated in the 1747 edition by the sign *tr* . A single *tr* in meas. 5, necessary on account of the sequence, is missing.

All shakes occur on dotted notes followed by rests or shorter notes that are not simply ending patterns belonging to the shakes. All shakes must accordingly end with a hold. The shakes in meas. 4 and 5 should clearly bridge over the leap of a third, by accentuation of the passing note; this might be done with either a slight *tenuto* or a full *appoggiatura*. Both possibilities have been written out; in the second, comparatively short appoggiaturas have been chosen to avoid the appearance of parallel fifths in meas. 5. (*Cf.* chapter VI, pp. 73-74.)

No. 6. Canon a 2 per Tonos (Modulating Canon)

The abbreviated notation in the original edition, for obvious practical reasons, does not employ flats in the key-signature. As the second canonic voice follows at the higher fifth, the key-signature would read more accurately if written with a sharp for the second clef:

The only editorial problem encountered in this number was the question where the necessary enharmonic change should be carried out. The editor has assumed that a combination of G-sharp minor and D-sharp minor will be read more easily than that of A-flat minor and E-flat minor, and has therefore introduced the enharmonic change at the end of the fifth appearance of the theme. The change is so placed that it is made during rests in each part rather than at the end of a full repetition.[1]

[1] It may be recalled in this connection that Bach preferred, in the *Well-Tempered Clavier*, G-sharp minor to A-flat minor. In the First Part, he combined a *Praeludium* in E-flat minor with a Fugue in D-sharp minor; in the Second Part, the corresponding pieces are both written in E-flat minor. In major, Bach went even further in the ascending scale of fifths, for he used C-sharp major rather than D-flat major, and this although he introduced B-flat minor in both parts of the work.

No. 7. SONATA (TRIO SONATA)

THE SONATA as an early form is discussed in chapter III, pp. 31-33.

The original edition presents the Sonata, without title, in three separate parts, entitled *Traversa*, *Violino*, and *Continuo* (see p. 32, notes 2 and 3). The four movements are in all parts indicated as *Largo*, *Allegro*, *Andante*, and *Allegro*. The edition is generously, though somewhat inconsistently, phrased, and the Continuo is fully figured. A page from the *Traversa* part of the original edition is reproduced as a frontispiece to the present volume.

The instrumentation, as specified in the 1747 edition, is unquestionably Bach's own and should be preserved in representative performance, particularly of the work in its entirety. In informal presentation, the Flute may be replaced by another Violin, but no provision has been made in the parts for such substitution (see chapter V, pp. 47 and 48f.).

The realization of the Continuo for the first, second, and fourth movements has been taken from an anonymous eighteenth-century manuscript; that for the third is by Kirnberger (see chapter VII, pp. 100f.).

LARGO

THE NOTES are evidently correct in the 1747 edition, with the possible exception of Flute, meas. 7, where Bach may have written *c'* rather than *d'*. There are two omissions: the ♮ before the small first *d''*♭ in the Flute, meas. 17, and the dot in the last measure of the Continuo. The end of the Flute part is ornamented by a *da capo* sign on the top and a fermata at the bottom of the double bar.

Dynamic markings are restricted in the 1747 edition to the single *piano* in the Violin, meas. 7. Corresponding markings have been added to the other appearances of the same figure (Flute, meas. 6, 21, and 43; Violin, meas. 22 and 44).

The ornaments include an appoggiatura in the Flute, meas. 43, which evidently was meant only to indicate that the upper tone of the trill should be the minor second; in the suggested execution, it has been given the value of a regular fast beat within the trill.[1]

The marks of phrasing are neither consistent nor entirely clear in the 1747 edition. Adjustments have been made wherever they were evidently necessary. The following notes discuss places where Bach's intentions are not obvious or not consistently presented.

The second measure of the first principal motif, in its fourth appearance, Violin, meas. 36, slurs the last two sixteenth-notes. As no similar slur appears at the corresponding places, the editor has assumed that it was inserted in the 1747 edition by mistake.

The second principal motif, first introduced in meas. 6-8, usually bears a slur of three notes in the first quarter when it appears in the Flute, but none in the Violin and Continuo. Bach must have felt that a slur would sound better in the Flute, a *non legato* in the other instruments. However, it seems that he did not start out with the intention of differentiating the wind instrument from the strings; for the Violin has a slur in meas. 6 exactly as the Flute has in meas. 7; and the slur is absent in Flute, meas. 11, exactly as in Violin, meas. 12. In order to arrive at a consistent treatment, the editor has eliminated the slur from the Violin, meas. 6, and added a slur to the Flute, meas. 11. If the Flute part is taken over by a Violin, no reason remains for a distinction between the higher instruments; in that case, the slurs in meas. 11, 37, 39, and 44 of the Flute should be eliminated. The variation of the motif, Flute, meas. 7 and 18, and Violin, meas. 20, which replaces the skip of a third by that of a second, requires a slur in the first quarter in both instruments. The Violin, meas. 6, and the Flute, meas. 37 and 44, originally began with slurs covering the entire first quarter, presumably by mistake.

The third principal motif, first introduced in meas. 13 and 14, is at several places phrased in the original edition as: ♪ ♫♩ , but the phrasing:

♪ ♫♩ prevails and it is established as authentic by *staccato* marks in the Violin, meas. 14 and 29. The Flute, meas. 31 and 32, begins with a slur embracing (though not clearly) the entire first quarter.

The slur in the Flute, meas. 36, covers only the first three sixteenth-notes; if Bach should have felt the element of variation as stronger than that of analogy, this phrasing might be correct.

In the Flute, meas. 14, and the Violin, meas. 46, the opening slur is not

[1] Landshoff interprets the appoggiatura in the opening motif similarly, but his reasons for doing so are not convincing. Earlier editions suggest—in accordance with certain eighteenth-century copies of the Sonata—that the appoggiatura in the opening motif be held for a full quarter, which sounds very pedantic and apparently does not correspond to Bach's intention (see chapter V, pp. 73ff.).

quite clearly drawn and may originally have been meant to cover four eighth-notes.

The *quasi legato* repetition of eighth-notes in the Continuo is indicated in the 1747 edition, according to the custom of the time, simply by slurs; the *staccato* dots for the Violoncello and the *tenuto* dashes for the keyboard instrument have been added by the editor. Not a single measure in eighth-note motion is given more than one slur in the old edition. The slurs in meas. 4, 34, and 36, however, begin with the second quarter, indicating that Bach wanted the thematic skip of a diminished seventh emphasized by a break. Similar phrasing is suggested for meas. 21 and 23. In all of these, the intended phrasing has been made evident by the addition of a slur for the first two eighth-notes; meas. 35, however, which erroneously received the treatment of meas. 34 and 36 in the 1747 edition, has been treated like meas. 33, of which it is the sequential counterpart. Slurs in meas. 7 and 19 have been added as a matter of course. A slur covering meas. 42 has been eliminated, for apparently Bach wanted the cadences emphasized by full strokes of the bow, as can be seen in meas. 15, 28, and 47, and also 30 and 32, none of which are slurred in the original edition.

The figuring of the Continuo in the 1747 edition contains two errors which, in the only known copy, are corrected in an eighteenth-century hand, possibly that of the printer himself. In meas. 24 the second quarter, which begins a new line in the old print, read originally $\sharp\begin{smallmatrix}6\\4+\end{smallmatrix}$; this is corrected to $\begin{smallmatrix}4+6\\2\;2\end{smallmatrix}$, not quite properly, for the second harmony is actually $\begin{smallmatrix}6\\4+\\2+\end{smallmatrix}$. In meas. 40 the second figure is blotted out and the correct figure 8 added. It may be mentioned also that in meas. 7 the second harmony is indicated as $\begin{smallmatrix}7\\4\\2\end{smallmatrix}$; probably this should have read $\begin{smallmatrix}7\\4\\2+\end{smallmatrix}$, which is given in the old figured-bass realization, replacing the augmented-sixth chord specified in the figuration. It should be noted, however, that such an augmented-sixth chord appears in the further course of the Sonata (*Allegro*, meas. 48 and 69).

The old realization of the figured bass reproduced in the edition contains five-tone harmonies at two places, in meas. 7 and 26; at the first place, the unknown corrector remarked disapprovingly: "4 tones".

All appoggiaturas were written in small quarter-notes. In order to avoid discrepancies in performance, they have been notated as full-sized eighth-notes followed by the principal notes in dotted quarters. Such appoggiaturas occur in meas. 1, 3, 15, 33, 35, 41, and 47. Those in meas. 15 (g'), 35, 41, and 47 (e'♭) have been added by the editor. The appoggiaturas in meas. 28 and 42, written out in full in the obbligato voices, are clearly indicated by figures.

ALLEGRO

THE NOTES are correct in the 1747 edition. A single ♮ is missing in the Continuo, meas. 95.[1]

The recapitulation was indicated by *Da capo al Segno* after meas. 172, and a corresponding mark at the beginning of meas. 12. The end was indicated by a hold in meas. 88. In order to fill the last measure properly, the editor has added a dot to the last note. The recapitulation has been printed in full, without differentiation between original marks of phrasing and additions by the editor.

The ornaments used in this movement include a necessarily short appoggiatura (Flute, meas. 30, see chapter V, p. 74).

The marks of phrasing again contain a number of problems.

The phrasing of the first subject is consistent in the 1747 edition as far as the first two measures and the middle section—the fifth to seventh measures—are concerned. Of the five entries written out in the upper voices, one slurs the first three notes in the third measure, apparently by mistake; all five slur three notes in the second quarter of the same measure, although one inappropriately slurs the last three. Three slur the entire first quarter of the fourth measure, and one the first three notes of the second quarter; the last slur probably was intended for the first quarter, which, in this instance, is without slur. If one follows the majority of markings in each case, an excellent phrasing results—presumably the one intended by Bach himself. The Continuo, in its only entry (meas. 117 ff.), slurs fully the two quarters of the third measure and the first quarter of the fourth. There is a certain possibility that Bach considered the string bass as less agile than the higher instruments, or the harpsichord as less in need of a more detailed phrasing, in which case the 1747 edition might represent Bach's own phrasing; the editor has preferred consistency throughout the movement to the acceptance of a differentiation the authenticity of which is possible but not probable.

The motif at the end of the first subject, in the ninth measure, is given with two slurs in the first entry of the Flute (meas. 19) and throughout the elaboration in the second part of the middle section (meas. 126-159).

[1] The editor of the *Bach-Gesellschaft* edition, in his Preface, discusses a few variants. Since he relies chiefly on an unsatisfactory copy, most of his decisions are wrong. The *Traversa*, meas. 79, clearly reads G, not F (see also Violin, meas. 36). The Violin, meas. 84, specifies the beginning of the second quarter as B♮, not B♭ (see also *Traversa*, meas. 41). The Violin, meas. 151, has a somewhat blurred sixth note, but evidently F is meant, not G (see *Traversa*, meas. 110). The Continuo, meas. 169, clearly indicates A♮, not A♭.

It is nowhere slurred in the Violin part. We may assume, however, that the 32nd-notes after the trill were understood to form a part of the ornament and therefore to be slurred as a matter of course.

The little figure following the end of the subject (and forming the tenth measure) is rather consistently phrased in the upper voices as:

In the first entry of the Violin (meas. 10) and in the second of the Flute (meas. 76), the slurs are missing. Full quarters appear for this figure in the Continuo (meas. 28-31) and, in accordance with these, in the Violin as well (meas. 28 and 31); here, too, possible authenticity has been disregarded in favor of complete consistency.

The Violin has full quarter slurs at the beginning of the first episode (meas. 34-36); the phrasing of the corresponding place in the Flute (meas. 77-79) has seemed preferable and been taken over. The phrasing in the opening of the concluding line in the Flute (meas. 41), on the other hand, has seemed superior to that in the corresponding place in the Violin (meas. 84), which ends with two slurs of two notes each, the first of which bridges over an augmented second.

The first counterpoint to the combined subjects, in the Flute, contains suspensions slurred to their resolutions (meas. 49-52), and a dotted slur has therefore been added to a number of corresponding suspensions in the Flute (meas. 55-56, 64-66, 104-106, and 121-122) as well as the Violin (meas. 59-61, 62-63, 70-73, and 145-147). An equally consistent phrasing, which may seem preferable to some players, can be achieved if the isolated slurs appearing in the original Flute part (meas. 49-52) are disregarded, and no slurs added to any of the following suspensions. Which of the two solutions represents Bach's intention is hard to determine since the original edition is so inconsistent in this respect. The editor has therefore used dotted slurs in the parts so that either interpretation may be carried out.

The Flute begins meas. 53 with a full quarter slur; the phrasing of the Violin at the corresponding place (meas. 74) is preferable and has been used for the Flute as well.

The imitation in contrary motion at the beginning of the center section is not accurately phrased in the 1747 edition. The Violin introduces in its third and seventh measures (91 and 95) four pairs of slurred sixteenth-notes, whereas the Flute answers with a single larger slur, instead of the two small ones, on the second quarter (meas. 92 and 96); the Continuo, which for a moment imitates the Violin in parallel motion (meas. 96, second quarter) also uses one slur instead of two. The phrasing of the Violin has been applied throughout.

The slur in the Violin, meas. 100, has been added in analogy to that in the Flute, meas. 141; on account of the sequence, a slur of three notes is preferable to the full quarter slur appearing in the Flute part of the

1747 edition. That edition gives also a quarter slur at the beginning of meas. 141 in the Continuo; the unslurred playing of the run in meas. 100 has been considered more appropriate.

The motif from the episode, derived from one in the preceding *Largo* (see the analysis in chapter VIII) is phrased differently as it resumes more and more clearly its original shape (compare meas. 107-116, 124, 133-137, and 148-157). The phrasing of the original edition is entirely convincing except for two minor details: the Flute in meas. 107 does not slur the first two notes, whereas the Violin in meas. 148 does; and the Flute in meas. 133 slurs full quarters, whereas its canonic imitation slurs pairs of sixteenth-notes. In both cases, the version of the Violin has been applied to the phrasing of the Flute.

In the original edition, the slur in the Flute, meas. 120, begins incorrectly with the third note.

It may be added that, as in the preceding movement, the *quasi legato* repetitions of eighth-notes in the Continuo (meas. 32, 97 ff., and 138 ff.) are indicated in the 1747 edition by slurs only, the *staccato* dots being an explanatory addition by the editor.

The figuring of the Continuo in the only known copy of the original edition shows the following handwritten corrections—possibly based on Bach's manuscript:

Meas. 9, third eighth, $5\flat$ added beneath the original 7.

Meas. 10, second eighth, an original 6 changed to 7.

Meas. 18, last eighth, $\sharp$ added.

Meas. 44, first eighth, $\frac{5}{3}$ added.

Meas. 48, last eighth, 6 changed to $\frac{6}{5\flat}$

Meas. 52, last eighth, $\frac{6}{4}$ added.

Meas. 53, first eighth, $\natural$ added beneath $\frac{6}{5}$

The realization of the figured bass again introduces a number of five-tone harmonies; after the first, the corrector ceases to mark them. The fifth part is at several places not properly introduced or concluded.

Meas. 87. E$\flat$ was originally held for a full quarter. The corrector remarked at the second eighth: "6 is missing". The measure is corrected in the manuscript.

Meas. 106. D was originally held for a full quarter. The corrector remarked at the second eighth: "7 does not resolve". The measure is corrected in Röllig's copy.

Meas. 112-113. The original read:

As the corrector stated at meas. 113, "the 7 does not resolve". The measures have been changed by the editor.

Meas. 120. The D was originally held an eighth-note longer. The
corrector remarked at the second eighth: "7 without 3". The B♮ has
accordingly been added by the editor.

Meas. 125. The original has in the top line: *c'' e''♭ f'' g''*. The second
voice forms parallel octaves to the bass. The parallel motion of all parts
sounds particularly bad at this exposed spot. The editor has accordingly
changed the voice-leading.

Meas. 126. The original indicates 4 instead of 4+ and accordingly
writes E♭ instead of the E♮ required by Bach. The editor has also added
a ♭ to D in the second half of the measure; the tonality is F minor, the
D descending and the figure 4 over an A♭ ambiguous.

Meas. 141. The figuration would require B♮ in the last eighth, whereas
no such anticipation is indicated in the corresponding meas. 100; therefore no change has been made in the realization.

Meas. 154. The corrector remarked: "*Das E ziehet in der Höhe gerne*",
which indicates either that he preferred the leading-tone to resolve upwards or, more probably, that he liked to see it in the top voice.

Meas. 158. $\frac{7}{5}$ is, probably correctly, interpreted as $\frac{7}{5}_{\natural 3}$

Meas. 249. As the recapitulation is not written out in the 1747 edition,
no indication for a close with the major third could be given; it is nevertheless likely that Bach expected the *tierce de Picardie* to be used at the
end of this extended movement.

ANDANTE

THE NOTES in this movement are correct in the 1747 edition. The *Bach-
Gesellschaft* edition presents meas. 7, quite wrongly, in minor up to the
end of the cadence.

Dynamic markings, consisting exclusively of the indications *pia.* and
for., are generously given to this movement in the 1747 edition (see the
reproduction of the Flute part, facing the title page). A strange gap
appears in the recapitulation, meas. 22-27. It is easy to mark meas. 22-23
in analogy to meas. 5-6. But whether Bach intended the contrast between
forte and *piano* to continue through the following two measures (24-25)
is hard to decide. A dynamic contrast between the appearances of the
ascending figure and those of the descending one has been suggested by
the editor; this suggestion, however, need not necessarily be followed,
the alternative being a straight *forte* from meas. 24 to meas. 28, interrupted, perhaps, by a *piano* at the last sixteenth of meas. 25.

The *piano* in the Violin, meas. 17, has been added in analogy to the original one in the Flute, meas. 16. But care should be taken that the Flute, playing *forte*, does not eclipse the Violin in *piano*.

No contrasts are indicated in the Continuo part and none can be introduced without destroying the continuous flow of the bass lines.

The ornaments include an unprepared appoggiatura in the Flute, meas. 11. In the 1747 edition it was written as a small eighth-note, but a comparatively short execution seems required so as not to obscure the imitation in contrary motion. The appoggiatura accordingly has been printed as a small sixteenth-note and a 32nd suggested for its realization. A similar appoggiatura has been added to the Violin in meas. 13.

The phrasing of this movement is fairly consistent in the 1747 edition. *Staccato* marks appear regularly only in the Flute; Bach probably added the marks only to the top line of his score, without any intention of treating the Violin differently from the Flute.

It seems that Bach phrased the Continuo differently from the upper voices. Meas. 3 and 4 appear in the Continuo exactly as they are reproduced here; the motif itself being altered, there is no reason why the difference in phrasing should not be retained. In meas. 20 and 21, only the eighth-notes and the second pair of sixteenth-notes are slurred in the original part; the phrasing has been made exactly like that in meas. 3 and 4.

In the Flute, meas. 26, last quarter, a slur appears in the 1747 edition between F and F♭; but this must have been added by mistake, as can be seen from the next measure in the Flute and from meas. 15 and 16 in the Violin.

The figuring of the Continuo in the only known copy of the original edition contains a manuscript $\frac{6}{5}$ in meas. 9, fourth eighth. A slight rhythmic variation is suggested by the placement of the figures in the corresponding measures 11 and 13.

The realization of the figured bass by Kirnberger (see chapter VII, p. 100) includes five-tone harmonies, which seems to confirm the conclusion that he was not the corrector of the unknown author's realization of the figured bass to the Sonata and the Mirror Canon (*ibid.*).

Kirnberger added a few figures like 5, 3, and ♮, in order to be more explicit. In meas. 9, second quarter, he replaced the dash by $\frac{7}{3}$. In meas. 11, he added a 2 to the fifth eighth. In meas. 13, seventh eighth, he replaced the 5 by a ♭3. The slight inconsistency in the treatment of the figures in the meas. 11 and 13 is clearly expressed in Kirnberger's rhythm; the variation adds to the improvisatory charm of the accompaniment and has therefore been preserved. In meas. 21, first quarter, Kirnberger changes the short suspension indicated by Bach to a long one, by leaving out the $\frac{8}{3}$, adding a $\frac{6}{4}$ to the second eighth-note, and

giving the solution thus: [musical notation] ; this has been changed by

the editor in compliance with the original figuration. It should be noted, furthermore, that the dashes in the first half of measures 3, 4, 20, and 21 of the original edition suggest harmonies held through half a measure rather than the rests chosen by Kirnberger.

ALLEGRO

THE NOTES are correct in the original edition of this movement. In the Continuo, meas. 20, the quarter is not dotted. In the Flute, meas. 41, a ♭ is printed before A instead of the ♮ required by the context (see Flute, meas. 44, and Violin, meas. 40 and 43) and specified in the figured bass.

In the last measure, the eighth-rest is missing in the Flute and Continuo parts.

In the *Bach-Gesellschaft* edition, there are mistakes affecting the rhythm and accidentals in Violin, meas. 109.

The ornaments again include an unprepared appoggiatura in the Violin, meas. 66; if executed as an eighth-note, this would produce parallel fifths with the Flute. This place, like one in the first *Allegro* (Flute, meas. 30), seems to prove that Bach wanted appoggiaturas of this kind short.

The edition of the *Bach-Gesellschaft* erroneously eliminates the *tr* in meas. 83.

The phrasing offers puzzles at various places.

The Royal theme begins with a slur covering six eighth-notes in five of its eight entries (all the entries in the Flute, the last entry in the Violin, and the first in the Continuo); in the other three entries, however, with a slur covering only five eighth-notes. The prevailing phrasing has been used here for all entries. The long slur reaching from the fifth into the seventh measure does not appear in the two entries of the Continuo; as a *non legato* gives more strength to the entry in the bass, the editor has not added slurs at these places.

The four-note allusions to the opening of the theme are not slurred in the Continuo (meas. 2, 44-45, and 54), whereas those in the Flute (meas. 24 and 70) are; the editor has preferred not to change this relation, which makes the thematic material in the bass easier to hear.

The opening measure of the first counterpoint is given in the Flute (meas. 11 and 46) with *staccato* marks for the first part of the scale run, but without marks for the three last notes of the run. Apparently Bach wanted an effect like this: . In the

Violin, meas. 55, the first part of the run is slurred; the slur has been replaced here by the *staccato* marking found in the other entries of the counterpoint.

The third measure of the counterpoint has *staccato* marks for the second and third eighth-notes in its first appearance (Flute, meas. 13); later it appears with a slur (Flute, meas. 48, and Violin, meas. 57); the latter version has been adopted for the first entry as well.

The fifth measure of the counterpoint (Flute, meas. 15) is not slurred in the first three of the five entries in which it appears (see Violin, meas. 29, and Flute, meas. 50); the slurs in the last two (Violin, meas. 59, and Flute, meas. 75) have accordingly been eliminated.

The second counterpoints, to the bass entry of the subject (meas. 23 ff.), include two measures with sixteenth-note figures not slurred in the 1747 edition (Violin, meas. 23, second beat, and meas. 25, second beat; Flute meas. 25, both beats; meas. 25 also returning in both instruments as meas. 71). These are difficult to play and do not seem to match the slurred sixteenth-note figures appearing in the same phrase (meas. 23, first beat, and meas. 24) and in the further course of the movement. Additional slurs have been suggested by the editor, in analogy to the phrasing prevailing from meas. 86 on. Players who are able to perform the lines smoothly without the slurs may do so.

In the sixth measure of the counterpoint in the Flute (meas. 28) the second and third notes are slurred, while the corresponding notes in the Violin (meas. 74) are not; a slur has been added in the latter place.

The second half of the movement opens with imitations between the upper voices in which a differentiation of phrasing is clearly indicated: the Flute slurs larger portions of the main motif than the Violin (compare meas. 62 and 64). The same contrast appears in the recapitulation of the episode (see meas. 78 and 80). If the Flute is replaced by another Violin, that distinction, no more justified by the contrast of tone color and tone production, should be abandoned.

A similar contrast is maintained for the extension of the episode (Violin, meas. 83-85, against Flute, meas. 86-88). In the following counterpoints to the subject, however, Bach apparently intended a return to equal treatment of the two instruments; the Violin, which has a rather indefinite or defective marking in the original part (meas. 91-94), has been adjusted to the Flute (meas. 97-100), the marking of which is fairly clear. In determining the phrasing of the passage, the *staccato* marks in the 1747 edition are of considerable help; one of these, however (Violin, meas. 91, second beat, first note) was apparently added by mistake. A possibly authentic alternative remains only for the last quarter of the counterpoint (second quarter of Violin, meas. 94, and Flute, meas. 100),

which may have been intended as: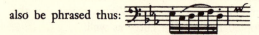

The Continuo part is properly slurred in meas. 95, but in the following measure, the slurs are lacking; the second quarter of that measure may

also be phrased thus:

The following minor inaccuracies of the original edition have been adjusted:

Flute, meas. 43-44, a single slur covering two measures, instead of two slurs as required by the context.

Violin, meas. 50, last note, a superfluous *staccato* mark.

Violin, meas. 53, a slur split into two parts on account of a page turn.

Continuo, meas. 55, a slur not clearly drawn; the measure has been phrased like the corresponding meas. 46, the alternative being the introduction of separate slurs, the second starting on the second sixteenth-note.

Continuo, meas. 65, a slur lacking, needed in anticipation of the slurs in the two following measures.

Continuo, meas. 88, slur beginning on D instead of C.

Flute, meas. 89, slur beginning with the first note, instead of the second, as in Violin, meas. 88.

Continuo, meas. 101, second beat, a slur missing.

Flute, a slur missing in meas. 103 and two slurs in meas. 105, needed in accordance with slurs in the Violin, meas. 105 and 103; the contrast between Flute, meas. 104, and Violin, meas. 106, has been preserved on account of the differences in the other voices.

Violin, meas. 109, second beat, phrasing not clear; the phrasing of the Flute has been used as a model.

Continuo, meas. 111, two slurs missing; no slur is given or needed in the following measure, although one might slur the second to sixth sixteenth-notes.

The figuring of the Continuo shows possibly authentic manuscript additions at two places: in meas. 102 a 6 is added to each of the last two eighth-notes, and in meas. 111, a ♮ is added to the fifth sixteenth-note.

In the course of this movement, a number of errors appear in the figuring. Almost all of them concern the exact sizes of intervals (♮ instead of 6, 4 instead of 4+ etc.). Most of them were already corrected by the unknown author of the figured-bass realization, which is no mean proof of his musicianship. The corrections have been taken over here—without discussion, since none of them is questionable.

The realization of the figured bass has fared better with the corrector in this movement than in the first *Allegro*. He criticizes only two places. The first, meas. 9, originally had a C held as top voice throughout the measure; at the third eighth, the corrector remarks: "the 6 is missing"; the change has been carried out by the present editor.

The other objection to the original text of the realization concerns meas. 78 and its sequence, meas. 80; here the corrector objects to the omission of the 4 in the second half of the measure, which, however, seems an entirely legitimate liberty.

In meas. 11, a slur connected the two notes A♮; as they belong to different voices, the slur has been eliminated.

In meas. 26, last eighth, the figuring is supplemented by a ♮. But the tonality should change at this place back to C minor and the A is descending; the editor has changed the A♮ to A♭, considering the clash with the sixteenth-note A♮ in the Violin as negligible.

In meas. 68, the editor has assumed that the ⁶ chord is supposed to enter on the fifth eighth, not on the sixth, and has accordingly changed

the rhythm of the two moving voices from: ♩ ♪ to: ♪♩

In meas. 110, the second note of the top part, originally a quarter, has been split into two eighth-notes.

THEMATIS REGII ELABORATIONES CANONICAE (CANONIC ELABORATIONS OF THE ROYAL THEME)

The titles of the canon group as well as of the single pieces are discussed in chapter III, pp. 22-28.

The original edition presents the first canon of this group in parts, following the Sonata; the others appear in abbreviated notation on the canon sheets and the last page of the *Ricercar a 6*. The original notation of No. 9 is reproduced on p. 12, top; of Nos. 10 and 11, on p. 14, bottom; and of No. 12 on p. 12, bottom, and p. 13. The distribution in the 1747 edition is discussed in chapter VII, pp. 92-93.

The interpretation of these canons is discussed in chapter V, pp. 77-82.

The solution of the canons has been indicated in the original edition for No. 8, which is printed in full, and No. 12. The Nos. 9-11 are treated as puzzle canons; for sources of written-out solutions, see chapter VII, pp. 96-99.

No. 8. Canon perpetuus (Mirror Canon)

The instrumentation of this composition as given in the 1747 edition invites a critical note. The canon proper cannot very well be presented

in abbreviated notation (see chapter III, p. 26). Bach, therefore, must
have written it down in full score, exactly as he did the Sonata which it
followed. Schübler inserted the parts of the canon in the partbooks of
the Sonata and thus presented the piece as one for Flute, Violin, and
Continuo. Such specification is appropriate, and the presence of the figures
in the bass makes it actually probable that Bach had a specific combination in mind for this movement. However, we cannot prove that the
specification appeared in Bach's manuscript, and the possibility remains
that Bach had simply offered a score to be executed by any suitable
instruments and that the inclusion of the canon in the Sonata parts
effected a specification not originally given by Bach. The Flute has
been retained in the instrumentation suggested for complete performance
of the work, while the canon by itself might just as well be performed
by two Violins and Continuo.[1]

The phrasing of the Mirror Canon contains another problem that cannot be solved definitely in the absence of Bach's autograph. The original
edition contains a considerable number of slurs in the *Violino* part, but
hardly any in the *Traversa*. This difference in treatment may be considered justified to a certain degree by the fact that the parts move in
contrary motion; and it sounds perfectly convincing if one canonic part
is played by a Flute, the other by a Violin. Bach introduced, in the
Sonata, an apparently deliberate contrast in phrasing between Flute
and Violin (see above, p. 169 f.), and it is probable that the contrast
found here was also introduced deliberately. But there is also a chance
that Bach indicated in his score the phrasing for only one of the canonic
parts, assuming that the corresponding phrasing would be added to the
following part; in this case, the Violin must have formed the top part
of the score and the slurs found in the *Traversa* (meas. 10 and 27-28)
would have been added by Bach somewhat at random, without the
intention of having these places treated differently from the rest of the
part. The edition of the *Bach-Gesellschaft* makes the phrasing of the
Flute conform, though not with complete accuracy, to that of the Violin;
Landshoff, on the contrary, reproduces the phrasing of the original edition without change. To arrive at a practical solution, one may retain the
phrasing of the original edition if the canon is performed with Flute
and Violin; but if it is performed by two Violins, the parts should be
phrased alike, since a differentiation would sound artificial in that case.
The parts have been treated accordingly in the present edition.

A few slurs have been added in the Violin part to make the phrasing
of the theme equal to that of its inversion (*cf.* meas. 8 and 25, 11 and 29).

[1] Such performance has been provided for by insertion of the original Flute
part in the partbook of Violin II.

The slurs in meas. 29-30 were incorrectly given in the original part as:

The original Continuo part does not include slurs. Slurs have been suggested by the editor in order to provide for a proper moulding of this line which is difficult to phrase convincingly in a continuous *détaché*.

The ornamentation of this number contains another tricky, though minor, problem. The theme in its original motion is not embellished in the first appearance (Flute, meas. 1 ff.) and its return (Flute, meas. 31 ff.), but a ✿ is added to the opening motif in the second appearance (Violin, meas. 21) and to the isolated appearance of the opening motif in the Continuo (meas. 30). The theme in inversion does not contain a corresponding ornament, and should not, for the inversion would require a mordent which anticipates the leading tone and thus weakens the melodic line. However, the appearance of the ornament in the Continuo (meas. 30) immediately precedes the return of the theme in the Flute, and accordingly an ornament is clearly expected in the Flute at that place (meas. 32), though missing in the original edition. Now, this appearance of the theme in the Flute marks the beginning of the recapitulation, and one might thus be inclined to turn back and add a trill to the opening motif in its first appearance (meas. 2); but that addition would let the following entrance of the necessarily unembellished inversion of the theme appear somewhat as an anticlimax and should therefore be avoided, while later on the difference in treatment will hardly be noticed.

The figuring of the Continuo contains three errors which have been corrected. Meas. 14 in the original edition offers a $\frac{7}{5+}$ with the first note, which does not seem logical. In meas. 22, a 2 instead of a 3 is given with the $\frac{6}{4+}$ In meas. 24, the first quarter is figured 6♮ instead of $\frac{6}{♮}$

Meas. 18, last quarter, shows the figuring reproduced in the text, requiring F♯ and A♭; this was considered erroneous by previous editors, but seems entirely convincing since the bass has the character of a dominant while the A♭ in the Violin is required by the canon. It may be noted that a corresponding progression, which is undoubtedly correct, appears in the last movement of the Sonata, meas. 108.

The figured-bass realization of this number comes from the same source as does that of the Sonata (see chapter VII, pp. 100 f.). The unknown scholar acquitted himself rather well, considering the intricacies of the harmonic setting. A few slurs have been added, as dotted ones, by the editor. Furthermore the following places had to be changed:

Meas. 7, fourth eighth originally $f'g'b'\natural$, improperly resolved onto $c'e'\flat c''$.

Meas. 9, c'' originally entering on the first beat.

Meas. 10, third quarter, d' originally held for two quarters.

Meas. 12, originally: *(musical notation)*

Meas. 18, last quarter, read originally: *(musical notation)*

The change has been made in order to make the clash between F$\sharp$ and A$\flat$ less conspicuous.

Meas. 19, second quarter, a third voice $(a'd')$ supplied by the editor.

Meas. 20, originally disregarding the 6: *(musical notation)*

Meas. 22, last quarter, originally $a'd''f''\sharp$, going to $b'd''g''$; the jump into a $\begin{smallmatrix}7\sharp\\5\sharp\\3\end{smallmatrix}$ which changes into $\begin{smallmatrix}6\\4\end{smallmatrix}$ does not sound good.

Meas. 23, the last eighth-note has been added by the editor.

Meas. 30, last quarter, originally $f'b'\natural d''$, improperly resolving into $g'c''g''$, which was held for three quarters.

No. 9. Canon a 2 (Crab Canon)

The original edition gives the time signature as **C** at the beginning and as **¢** at the end; the latter evidently is correct.

Retrograde motion, by inverting the order of the notes, inverts the direction of all intervals, changing ascending intervals into descending and *vice versa*. Thus the Crab Canon offers the same problems of accidental-setting as a canon in contrary motion. All previous editions present the second voice as an exact reversion, which produces a stiff and unsatisfactory solution—as in the case of the Canons in Contrary Motion, Nos. 4 and 5, only a tonal answer can result in a convincing realization.

In a crab canon in the minor mode, a tonal answer would ordinarily include a minor third throughout, a major seventh and a major sixth in the ascent, a minor sixth and preferably a minor seventh in the descent. In the present example, there is no question about the size of any interval in the reverse theme, while a decision is required about the sixth and seventh scale degrees as used in the counterpoint. Bach's original line introduces major intervals in the ascent and minor ones in the descent, as might be expected, though only in the opening measures of the counterpoint (meas. 9-11) and for its conclusion (meas. 16-18); inserted between these groups of measures are modulations making freer use of the intervals. In the reverse part, a straight tonal answer can be maintained for four measures; then the chromatic sequence of the theme must be accompanied by modulatory scales in the retrograde part. The original C minor tonality is restored in meas. 7, and from that point on, to the end of the counterpoint, one might again follow the principle of tonal answer within the C minor scale. In meas. 8, however, *b'♮* and *a'♮* seem preferable to *b'♭* and *a'♭* in consideration of the cadence quality of the measure and as a preparation for the isolated *c''* in the following measure.[2]

A note on the reversion of the entire canon is given in chapter III, p. 26 and note 7. The inscription *Quaerendo invenietis*, which is given in the 1747 edition to the following piece, may originally have referred to the present number as well; see chapter VII, pp. 92-93.

No. 10. Canon a 2 (Canon in Contrary Motion)

In the original edition, we find the words *Quaerendo invenietis* instead of an explanatory title for this number. Since the second part enters at the unusual distance of five half-measures, the canon forms a particularly attractive puzzle.

The theme contains so many chromatic passing-notes that Bach preferred to present this number without flats in the key-signature, as he had done with the Modulating Canon, No. 6.

This is the last canon in contrary motion in the *Musical Offering*. Since the pivot of the inversion is the dominant, an initial tonic chord in minor (C E♭ G) is answered in the inverted part by the dominant major chord (D B♮ G). Accordingly the inversion can be made "real" or exact without difficulty, and this was evidently Bach's intention. It is interesting to note that Bach used, in meas. 15, an augmented second E♭ F♯, which points forward to a descending augmented second B♮ A♭ in the inversion. A single passage might be found smoother if handled as a tonal answer rather than a real one (B♭ instead of B♮ in the lower voice, meas. 14, last note; likewise in the upper voice, meas. 12, of the inverted version); consistency, however, has seemed more valuable than the slight melodic improvement which could be gained by the introduction of an isolated tonal element into the otherwise strict answer.

As the composition contains neither a *cantus firmus* (as did two of the preceding canons in contrary motion: Nos. 4 and 5) nor an accom-

---

[2] That a descending minor scale with a major seventh and sixth was not foreign to Bach, may be seen from the opening of the *Duetto* in E minor from the Third Part of the *Clavier-Übung:*

[3] The solution of the present number is not difficult since two clefs are given and the parts enter simultaneously. However, the fact that Bach neither gives a specific title to the piece nor indicates that the parts enter simultaneously may be considered sufficient to establish the piece as a puzzle canon.

panying bass (as No. 8), it can be inverted completely. In the strictly inverted version, the lower part begins, descending, and the higher follows, ascending, after five half-measures. This solution was first realized by Agricola (see chapter VII, p. 97) together with the correct solution, though with slight errors; someone, possibly Kirnberger, remarked in Agricola's manuscript that the inverted version, as opposed to the "true solution", did not represent the author's intention.[4] The inversion in double counterpoint included in our edition corresponds, in principle, to Agricola's second solution; however, the parts have been exchanged in double counterpoint at the octave so that each player may perform the inversion of his own original part. This inversion contains a few minor liberties of harmonic and contrapuntal progression, but it seemed preferable to Agricola's inversion, for it offers greater interest to both player and performer, and it creates a fuller correspondence between this and the preceding Crab Canon.

The original canonic line embellishes the end of the theme (meas. 8) with a trill. It should be noted that the shake must be replaced by a mordent in the inverted part.

No. 11. Canon a 4 (Four-Part Canon)

The abbreviated notation of this canon in the original edition is in the key of G minor, and all solutions of the piece have been given in that key. The idea of the *Musical Offering*, however, was to present a series of compositions as a whole, relying on unity of tonality as one of the means to keep the various pieces together. The *Andante*, it is true, is written in E-flat major; but it forms part of the Sonata, a larger unit which begins and ends in C minor, the basic tonality of the complete work. The Four-Part Canon, on the other hand, is a composition complete in itself; if it is to be acknowledged as an integral part of the *Musical Offering*, it must be presented in C minor, and it is so presented in the new edition.

Why did Bach write this Canon in G minor? To indicate a canon at the double octave in abbreviated notation he used the combination of a G clef and a C clef—the only combination at his disposal, as will be shown below. Now, the canonic line has the unusually wide range of

---

[4] Dörffel, in the edition of the *Bach-Gesellschaft*, quotes two more solutions according to suggestions made in the *Allgemeine Musikalische Zeitung* of Leipzig, one by Fischer, the other by the anonymous *Kontrapunktist* (see above, p. 97). The second part enters in both at the second quarter of meas. 19. In the first, the higher voice begins, ascending; in the other, the lower voice, descending. The first is, in its entire two-part center, identical with Agricola's second, inverted version; the other, with the original "true solution". Thus these "solutions" are only variants of those mentioned above—inferior ones, for the second voice enters in both only after the first has exposed episodic material in addition to the full theme.

two full octaves. If Bach had written it down in C minor, he would have been forced to use as many as three upper leger lines without making full use of the lower part of the staff. Leger lines, however, were still avoided as far as possible in Bach's time. Apparently this is why he resorted to a transposition which centered the canonic line exactly on the middle of the staff, sacrificing consistency to elegance of appearance. Bach introduced two clefs to indicate four voices. Taken literally, the abbreviated notation leads to a combination of two high voices in unison and two low voices in unison (employed by Dörffel) or of three high voices in unison against a single bass (employed by Oley and Landshoff). In the first case, the voices would preferably enter in alternation: e.g. Violin I, Violoncello I, Violin II, Violoncello II, in succession. In the second type of solution, the three voices in unison would first be introduced successively, and followed by the single low entrance. None of these solutions, however, provides a thoroughly satisfactory distribution of sonorities.

The clefs Bach had at his disposal marked certain lines on the staff as g', c', or f. Each of these clefs could be attached to various lines on the staff, but never to a space between two lines. The distance between any two clefs was accordingly a third, a fifth, or a multiple of thirds. Middle C, for instance, could be expressed in the following ways:

An abbreviated notation, therefore, could be applied only to canons at the distance of a third, a fifth, or a multiple of thirds, as can be seen more clearly from the following tabulation of the meanings a note on the bottom line of the staff would acquire through change of clefs:

Original notation

Modern notation

Now, the double octave can be expressed as a multiple of thirds, but not the single octave. Bach, then, could not possibly have written down a canon at a single octave in abbreviated notation. Thus it is entirely possible, and, if one considers the structure of the Four-Part Canon, even probable, that Bach used the distance of a double octave to indicate the distance of the outer voices—that is, the compass of the composition—

rather than the actual distance of all the parts to be derived from the original line. The solution given here introduces a single part between the highest and the lowest parts specified by Bach, at an octave's distance from either. Dörffel was the first to mention the possibility of such treatment; it complies in all probability with Bach's intention or at least would have met with his approval. Lenzewsky, carrying out Dörffel's suggestion, introduced the parts in the order: high, middle, high, low. But this creates a sequence which might and should go on, exactly as any form of the pattern A B A C seems to require a continuation with A D A E etc. The same formal shortcoming would result if one were to introduce the parts in the order: high, high, middle, low. The order adapted in our edition closes a series of descending entrances with a return to the pitch of the first entrance: Violin, Viola, Violoncello, Violin—creating a formal pattern A B C A, which necessarily cannot be continued. This solution, first set forth by Busoni, seems the only solution satisfactory from the points of view of both structure and sonority.

In meas. 8 of the abbreviated notation a ♯ is found before the seventh sixteenth (F♯, corresponding to B♮ here). It is highly improbable, however, that an augmented second was intended for a fast descending run like this. Perhaps a ♮ before the eighth sixteenth (E♮, corresponding to A♮ here) was left out in the original edition, or the ♯ was a misprint for a ♮. As the descent C B♭ A♭ sounds most natural, it has been chosen here, in accordance with Müller's and Dörffel's editions.

No. 12. *Fuga canonica in Epidiapente (Canonic Fugue)*

The abbreviated notation of this canon in the 1747 edition specifies the interval between the canonic parts not only in the title but also by a double clef. The lower first part has a single ♭ in the key signature while the higher second has no accidental; thus an exact answer is implied. The bass shows the regular C-minor signature of three flats.

The original edition supplies in the text itself the flats left out in the key signature of the canonic parts, but a few are omitted by mistake. Thus no flat is given before E♭ in meas. 53 and before A♭ in meas. 67 of the canonic line. In the dedicatory copy, a ♮ is also missing before the seventh eighth-note of meas. 74; it was added on the engraved plate after the first printing.

The entrance of the second part is indicated by a manuscript sign in the dedicatory copy; other copies of the original edition lack such an indication. The place in the first canonic part which is to become the end in the second is marked by a *fermata* in the original, according to old practice; this *fermata* does not, of course, signify a hold in the first canonic part.

In order to emphasize the correspondence between the Mirror Canon, No. 8, and the Canonic Fugue, identical instrumentation has been suggested for both pieces. If the work is presented in its entirety, the Flute and the keyboard instrument required for the Sonata should be used for the Canonic Fugue as well. The original edition, however, fails to specify instruments for the present number and does not include figures in the bass; accordingly one may perform the Canonic Fugue as a separate piece with a Violin instead of the Flute and without a keyboard instrument.[5] The realization of the Continuo has been supplied by the editor.

Slurs appear at a single place in the original edition, meas. 60-61. Additional slurs have been suggested as an essential help in phrasing both for the canonic parts and for the Violoncello; similar markings for the keyboard instrument did not seem necessary.

[5] In order to facilitate execution without a Flute, the Flute part has been duplicated in the part-book of Violin I, and the part of the first Violin in the part-book of Violin II.

No. 13. RICERCAR A 6 (SIX-PART RICERCAR)

BACH'S HOLOGRAPH of this number is written in keyboard notation.

The 1747 edition presents the composition in score, using the clefs:

The relation between the two sources is discussed in chapter VII, pp. 83f. and 89; the evaluation given there summarizes the conclusions drawn from the variants mentioned below. The holograph is completely reproduced on pp. 85-88. The last page of the composition as it appears in the original edition is reproduced on p. 14.

The title of this *Ricercar* includes, in the 1747 edition, the indication *a 6*, while the corresponding *a 3* is lacking in the title of the other *Ricercar*. The holograph has no title in Bach's hand.

The time signature in both sources is ¢ . Both are written in true *alla breve*, that is with four half-notes to a measure. The reprints of the keyboard version in Dörffel's and Landshoff's editions, supposedly according to Bach's holograph, reproduce the composition incorrectly in 2/2 meter.

The readings concern mostly variants between the holograph and the 1747 edition. In the following discussion, the parts are numbered in descending order as i to vi.

Meas. 49. The holograph gives vi as:

Bach may originally have written: ◯ ◯ , and, in changing the first note to a *brevis*, forgotten to eliminate the second whole-note. The *brevis*, which seems to represent Bach's final version, is preferable and has been used in agreement with the original edition.

Meas. 50. In the holograph, the second quarter of iii is missing. The missing note can only be a D. The 1747 edition adds *d'*, which has been used for the keyboard version because it can be played without splitting the *d''* in i. In the score, *d''* has been used, for it produces a better curved line and an imitation between i and iii, which probably was Bach's original intention.

Meas. 56-57. The version reproduced here for the first time is exactly the version of the holograph. The 1747 edition and the so-called reprints of Bach's holograph lead iv: 𝄢 The change eliminates the somewhat strange progression E♭—D♭—C underneath a *d''♭*, and a $\begin{smallmatrix}6\\4\end{smallmatrix}$ chord reached and left with skips in the bass; it may, therefore, represent a change indicated by Bach. It produces, however, a chord with B♭ in three octaves in the three lower voices (last quarter of meas. 56); it cannot, therefore, be regarded as an improvement and has not been used.

Meas. 58. Bach had originally written the first note of v and vi as: 𝅗𝅥 Then he drew the slur between the two note-heads F in the bass and eliminated the down-stem. The resulting picture: 𝄢 is incorrect, but its interpretation in the 1747 edition, which has been taken over, is convincing.

Meas. 59. Close examination of this place, which is rather blurred in the holograph, reveals that Bach intended the lower voices to read as in our text. Landshoff reads the note-heads correctly, but leads iv and v thus: 𝄢 . The 1747 edition presents the three lower parts as follows:

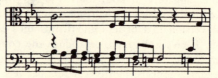

The change may have been made in order to insert an E♮ into the harmony on the third quarter, which would be a pedantic purpose, for the *e'♮* of the theme in iii has penetrating force and is still strongly felt after the note itself ceases. More probably the change was simply caused by an error in reading. The version of the 1747 edition destroys, in any case, the basic curve of the motif, which should appear in vi, and the imitation between ii in meas. 58 and v in 59.

Meas. 61. The 1747 edition and the so-called reprints of Bach's holograph have the following bass line: The change was apparently introduced in order to cover the ascent from the suspended B♭. The suspension, however, resolves properly on the third quarter, and the change, which introduces a $\frac{6}{4}$ chord through skips in the bass, cannot be considered an improvement.

Meas. 61, second half. In the 1747 edition, iv is changed to: The change, which eliminates consecutive twelfths between i and iv, may have been asked for by Bach. It impairs, however, the rhythmic smoothness of the cadence and has therefore not been accepted.

Meas. 72. Bach originally wrote the second group of eighth-notes in the bass as E♭ F G♭ E♮ F, but then erased the ♮ before the second E.

Meas. 76. The rhythm of the top voice was changed in the original edition, evidently by mistake, to:

Meas. 78. The last note in iii is given in the 1747 edition as a quarter. The original version, which has greater continuity, has been restored.

Meas. 79. Bach's holograph opens the imitations between v and vi as indicated in the keyboard version while the 1747 edition uses the version given in the score. Whether the change was according to Bach's instructions is difficult to determine. The original version is more logical, while the version of the 1747 edition gives greater weight to the beginning of the imitative sequence. Possibly Bach made the change in order to recall more clearly the ascent in meas. 29. The version of the old edition has been used for the score because it avoids the single B♭, below the range of the Viola.

Meas. 85, second half, and 86. The holograph, not clearly legible, seems to have been misinterpreted in the 1747 edition as well as in the reprints of the holograph itself, which read parts iii and iv as follows:

Meas. 89. Part iii reads in the 1747 edition: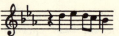

The change, which blurs the otherwise clear harmonic structure, cannot be accounted for by any musical reason.

Meas. 92. Part iii is given in the 1747 edition as:

The change may have been made in order to avoid the consecutive fifths between ii and iii, or to make the harmony clearer. The original version is rhythmically more natural and harmonically more piquant, while the progression from a diminished fifth to a perfect one is not at all disturbing.

Meas. 96. Bach's holograph, though none too legible in the entire passage, indicates for ii clearly enough the second $b'\flat$ and the quarter-rests in the second half of the measure, while the second stem of the $a'\natural$ is missing or hardly visible. The 1747 edition interprets the line, without doubt erroneously, as:

Meas. 102, second half and 103. Bach's holograph indicates v as:

The 1747 edition places a $\natural$ before both E's.

The original version refers more clearly back to that employed at the corresponding place, meas. 51, and strikingly emphasizes the final chord by reserving the *tierce de Picardie* for the last measure.

Meas. 103. Bach indicated the last note of each part as a *longa*, by writing it in the form of two connected *breves*. The 1747 edition and the reprints of the holograph reproduce the last note as *brevis* with *fermata*. The notation chosen by Bach conveys much more clearly his intention that the note should be held very long or, indeed, as long as possible.

Ornaments are not found in either the holograph or the 1747 edition, and apparently none were supposed to be added.

The phrasing of the originals has been retained in the keyboard version; it will be seen that the original manuscript contains no marks of phrasing except single slurs in meas. 5, 9, and 13. The 1747 edition omits these slurs, but offers corresponding slurs in meas. 19, parts iii and iv (see p. 84) and an additional slur in i, meas. 93, second half. The last is drawn inaccurately as: . It should

either cover the entire second half of the measure, or be split as has been suggested in the text.

Octave-transpositions of entire phrases are not necessary in this composition, whether it is to be performed by modern strings or by a combination of reed instruments and strings. A single $'B\flat$ in vi, meas. 67, and a single $A\flat$ in iv, meas. 82, have been transposed up an octave in the open score and the parts. The restoration of the original version in iv, meas. 56-57, eliminates another descent, found in the original edition, beyond the range of the Viola. The choice of the version of the 1747 edition for the ensemble version in meas. 79 makes iv completely playable on the Viola; whoever prefers to use the version of the holograph must have the Viola play an octave higher than written from the second note of meas. 79 to the second note of meas. 82. The last note of vi, if played by a Violoncello alone, may be played an octave lower than written, or doubled in the lower octave.

INDEX

Entries that might have formed sub-headings to Bach, J. S.,
or Musical Offering *have been distributed through the Index.
Works by Bach are given in italics while all other entries
appear in roman type. Exclusive references to the* Musical
Offering *are marked by asterisks. The principal references
to movements from the* Musical Offering *are indicated by
page numbers in italics.*

**A CATALOGUE OF SELECTED DOVER BOOKS
IN ALL FIELDS OF INTEREST**

A CATALOGUE OF SELECTED DOVER BOOKS
IN ALL FIELDS OF INTEREST

AMERICA'S OLD MASTERS, James T. Flexner. Four men emerged unexpectedly from provincial 18th century America to leadership in European art: Benjamin West, J. S. Copley, C. R. Peale, Gilbert Stuart. Brilliant coverage of lives and contributions. Revised, 1967 edition. 69 plates. 365pp. of text.
21806-6 Paperbound $3.00

FIRST FLOWERS OF OUR WILDERNESS: AMERICAN PAINTING, THE COLONIAL PERIOD, James T. Flexner. Painters, and regional painting traditions from earliest Colonial times up to the emergence of Copley, West and Peale Sr., Foster, Gustavus Hesselius, Feke, John Smibert and many anonymous painters in the primitive manner. Engaging presentation, with 162 illustrations. xxii + 368pp.
22180-6 Paperbound $3.50

THE LIGHT OF DISTANT SKIES: AMERICAN PAINTING, 1760-1835, James T. Flexner. The great generation of early American painters goes to Europe to learn and to teach: West, Copley, Gilbert Stuart and others. Allston, Trumbull, Morse; also contemporary American painters—primitives, derivatives, academics—who remained in America. 102 illustrations. xiii + 306pp.
22179-2 Paperbound $3.00

A HISTORY OF THE RISE AND PROGRESS OF THE ARTS OF DESIGN IN THE UNITED STATES, William Dunlap. Much the richest mine of information on early American painters, sculptors, architects, engravers, miniaturists, etc. The only source of information for scores of artists, the major primary source for many others. Unabridged reprint of rare original 1834 edition, with new introduction by James T. Flexner, and 394 new illustrations. Edited by Rita Weiss. 6⅝ x 9⅝.
21695-0, 21696-9, 21697-7 Three volumes, Paperbound $13.50

EPOCHS OF CHINESE AND JAPANESE ART, Ernest F. Fenollosa. From primitive Chinese art to the 20th century, thorough history, explanation of every important art period and form, including Japanese woodcuts; main stress on China and Japan, but Tibet, Korea also included. Still unexcelled for its detailed, rich coverage of cultural background, aesthetic elements, diffusion studies, particularly of the historical period. 2nd, 1913 edition. 242 illustrations. lii + 439pp. of text.
20364-6, 20365-4 Two volumes, Paperbound $6.00

THE GENTLE ART OF MAKING ENEMIES, James A. M. Whistler. Greatest wit of his day deflates Oscar Wilde, Ruskin, Swinburne; strikes back at inane critics, exhibitions, art journalism; aesthetics of impressionist revolution in most striking form. Highly readable classic by great painter. Reproduction of edition designed by Whistler. Introduction by Alfred Werner. xxxvi + 334pp.
21875-9 Paperbound $2.50

ALPHABETS AND ORNAMENTS, Ernst Lehner. Well-known pictorial source for decorative alphabets, script examples, cartouches, frames, decorative title pages, calligraphic initials, borders, similar material. 14th to 19th century, mostly European. Useful in almost any graphic arts designing, varied styles. 750 illustrations. 256pp. 7 x 10.   21905-4 Paperbound $4.00

PAINTING: A CREATIVE APPROACH, Norman Colquhoun. For the beginner simple guide provides an instructive approach to painting: major stumbling blocks for beginner; overcoming them, technical points; paints and pigments; oil painting; watercolor and other media and color. New section on "plastic" paints. Glossary. Formerly *Paint Your Own Pictures*. 221pp.   22000-1 Paperbound $1.75

THE ENJOYMENT AND USE OF COLOR, Walter Sargent. Explanation of the relations between colors themselves and between colors in nature and art, including hundreds of little-known facts about color values, intensities, effects of high and low illumination, complementary colors. Many practical hints for painters, references to great masters. 7 color plates, 29 illustrations. x + 274pp.
20944-X Paperbound $2.50

THE NOTEBOOKS OF LEONARDO DA VINCI, compiled and edited by Jean Paul Richter. 1566 extracts from original manuscripts reveal the full range of Leonardo's versatile genius: all his writings on painting, sculpture, architecture, anatomy, astronomy, geography, topography, physiology, mining, music, etc., in both Italian and English, with 186 plates of manuscript pages and more than 500 additional drawings. Includes studies for the Last Supper, the lost Sforza monument, and other works. Total of xlvii + 866pp. 7⅞ x 10¾.
22572-0, 22573-9 Two volumes, Paperbound $10.00

MONTGOMERY WARD CATALOGUE OF 1895. Tea gowns, yards of flannel and pillow-case lace, stereoscopes, books of gospel hymns, the New Improved Singer Sewing Machine, side saddles, milk skimmers, straight-edged razors, high-button shoes, spittoons, and on and on . . . listing some 25,000 items, practically all illustrated. Essential to the shoppers of the 1890's, it is our truest record of the spirit of the period. Unaltered reprint of Issue No. 57, Spring and Summer 1895. Introduction by Boris Emmet. Innumerable illustrations. xiii + 624pp. 8½ x 11⅝.
22377-9 Paperbound $6.95

THE CRYSTAL PALACE EXHIBITION ILLUSTRATED CATALOGUE (LONDON, 1851). One of the wonders of the modern world—the Crystal Palace Exhibition in which all the nations of the civilized world exhibited their achievements in the arts and sciences—presented in an equally important illustrated catalogue. More than 1700 items pictured with accompanying text—ceramics, textiles, cast-iron work, carpets, pianos, sleds, razors, wall-papers, billiard tables, beehives, silverware and hundreds of other artifacts—represent the focal point of Victorian culture in the Western World. Probably the largest collection of Victorian decorative art ever assembled—indispensable for antiquarians and designers. Unabridged republication of the Art-Journal Catalogue of the Great Exhibition of 1851, with all terminal essays. New introduction by John Gloag, F.S.A. xxxiv + 426pp. 9 x 12.
22503-8 Paperbound $4.50

THE ARCHITECTURE OF COUNTRY HOUSES, Andrew J. Downing. Together with Vaux's *Villas and Cottages* this is the basic book for Hudson River Gothic architecture of the middle Victorian period. Full, sound discussions of general aspects of housing, architecture, style, decoration, furnishing, together with scores of detailed house plans, illustrations of specific buildings, accompanied by full text. Perhaps the most influential single American architectural book. 1850 edition. Introduction by J. Stewart Johnson. 321 figures, 34 architectural designs. xvi + 560pp.
22003-6 Paperbound $4.00

LOST EXAMPLES OF COLONIAL ARCHITECTURE, John Mead Howells. Full-page photographs of buildings that have disappeared or been so altered as to be denatured, including many designed by major early American architects. 245 plates. xvii + 248pp. 7⅞ x 10¾. 21143-6 Paperbound $3.50

DOMESTIC ARCHITECTURE OF THE AMERICAN COLONIES AND OF THE EARLY REPUBLIC, Fiske Kimball. Foremost architect and restorer of Williamsburg and Monticello covers nearly 200 homes between 1620-1825. Architectural details, construction, style features, special fixtures, floor plans, etc. Generally considered finest work in its area. 219 illustrations of houses, doorways, windows, capital mantels. xx + 314pp. 7⅞ x 10¾. 21743-4 Paperbound $4.00

EARLY AMERICAN ROOMS: 1650-1858, edited by Russell Hawes Kettell. Tour of 12 rooms, each representative of a different era in American history and each furnished, decorated, designed and occupied in the style of the era. 72 plans and elevations, 8-page color section, etc., show fabrics, wall papers, arrangements, etc. Full descriptive text. xvii + 200pp. of text. 8⅜ x 11¼.
21633-0 Paperbound $5.00

THE FITZWILLIAM VIRGINAL BOOK, edited by J. Fuller Maitland and W. B. Squire. Full modern printing of famous early 17th-century ms. volume of 300 works by Morley, Byrd, Bull, Gibbons, etc. For piano or other modern keyboard instrument; easy to read format. xxxvi + 938pp. 8⅜ x 11.
21068-5, 21069-3 Two volumes, Paperbound $10.00

KEYBOARD MUSIC, Johann Sebastian Bach. Bach Gesellschaft edition. A rich selection of Bach's masterpieces for the harpsichord: the six English Suites, six French Suites, the six Partitas (Clavierübung part I), the Goldberg Variations (Clavierübung part IV), the fifteen Two-Part Inventions and the fifteen Three-Part Sinfonias. Clearly reproduced on large sheets with ample margins; eminently playable. vi + 312pp. 8⅛ x 11. 22360-4 Paperbound $5.00

THE MUSIC OF BACH: AN INTRODUCTION, Charles Sanford Terry. A fine, nontechnical introduction to Bach's music, both instrumental and vocal. Covers organ music, chamber music, passion music, other types. Analyzes themes, developments, innovations. x + 114pp. 21075-8 Paperbound $1.25

BEETHOVEN AND HIS NINE SYMPHONIES, Sir George Grove. Noted British musicologist provides best history, analysis, commentary on symphonies. Very thorough, rigorously accurate; necessary to both advanced student and amateur music lover. 436 musical passages. vii + 407 pp. 20334-4 Paperbound $2.75

JOHANN SEBASTIAN BACH, Philipp Spitta. One of the great classics of musicology, this definitive analysis of Bach's music (and life) has never been surpassed. Lucid, nontechnical analyses of hundreds of pieces (30 pages devoted to St. Matthew Passion, 26 to B Minor Mass). Also includes major analysis of 18th-century music. 450 musical examples. 40-page musical supplement. Total of xx + 1799pp.
(EUK) 22278-0, 22279-9 Two volumes, Clothbound $15.00

MOZART AND HIS PIANO CONCERTOS, Cuthbert Girdlestone. The only full-length study of an important area of Mozart's creativity. Provides detailed analyses of all 23 concertos, traces inspirational sources. 417 musical examples. Second edition.
509pp. (USO) 21271-8 Paperbound $3.50

THE PERFECT WAGNERITE: A COMMENTARY ON THE NIBLUNG'S RING, George Bernard Shaw. Brilliant and still relevant criticism in remarkable essays on Wagner's Ring cycle, Shaw's ideas on political and social ideology behind the plots, role of Leitmotifs, vocal requisites, etc. Prefaces. xxi + 136pp.
21707-8 Paperbound $1.50

DON GIOVANNI, W. A. Mozart. Complete libretto, modern English translation; biographies of composer and librettist; accounts of early performances and critical reaction. Lavishly illustrated. All the material you need to understand and appreciate this great work. Dover Opera Guide and Libretto Series; translated and introduced by Ellen Bleiler. 92 illustrations. 209pp.
21134-7 Paperbound $1.50

HIGH FIDELITY SYSTEMS: A LAYMAN'S GUIDE, Roy F. Allison. All the basic information you need for setting up your own audio system: high fidelity and stereo record players, tape records, F.M. Connections, adjusting tone arm, cartridge, checking needle alignment, positioning speakers, phasing speakers, adjusting hums, trouble-shooting, maintenance, and similar topics. Enlarged 1965 edition. More than 50 charts, diagrams, photos. iv + 91pp. 21514-8 Paperbound $1.25

REPRODUCTION OF SOUND, Edgar Villchur. Thorough coverage for laymen of high fidelity systems, reproducing systems in general, needles, amplifiers, preamps, loudspeakers, feedback, explaining physical background. "A rare talent for making technicalities vividly comprehensible," R. Darrell, *High Fidelity*. 69 figures.
iv + 92pp. 21515-6 Paperbound $1.00

HEAR ME TALKIN' TO YA: THE STORY OF JAZZ AS TOLD BY THE MEN WHO MADE IT, Nat Shapiro and Nat Hentoff. Louis Armstrong, Fats Waller, Jo Jones, Clarence Williams, Billy Holiday, Duke Ellington, Jelly Roll Morton and dozens of other jazz greats tell how it was in Chicago's South Side, New Orleans, depression Harlem and the modern West Coast as jazz was born and grew. xvi + 429pp.
21726-4 Paperbound $2.50

FABLES OF AESOP, translated by Sir Roger L'Estrange. A reproduction of the very rare 1931 Paris edition; a selection of the most interesting fables, together with 50 imaginative drawings by Alexander Calder. v + 128pp. 6½x9¼.
21780-9 Paperbound $1.25

POEMS OF ANNE BRADSTREET, edited with an introduction by Robert Hutchinson. A new selection of poems by America's first poet and perhaps the first significant woman poet in the English language. 48 poems display her development in works of considerable variety—love poems, domestic poems, religious meditations, formal elegies, "quaternions," etc. Notes, bibliography. viii + 222pp.

22160-1 Paperbound $2.00

THREE GOTHIC NOVELS: THE CASTLE OF OTRANTO BY HORACE WALPOLE; VATHEK BY WILLIAM BECKFORD; THE VAMPYRE BY JOHN POLIDORI, WITH FRAGMENT OF A NOVEL BY LORD BYRON, edited by E. F. Bleiler. The first Gothic novel, by Walpole; the finest Oriental tale in English, by Beckford; powerful Romantic supernatural story in versions by Polidori and Byron. All extremely important in history of literature; all still exciting, packed with supernatural thrills, ghosts, haunted castles, magic, etc. xl + 291pp.

21232-7 Paperbound $2.00

THE BEST TALES OF HOFFMANN, E. T. A. Hoffmann. 10 of Hoffmann's most important stories, in modern re-editings of standard translations: Nutcracker and the King of Mice, Signor Formica, Automata, The Sandman, Rath Krespel, The Golden Flowerpot, Master Martin the Cooper, The Mines of Falun, The King's Betrothed, A New Year's Eve Adventure. 7 illustrations by Hoffmann. Edited by E. F. Bleiler. xxxix + 419pp.

21793-0 Paperbound $2.50

GHOST AND HORROR STORIES OF AMBROSE BIERCE, Ambrose Bierce. 23 strikingly modern stories of the horrors latent in the human mind: The Eyes of the Panther, The Damned Thing, An Occurrence at Owl Creek Bridge, An Inhabitant of Carcosa, etc., plus the dream-essay, Visions of the Night. Edited by E. F. Bleiler. xxii + 199pp.

20767-6 Paperbound $1.50

BEST GHOST STORIES OF J. S. LEFANU, J. Sheridan LeFanu. Finest stories by Victorian master often considered greatest supernatural writer of all. Carmilla, Green Tea, The Haunted Baronet, The Familiar, and 12 others. Most never before available in the U. S. A. Edited by E. F. Bleiler. 8 illustrations from Victorian publications. xvii + 467pp.

20415-4 Paperbound $2.50

THE TIME STREAM, THE GREATEST ADVENTURE, AND THE PURPLE SAPPHIRE— THREE SCIENCE FICTION NOVELS, John Taine (Eric Temple Bell). Great American mathematician was also foremost science fiction novelist of the 1920's. *The Time Stream*, one of all-time classics, uses concepts of circular time; *The Greatest Adventure*, incredibly ancient biological experiments from Antarctica threaten to escape; *The Purple Sapphire*, superscience, lost races in Central Tibet, survivors of the Great Race. 4 illustrations by Frank R. Paul. v + 532pp.

21180-0 Paperbound $3.00

SEVEN SCIENCE FICTION NOVELS, H. G. Wells. The standard collection of the great novels. Complete, unabridged. *First Men in the Moon, Island of Dr. Moreau, War of the Worlds, Food of the Gods, Invisible Man, Time Machine, In the Days of the Comet*. Not only science fiction fans, but every educated person owes it to himself to read these novels. 1015pp.

20264-X Clothbound $5.00

AMERICAN FOOD AND GAME FISHES, David S. Jordan and Barton W. Evermann. Definitive source of information, detailed and accurate enough to enable the sportsman and nature lover to identify conclusively some 1,000 species and sub-species of North American fish, sought for food or sport. Coverage of range, physiology, habits, life history, food value. Best methods of capture, interest to the angler, advice on bait, fly-fishing, etc. 338 drawings and photographs. 1 + 574pp. 6⅝ x 9⅜.
22383-1 Paperbound $4.50

THE FROG BOOK, Mary C. Dickerson. Complete with extensive finding keys, over 300 photographs, and an introduction to the general biology of frogs and toads, this is the classic non-technical study of Northeastern and Central species. 58 species; 290 photographs and 16 color plates. xvii + 253pp.
21973-9 Paperbound $4.00

THE MOTH BOOK: A GUIDE TO THE MOTHS OF NORTH AMERICA, William J. Holland. Classical study, eagerly sought after and used for the past 60 years. Clear identification manual to more than 2,000 different moths, largest manual in existence. General information about moths, capturing, mounting, classifying, etc., followed by species by species descriptions. 263 illustrations plus 48 color plates show almost every species, full size. 1968 edition, preface, nomenclature changes by A. E. Brower. xxiv + 479pp. of text. 6½ x 9¼.
21948-8 Paperbound $5.00

THE SEA-BEACH AT EBB-TIDE, Augusta Foote Arnold. Interested amateur can identify hundreds of marine plants and animals on coasts of North America; marine algae; seaweeds; squids; hermit crabs; horse shoe crabs; shrimps; corals; sea anemones; etc. Species descriptions cover: structure; food; reproductive cycle; size; shape; color; habitat; etc. Over 600 drawings. 85 plates. xii + 490pp.
21949-6 Paperbound $3.50

COMMON BIRD SONGS, Donald J. Borror. 33⅓ 12-inch record presents songs of 60 important birds of the eastern United States. A thorough, serious record which provides several examples for each bird, showing different types of song, individual variations, etc. Inestimable identification aid for birdwatcher. 32-page booklet gives text about birds and songs, with illustration for each bird.
21829-5 Record, book, album. Monaural. $2.75

FADS AND FALLACIES IN THE NAME OF SCIENCE, Martin Gardner. Fair, witty appraisal of cranks and quacks of science: Atlantis, Lemuria, hollow earth, flat earth, Velikovsky, orgone energy, Dianetics, flying saucers, Bridey Murphy, food fads, medical fads, perpetual motion, etc. Formerly "In the Name of Science." x + 363pp.
20394-8 Paperbound $2.00

HOAXES, Curtis D. MacDougall. Exhaustive, unbelievably rich account of great hoaxes: Locke's moon hoax, Shakespearean forgeries, sea serpents, Loch Ness monster, Cardiff giant, John Wilkes Booth's mummy, Disumbrationist school of art, dozens more; also journalism, psychology of hoaxing. 54 illustrations. xi + 338pp.
20465-0 Paperbound $2.75

THE PRINCIPLES OF PSYCHOLOGY, William James. The famous long course, complete and unabridged. Stream of thought, time perception, memory, experimental methods—these are only some of the concerns of a work that was years ahead of its time and still valid, interesting, useful. 94 figures. Total of xviii + 1391pp.
20381-6, 20382-4 Two volumes, Paperbound $6.00

THE STRANGE STORY OF THE QUANTUM, Banesh Hoffmann. Non-mathematical but thorough explanation of work of Planck, Einstein, Bohr, Pauli, de Broglie, Schrödinger, Heisenberg, Dirac, Feynman, etc. No technical background needed. "Of books attempting such an account, this is the best," Henry Margenau, Yale. 40-page "Postscript 1959." xii + 285pp.
20518-5 Paperbound $2.00

THE RISE OF THE NEW PHYSICS, A. d'Abro. Most thorough explanation in print of central core of mathematical physics, both classical and modern; from Newton to Dirac and Heisenberg. Both history and exposition; philosophy of science, causality, explanations of higher mathematics, analytical mechanics, electromagnetism, thermodynamics, phase rule, special and general relativity, matrices. No higher mathematics needed to follow exposition, though treatment is elementary to intermediate in level. Recommended to serious student who wishes verbal understanding. 97 illustrations. xvii + 982pp.
20003-5, 20004-3 Two volumes, Paperbound $5.50

GREAT IDEAS OF OPERATIONS RESEARCH, Jagjit Singh. Easily followed non-technical explanation of mathematical tools, aims, results: statistics, linear programming, game theory, queueing theory, Monte Carlo simulation, etc. Uses only elementary mathematics. Many case studies, several analyzed in detail. Clarity, breadth make this excellent for specialist in another field who wishes background. 41 figures. x + 228pp.
21886-4 Paperbound $2.25

GREAT IDEAS OF MODERN MATHEMATICS: THEIR NATURE AND USE, Jagjit Singh. Internationally famous expositor, winner of Unesco's Kalinga Award for science popularization explains verbally such topics as differential equations, matrices, groups, sets, transformations, mathematical logic and other important modern mathematics, as well as use in physics, astrophysics, and similar fields. Superb exposition for layman, scientist in other areas. viii + 312pp.
20587-8 Paperbound $2.25

GREAT IDEAS IN INFORMATION THEORY, LANGUAGE AND CYBERNETICS, Jagjit Singh. The analog and digital computers, how they work, how they are like and unlike the human brain, the men who developed them, their future applications, computer terminology. An essential book for today, even for readers with little math. Some mathematical demonstrations included for more advanced readers. 118 figures. Tables. ix + 338pp.
21694-2 Paperbound $2.25

CHANCE, LUCK AND STATISTICS, Horace C. Levinson. Non-mathematical presentation of fundamentals of probability theory and science of statistics and their applications. Games of chance, betting odds, misuse of statistics, normal and skew distributions, birth rates, stock speculation, insurance. Enlarged edition. Formerly "The Science of Chance." xiii + 357pp.
21007-3 Paperbound $2.00

PLANETS, STARS AND GALAXIES: DESCRIPTIVE ASTRONOMY FOR BEGINNERS, A. E. Fanning. Comprehensive introductory survey of astronomy: the sun, solar system, stars, galaxies, universe, cosmology; up-to-date, including quasars, radio stars, etc. Preface by Prof. Donald Menzel. 24pp. of photographs. 189pp. 5¼ x 8¼.
21680-2 Paperbound $1.50

TEACH YOURSELF CALCULUS, P. Abbott. With a good background in algebra and trig, you can teach yourself calculus with this book. Simple, straightforward introduction to functions of all kinds, integration, differentiation, series, etc. "Students who are beginning to study calculus method will derive great help from this book." Faraday House Journal. 308pp. 20683-1 Clothbound $2.00

TEACH YOURSELF TRIGONOMETRY, P. Abbott. Geometrical foundations, indices and logarithms, ratios, angles, circular measure, etc. are presented in this sound, easy-to-use text. Excellent for the beginner or as a brush up, this text carries the student through the solution of triangles. 204pp. 20682-3 Clothbound $2.00

TEACH YOURSELF ANATOMY, David LeVay. Accurate, inclusive, profusely illustrated account of structure, skeleton, abdomen, muscles, nervous system, glands, brain, reproductive organs, evolution. "Quite the best and most readable account,' *Medical Officer.* 12 color plates. 164 figures. 311pp. 4¾ x 7.
21651-9 Clothbound $2.50

TEACH YOURSELF PHYSIOLOGY, David LeVay. Anatomical, biochemical bases; digestive, nervous, endocrine systems; metabolism; respiration; muscle; excretion; temperature control; reproduction. "Good elementary exposition," *The Lancet.* 6 color plates. 44 illustrations. 208pp. 4¼ x 7. 21658-6 Clothbound $2.50

THE FRIENDLY STARS, Martha Evans Martin. Classic has taught naked-eye observation of stars, planets to hundreds of thousands, still not surpassed for charm, lucidity, adequacy. Completely updated by Professor Donald H. Menzel, Harvard Observatory. 25 illustrations. 16 x 30 chart. x + 147pp. 21099-5 Paperbound $1.25

MUSIC OF THE SPHERES: THE MATERIAL UNIVERSE FROM ATOM TO QUASAR, SIMPLY EXPLAINED, Guy Murchie. Extremely broad, brilliantly written popular account begins with the solar system and reaches to dividing line between matter and nonmatter; latest understandings presented with exceptional clarity. Volume One: Planets, stars, galaxies, cosmology, geology, celestial mechanics, latest astronomical discoveries; Volume Two: Matter, atoms, waves, radiation, relativity, chemical action, heat, nuclear energy, quantum theory, music, light, color, probability, antimatter, antigravity, and similar topics. 319 figures. 1967 (second) edition. Total of xx + 644pp. 21809-0, 21810-4 Two volumes, Paperbound $5.00

OLD-TIME SCHOOLS AND SCHOOL BOOKS, Clifton Johnson. Illustrations and rhymes from early primers, abundant quotations from early textbooks, many anecdotes of school life enliven this study of elementary schools from Puritans to middle 19th century. Introduction by Carl Withers. 234 illustrations. xxxiii + 381pp.
21031-6 Paperbound $2.50

THE PHILOSOPHY OF THE UPANISHADS, Paul Deussen. Clear, detailed statement of upanishadic system of thought, generally considered among best available. History of these works, full exposition of system emergent from them, parallel concepts in the West. Translated by A. S. Geden. xiv + 429pp.

21616-0 Paperbound $3.00

LANGUAGE, TRUTH AND LOGIC, Alfred J. Ayer. Famous, remarkably clear introduction to the Vienna and Cambridge schools of Logical Positivism; function of philosophy, elimination of metaphysical thought, nature of analysis, similar topics. "Wish I had written it myself," Bertrand Russell. 2nd, 1946 edition. 160pp.

20010-8 Paperbound $1.35

THE GUIDE FOR THE PERPLEXED, Moses Maimonides. Great classic of medieval Judaism, major attempt to reconcile revealed religion (Pentateuch, commentaries) and Aristotelian philosophy. Enormously important in all Western thought. Unabridged Friedländer translation. 50-page introduction. lix + 414pp.

(USO) 20351-4 Paperbound $2.50

OCCULT AND SUPERNATURAL PHENOMENA, D. H. Rawcliffe. Full, serious study of the most persistent delusions of mankind: crystal gazing, mediumistic trance, stigmata, lycanthropy, fire walking, dowsing, telepathy, ghosts, ESP, etc., and their relation to common forms of abnormal psychology. Formerly *Illusions and Delusions of the Supernatural and the Occult.* iii + 551pp.   20503-7 Paperbound $3.50

THE EGYPTIAN BOOK OF THE DEAD: THE PAPYRUS OF ANI, E. A. Wallis Budge. Full hieroglyphic text, interlinear transliteration of sounds, word for word translation, then smooth, connected translation; Theban recension. Basic work in Ancient Egyptian civilization; now even more significant than ever for historical importance, dilation of consciousness, etc. clvi + 377pp. 6½ x 9¼.

21866-X Paperbound $3.95

PSYCHOLOGY OF MUSIC, Carl E. Seashore. Basic, thorough survey of everything known about psychology of music up to 1940's; essential reading for psychologists, musicologists. Physical acoustics; auditory apparatus; relationship of physical sound to perceived sound; role of the mind in sorting, altering, suppressing, creating sound sensations; musical learning, testing for ability, absolute pitch, other topics. Records of Caruso, Menuhin analyzed. 88 figures. xix + 408pp.

21851-1 Paperbound $2.75

THE I CHING (THE BOOK OF CHANGES), translated by James Legge. Complete translated text plus appendices by Confucius, of perhaps the most penetrating divination book ever compiled. Indispensable to all study of early Oriental civilizations. 3 plates. xxiii + 448pp.   21062-6 Paperbound $3.00

THE UPANISHADS, translated by Max Müller. Twelve classical upanishads: Chandogya, Kena, Aitareya, Kaushitaki, Isa, Katha, Mundaka, Taittiriyaka, Brhadaranyaka, Svetasvatara, Prasna, Maitriyana. 160-page introduction, analysis by Prof. Müller. Total of 826pp.   20398-0, 20399-9 Two volumes, Paperbound $5.00

CATALOGUE OF DOVER BOOKS

JIM WHITEWOLF: THE LIFE OF A KIOWA APACHE INDIAN, Charles S. Brant, editor. Spans transition between native life and acculturation period, 1880 on. Kiowa culture, personal life pattern, religion and the supernatural, the Ghost Dance, breakdown in the White Man's world, similar material. 1 map. xii + 144pp.
22015-X Paperbound $1.75

THE NATIVE TRIBES OF CENTRAL AUSTRALIA, Baldwin Spencer and F. J. Gillen. Basic book in anthropology, devoted to full coverage of the Arunta and Warramunga tribes; the source for knowledge about kinship systems, material and social culture, religion, etc. Still unsurpassed. 121 photographs, 89 drawings. xviii + 669pp.
21775-2 Paperbound $5.00

MALAY MAGIC, Walter W. Skeat. Classic (1900) ; still the definitive work on the folklore and popular religion of the Malay peninsula. Describes marriage rites, birth spirits and ceremonies, medicine, dances, games, war and weapons, etc. Extensive quotes from original sources, many magic charms translated into English. 35 illustrations. Preface by Charles Otto Blagden. xxiv + 685pp.
21760-4 Paperbound $4.00

HEAVENS ON EARTH: UTOPIAN COMMUNITIES IN AMERICA, 1680-1880, Mark Holloway. The finest nontechnical account of American utopias, from the early Woman in the Wilderness, Ephrata, Rappites to the enormous mid 19th-century efflorescence; Shakers, New Harmony, Equity Stores, Fourier's Phalanxes, Oneida, Amana, Fruitlands, etc. "Entertaining and very instructive." *Times Literary Supplement*. 15 illustrations. 246pp.
21593-8 Paperbound $2.00

LONDON LABOUR AND THE LONDON POOR, Henry Mayhew. Earliest (c. 1850) sociological study in English, describing myriad subcultures of London poor. Particularly remarkable for the thousands of pages of direct testimony taken from the lips of London prostitutes, thieves, beggars, street sellers, chimney-sweepers, street-musicians, "mudlarks," "pure-finders," rag-gatherers, "running-patterers," dock laborers, cab-men, and hundreds of others, quoted directly in this massive work. An extraordinarily vital picture of London emerges. 110 illustrations. Total of lxxvi + 1951pp. 6⅝ x 10.
21934-8, 21935-6, 21936-4, 21937-2 Four volumes, Paperbound $14.00

HISTORY OF THE LATER ROMAN EMPIRE, J. B. Bury. Eloquent, detailed reconstruction of Western and Byzantine Roman Empire by a major historian, from the death of Theodosius I (395 A.D.) to the death of Justinian (565). Extensive quotations from contemporary sources; full coverage of important Roman and foreign figures of the time. xxxiv + 965pp. 21829-5 Record, book, album. Monaural. $3.50

AN INTELLECTUAL AND CULTURAL HISTORY OF THE WESTERN WORLD, Harry Elmer Barnes. Monumental study, tracing the development of the accomplishments that make up human culture. Every aspect of man's achievement surveyed from its origins in the Paleolithic to the present day (1964) ; social structures, ideas, economic systems, art, literature, technology, mathematics, the sciences, medicine, religion, jurisprudence, etc. Evaluations of the contributions of scores of great men. 1964 edition, revised and edited by scholars in the many fields represented. Total of xxix + 1381pp. 21275-0, 21276-9, 21277-7 Three volumes, Paperbound $7.75

ADVENTURES OF AN AFRICAN SLAVER, Theodore Canot. Edited by Brantz Mayer. A detailed portrayal of slavery and the slave trade, 1820-1840. Canot, an established trader along the African coast, describes the slave economy of the African kingdoms, the treatment of captured negroes, the extensive journeys in the interior to gather slaves, slave revolts and their suppression, harems, bribes, and much more. Full and unabridged republication of 1854 edition. Introduction by Malcom Cowley. 16 illustrations. xvii + 448pp. 22456-2 Paperbound $3.50

MY BONDAGE AND MY FREEDOM, Frederick Douglass. Born and brought up in slavery, Douglass witnessed its horrors and experienced its cruelties, but went on to become one of the most outspoken forces in the American anti-slavery movement. Considered the best of his autobiographies, this book graphically describes the inhuman treatment of slaves, its effects on slave owners and slave families, and how Douglass's determination led him to a new life. Unaltered reprint of 1st (1855) edition. xxxii + 464pp. 22457-0 Paperbound $2.50

THE INDIANS' BOOK, recorded and edited by Natalie Curtis. Lore, music, narratives, dozens of drawings by Indians themselves from an authoritative and important survey of native culture among Plains, Southwestern, Lake and Pueblo Indians. Standard work in popular ethnomusicology. 149 songs in full notation. 23 drawings, 23 photos. xxxi + 584pp. 6⅝ x 9⅜. 21939-9 Paperbound $4.50

DICTIONARY OF AMERICAN PORTRAITS, edited by Hayward and Blanche Cirker. 4024 portraits of 4000 most important Americans, colonial days to 1905 (with a few important categories, like Presidents, to present). Pioneers, explorers, colonial figures, U. S. officials, politicians, writers, military and naval men, scientists, inventors, manufacturers, jurists, actors, historians, educators, notorious figures, Indian chiefs, etc. All authentic contemporary likenesses. The only work of its kind in existence; supplements all biographical sources for libraries. Indispensable to anyone working with American history. 8,000-item classified index, finding lists, other aids. xiv + 756pp. 9¼ x 12¾. 21823-6 Clothbound $30.00

TRITTON'S GUIDE TO BETTER WINE AND BEER MAKING FOR BEGINNERS, S. M. Tritton. All you need to know to make family-sized quantities of over 100 types of grape, fruit, herb and vegetable wines; as well as beers, mead, cider, etc. Complete recipes, advice as to equipment, procedures such as fermenting, bottling, and storing wines. Recipes given in British, U. S., and metric measures. Accompanying booklet lists sources in U. S. A. where ingredients may be bought, and additional information. 11 illustrations. 157pp. 5⅝ x 8⅛. (USO) 22090-7 Clothbound $3.50

GARDENING WITH HERBS FOR FLAVOR AND FRAGRANCE, Helen M. Fox. How to grow herbs in your own garden, how to use them in your cooking (over 55 recipes included), legends and myths associated with each species, uses in medicine, perfumes, etc.—these are elements of one of the few books written especially for American herb fanciers. Guides you step-by-step from soil preparation to harvesting and storage for each type of herb. 12 drawings by Louise Mansfield. xiv + 334pp. 22540-2 Paperbound $2.50

INCIDENTS OF TRAVEL IN YUCATAN, John L. Stephens. Classic (1843) exploration of jungles of Yucatan, looking for evidences of Maya civilization. Stephens found many ruins; comments on travel adventures, Mexican and Indian culture. 127 striking illustrations by F. Catherwood. Total of 669 pp.
20926-1, 20927-X Two volumes, Paperbound $5.00

INCIDENTS OF TRAVEL IN CENTRAL AMERICA, CHIAPAS, AND YUCATAN, John L. Stephens. An exciting travel journal and an important classic of archeology. Narrative relates his almost single-handed discovery of the Mayan culture, and exploration of the ruined cities of Copan, Palenque, Utatlan and others; the monuments they dug from the earth, the temples buried in the jungle, the customs of poverty-stricken Indians living a stone's throw from the ruined palaces. 115 drawings by F. Catherwood. Portrait of Stephens. xii + 812pp.
22404-X, 22405-8 Two volumes, Paperbound $6.00

A NEW VOYAGE ROUND THE WORLD, William Dampier. Late 17-century naturalist joined the pirates of the Spanish Main to gather information; remarkably vivid account of buccaneers, pirates; detailed, accurate account of botany, zoology, ethnography of lands visited. Probably the most important early English voyage, enormous implications for British exploration, trade, colonial policy. Also most interesting reading. Argonaut edition, introduction by Sir Albert Gray. New introduction by Percy Adams. 6 plates, 7 illustrations. xlvii + 376pp. 6½ x 9¼.
21900-3 Paperbound $3.00

INTERNATIONAL AIRLINE PHRASE BOOK IN SIX LANGUAGES, Joseph W. Bátor. Important phrases and sentences in English paralleled with French, German, Portuguese, Italian, Spanish equivalents, covering all possible airport-travel situations; created for airline personnel as well as tourist by Language Chief, Pan American Airlines. xiv + 204pp.
22017-6 Paperbound $2.00

STAGE COACH AND TAVERN DAYS, Alice Morse Earle. Detailed, lively account of the early days of taverns; their uses and importance in the social, political and military life; furnishings and decorations; locations; food and drink; tavern signs, etc. Second half covers every aspect of early travel; the roads, coaches, drivers, etc. Nostalgic, charming, packed with fascinating material. 157 illustrations, mostly photographs. xiv + 449pp.
22518-6 Paperbound $4.00

NORSE DISCOVERIES AND EXPLORATIONS IN NORTH AMERICA, Hjalmar R. Holand. The perplexing Kensington Stone, found in Minnesota at the end of the 19th century. Is it a record of a Scandinavian expedition to North America in the 14th century? Or is it one of the most successful hoaxes in history. A scientific detective investigation. Formerly *Westward from Vinland*. 31 photographs, 17 figures. x + 354pp.
22014-1 Paperbound $2.75

A BOOK OF OLD MAPS, compiled and edited by Emerson D. Fite and Archibald Freeman. 74 old maps offer an unusual survey of the discovery, settlement and growth of America down to the close of the Revolutionary war: maps showing Norse settlements in Greenland, the explorations of Columbus, Verrazano, Cabot, Champlain, Joliet, Drake, Hudson, etc., campaigns of Revolutionary war battles, and much more. Each map is accompanied by a brief historical essay. xvi + 299pp. 11 x 13¾.
22084-2 Paperbound $6.00

BASIC ELECTRICITY, U. S. Bureau of Naval Personel. Originally a training course, best non-technical coverage of basic theory of electricity and its applications. Fundamental concepts, batteries, circuits, conductors and wiring techniques, AC and DC, inductance and capacitance, generators, motors, transformers, magnetic amplifiers, synchros, servomechanisms, etc. Also covers blue-prints, electrical diagrams, etc. Many questions, with answers. 349 illustrations. x + 448pp. 6½ x 9¼.
20973-3 Paperbound $3.00

TENSORS FOR CIRCUITS, Gabriel Kron. The purpose of this volume was to develop a new mathematical method of analyzing engineering problems—through tensor analysis—which has since proven its usefulness especially in electrical and structural networks in computers. Introduction by Banesh Hoffmann. Formerly *A Short Course in Tensor Analysis.* Over 800 figures. xviii + 250pp.
60534-5 Paperbound $2.00

INFORMATION THEORY, Stanford Goldman. A thorugh presentation of the work of C. E. Shannon and to a lesser extent Norbert Weiner, at a mathematical level understandable to first-year graduate students in electrical engineering. In addition, the basic and general aspects of information theory are developed at an elementary level for workers in non-mathematical sciences. Table of logarithms to base 2. xiii + 385pp.
62209-6 Paperbound $3.50

INTRODUCTION TO THE STATISTICAL DYNAMICS OF AUTOMATIC CONTROL SYSTEMS, V. V. Solodovnikov. General theory of control systems subjected to random signals. Theory of linear analysis, statistics of random signals, theory of linear prediction and filtering. For advanced and graduate-level students. Translated by John B. Thomas and Lotfi A. Zadeh. xxi + 307pp.
60420-9 Paperbound $3.00

FUNDAMENTAL OF HYDRO- AND AEROMECHANICS, Ludwig Prandtl and O. G. Tietjens. Tietjens' famous expansion of Professor Prandtl's Kaiser Wilhelm Institute lectures. Much original material included in coverage of statics of liquids and gases, kinematics of liquids and gases, dynamics of non-viscous liquids. Proofs are rigorous and use vector analysis. Translated by L. Rosenhead. 186 figures. xvi + 270pp.
60374-1 Paperbound $2.25

MATHEMATICAL METHODS FOR SCIENTISTS AND ENGINEERS, L. P. Smith. Full investigation of methods, practical description of conditions where used: elements of real functions, differential and integral calculus, space geometry, residues, vectors and tensors, Bessel functions, etc. Many examples from scientific literature completely worked out. 368 problems for solution, 100 diagrams. x + 453pp.
60220-6 Paperbound $2.75

COMPUTATIONAL METHODS OF LINEAR ALGEBRA, V. N. Faddeeva. Only work in English to present classical and modern Russian computational methods of linear algebra, including the work of A. N. Krylov, A. M. Danilevsky, D. K. Faddeev and others. Detailed treatment of the derivation of numerical solutions to problems of linear algebra. Translated by Curtis D. Benster. 23 carefully prepared tables. New bibliography. x + 252pp.
60424-1 Paperbound $2.50

A Treatise on the Differential Geometry of Curves and Surfaces, Luther P. Eisenhart. Detailed, concrete introductory treatise on differential geometry, developed from author's graduate courses at Princeton University. Thorough explanation of the geometry of curves and surfaces, concentrating on problems most helpful to students. 683 problems, 30 diagrams. xiv + 474pp.
60667-8 Paperbound $2.75

An Essay on the Foundations of Geometry, Bertrand Russell. A mathematical and physical analysis of the place of the a priori in geometric knowledge. Includes critical review of 19th-century work in non-Euclidean geometry as well as illuminating insights of one of the great minds of our time. New foreword by Morris Kline. xx + 201pp.
60233-8 Paperbound $2.00

Introduction to the Theory of Numbers, Leonard E. Dickson. Thorough, comprehensive approach with adequate coverage of classical literature, yet simple enough for beginners. Divisibility, congruences, quadratic residues, binary quadratic forms, primes, least residues, Fermat's theorem, Gauss's lemma, and other important topics. 249 problems, 1 figure. viii + 183pp.
60342-3 Paperbound $2.00

An Elementary Introduction to the Theory of Probability, B. V. Gnedenko and A. Ya. Khinchin. Introduction to facts and principles of probability theory. Extremely thorough within its range. Mathematics employed held to elementary level. Excellent, highly accurate layman's introduction. Translated from the fifth Russian edition by Leo Y. Boron. xii + 130pp.
60155-2 Paperbound $1.75

Selected Papers on Noise and Stochastic Processes, edited by Nelson Wax. Six papers which serve as an introduction to advanced noise theory and fluctuation phenomena, or as a reference tool for electrical engineers whose work involves noise characteristics, Brownian motion, statistical mechanics. Papers are by Chandrasekhar, Doob, Kac, Ming, Ornstein, Rice, and Uhlenbeck. Exact facsimile of the papers as they appeared in scientific journals. 19 figures. v + 337pp. $6\frac{1}{8}$ x $9\frac{1}{4}$.
60262-1 Paperbound $3.00

Statistics Manual, Edwin L. Crow, Frances A. Davis and Margaret W. Maxfield. Comprehensive, practical collection of classical and modern methods of making statistical inferences, prepared by U. S. Naval Ordnance Test Station. Formulae, explanations, methods of application are given, with stress on use. Basic knowledge of statistics is assumed. 21 tables, 11 charts, 95 illustrations. xvii + 288pp.
60599-X Paperbound $2.00

Mathematical Foundations of Information Theory, A. I. Khinchin. Comprehensive introduction to work of Shannon, McMillan, Feinstein and Khinchin, placing these investigations on a rigorous mathematical basis. Covers entropy concept in probability theory, uniqueness theorem, Shannon's inequality, ergodic sources, the E property, martingale concept, noise, Feinstein's fundamental lemma, Shanon's first and second theorems. Translated by R. A. Silverman and M. D. Friedman. iii + 120pp.
60434-9 Paperbound $1.75

MATHEMATICAL PUZZLES FOR BEGINNERS AND ENTHUSIASTS, Geoffrey Mott-Smith. 189 puzzles from easy to difficult—involving arithmetic, logic, algebra, properties of digits, probability, etc.—for enjoyment and mental stimulus. Explanation of mathematical principles behind the puzzles. 135 illustrations. viii + 248pp.
20198-8 Paperbound $1.25

PAPER FOLDING FOR BEGINNERS, William D. Murray and Francis J. Rigney. Easiest book on the market, clearest instructions on making interesting, beautiful origami. Sail boats, cups, roosters, frogs that move legs, bonbon boxes, standing birds, etc. 40 projects; more than 275 diagrams and photographs. 94pp.
20713-7 Paperbound $1.00

TRICKS AND GAMES ON THE POOL TABLE, Fred Herrmann. 79 tricks and games— some solitaires, some for two or more players, some competitive games—to entertain you between formal games. Mystifying shots and throws, unusual caroms, tricks involving such props as cork, coins, a hat, etc. Formerly *Fun on the Pool Table*. 77 figures. 95pp.
21814-7 Paperbound $1.00

HAND SHADOWS TO BE THROWN UPON THE WALL: A SERIES OF NOVEL AND AMUSING FIGURES FORMED BY THE HAND, Henry Bursill. Delightful picturebook from great-grandfather's day shows how to make 18 different hand shadows: a bird that flies, duck that quacks, dog that wags his tail, camel, goose, deer, boy, turtle, etc. Only book of its sort. vi + 33pp. 6½ x 9¼. 21779-5 Paperbound $1.00

WHITTLING AND WOODCARVING, E. J. Tangerman. 18th printing of best book on market. "If you can cut a potato you can carve" toys and puzzles, chains, chessmen, caricatures, masks, frames, woodcut blocks, surface patterns, much more. Information on tools, woods, techniques. Also goes into serious wood sculpture from Middle Ages to present, East and West. 464 photos, figures. x + 293pp.
20965-2 Paperbound $2.00

HISTORY OF PHILOSOPHY, Julián Marias. Possibly the clearest, most easily followed, best planned, most useful one-volume history of philosophy on the market; neither skimpy nor overfull. Full details on system of every major philosopher and dozens of less important thinkers from pre-Socratics up to Existentialism and later. Strong on many European figures usually omitted. Has gone through dozens of editions in Europe. 1966 edition, translated by Stanley Appelbaum and Clarence Strowbridge. xviii + 505pp. 21739-6 Paperbound $3.00

YOGA: A SCIENTIFIC EVALUATION, Kovoor T. Behanan. Scientific but non-technical study of physiological results of yoga exercises; done under auspices of Yale U. Relations to Indian thought, to psychoanalysis, etc. 16 photos. xxiii + 270pp.
20505-3 Paperbound $2.50

Prices subject to change without notice.
Available at your book dealer or write for free catalogue to Dept. GI, Dover Publications, Inc., 180 Varick St., N. Y., N. Y. 10014. Dover publishes more than 150 books each year on science, elementary and advanced mathematics, biology, music, art, literary history, social sciences and other areas.